AF675653

Whose America?

Whose America?

The War of 1898 and the Battles to Define the Nation

Edited by
VIRGINIA M. BOUVIER

PRAEGER

Westport, Connecticut
London

Library of Congress Cataloging-in-Publication Data

Whose America? : the war of 1898 and the battles to define the nation / edited by Virginia M. Bouvier.
p. cm.
Includes bibliographical references and index.
ISBN 0-275-96794-8 (alk. paper)
1. Spanish-American War, 1898—Influence. 2. Spanish-American War, 1898—Social aspects. 3. Imperialism—History—19th century. 4. Intervention (International law)—History—19th century. I. Bouvier, Virginia Marie, 1958–
E735.W57 2001
973.8'9—dc21 00-049177

British Library Cataloguing in Publication Data is available.

Copyright © 2001 by Virginia M. Bouvier

All rights reserved. No portion of this book may be reproduced, by any process or technique, without the express written consent of the publisher.

Library of Congress Catalog Card Number: 00-049177
ISBN: 0-275-96794-8

First published in 2001

Praeger Publishers, 88 Post Road West, Westport, CT 06881
An imprint of Greenwood Publishing Group, Inc.
www.praeger.com

Printed in the United States of America

The paper used in this book complies with the Permanent Paper Standard issued by the National Information Standards Organization (Z39.48–1984).

10 9 8 7 6 5 4 3 2 1

Copyright Acknowledgments

The editor and publisher are grateful to the following for granting permission to reprint from their materials:

Material from chapter 4 is drawn from Virginia M. Bouvier, "Imperial Humor: U.S. Political Cartoons and the War of 1898," originally published in *Colonial Latin American Historical Review* 8, no 1 (1999): 5–41.

Material in chapter 5 is drawn from Kristin L. Hoganson, *Fighting for American Manhood: How Gender Politics Provoked the Spanish-American and Philippine-American Wars* (New Haven: Yale University Press, 1998).

Contents

Figures

Acknowledgments

An edited volume by its nature is a collaborative endeavor, even more so when many of the contributions originated in a conference. I am greatly indebted first of all to each of the participants who presented papers at the Challenges to Peace, 1898–1998: Visions from the Past, Lessons for the Future conference in October 1998. The conference and edited volume were great excuses to work with some of the intellectual luminaries in the field and to meet some of the shining stars of the next generation. To them I dedicate this volume. A special word of thanks to Sylvia L. Hilton, Louis A. Pérez, Jr., and Lester D. Langley for their comments on earlier drafts of this book and to each of the contributors for the promptness and good humor with which they responded to my innumerable queries.

The conference itself could not have happened without the sponsorship of the Department of Spanish and Portuguese and the Latin American Studies Center at the University of Maryland, College Park (UMCP), the Hispanic Division of the Library of Congress, the Consortium of Universities of the Washington Metropolitan Area, the Embassy of Spain, The American University, Georgetown University, George Washington University, The Catholic University of America, Howard University, Johns Hopkins University, and Trinity College.

Institutional support for the conference was provided by the following additional departments and individuals at UMCP: Charles S. Rutherford, associate dean for the College of Arts and Humanities; the College Academic Planning Advisory Committee; the Committee on Africa and the Americas; the Department of Women's Studies; the Department of Comparative Literature; the Sociology Department; the University Honors Program; the College Park Scholars program; and the Department of American Studies. Within those and other units, I am especially grateful for the support and suggestions given to me by John Caughey, Regina Harrison, Carla Peterson, Carmen Román, Martha Geores, Claire Moses, Lois Vietri, Patricio Korzeniewicz, and Sandy Mack. I would also like to thank my Honors students for their help in the execution of the conference program, and Christina Guidorizzi for her logistical and budgetary support. I owe a debt of gratitude particularly to Evelyn Canabal-Torres, whose sharp mind and unflagging enthusiasm nourished the roots of this project. Thank you also to Ana Patricia Rodríguez for her intellectual collaboration and moral support.

Colleagues at other institutions were also generous with their time and support for both the conference and the publication. I wish to acknowledge herein the generosity of Georgette Dorn and Barbara Tenenbaum of the Hispanic Division at the Library of Congress, who spent countless hours discussing the conceptualization and details of the program; Philip Brenner, director of the American University Latin American Studies Program; Cynthia McClintock, director of the George Washington University Latin American Studies Center; Arturo Valenzuela, director of the Center for Latin American Studies at Georgetown University; Michael Foley, from the Catholic University of America; Mary Hayes from Trinity College; and Amelia Mondragón from Howard University. Bill LeoGrande, at the American University School of Public Affairs, was a particularly generous intellectual collaborator. Many thanks also for the gracious hospitality of Spain's Ambassador Antonio Oyarzábal and his wife, Beatriz; cultural affairs officer Juan Romero de Terreros; and the staff at the Embassy of Spain.

In conceptualizing the conference, I benefited from the advice of many of the aforementioned individuals, as well as that of Mark Sullivan, Nina Serafino, and Larry Minnear, of the Congressional Research Service; Fernando Cepeda, former Colombian ambassador to the OAS; Lou Goodman, dean of the School of International Studies at the American University; Carlos Portales, Chilean ambassador to the OAS; Kelly McBride of the Unit for the Promotion of Democracy at the OAS; Cynthia Arnson and Joseph Tulchin of the Woodrow Wilson International Center for Scholars; Dana Priest at the *Washington Post*; Mark Schneider at the Agency for International Development; Margaret Keck, at Johns Hopkins University; Eileen Findlay of American University; and Eusebio Mujal-León, of Georgetown University. Thank you for logistical help to Judith Weir at the Institute for Policy Studies; Doug Reilly at the Center for International Policy; Hugh Byrne, Coletta Youngers, and Rachel Nield at the Washington Office on Latin America; and Joy Olson, of the Latin American Working Group. A word of thanks also to my editor at Praeger, Jim Sabin, my production editor, Nicole Cournoyer, and my copy editor, Liliane McCarthy.

Sue Goodwin, Marta Tannenhaus, Joseph Eldridge, Jo Marie Griesgraber,

Heather Foote, Cynthia Buhl, Bill Goodfellow, Cheryl Morden, Kathy Gille, Doug Tanner, Chris Krueger, George Rogers, and John Cavanagh continue to inspire me to search for ways to engage in scholarship that is relevant to the public policy debates. I thank my parents, Jane and Edouard Bouvier, for teaching me to persevere and their belief in my ability to do whatever I set my mind to do; and the rest of my siblings and their families for always being there for me. A final word of appreciation goes to my husband, Jim Lyons, who indulged me as I immersed myself in life one hundred years ago. I am grateful to him and to our daughter, Maya, for providing me with the balance and humor that sustained this "reading and writing lady" during the tenure of this project.

Introduction

Virginia M. Bouvier

Three decades ago, Henry Kissinger spoke frankly to Ambassador Gabriel Valdés, the Chilean ambassador to the United States: "History has never been produced in the South. The axis of history starts in Moscow, goes to Bonn, crosses over to Washington, and then goes to Tokyo. What happens in the South is of no importance."[1] Kissinger's view of history as something that is made only in the North is not uncommon. Scholars of American or world history often marginalize events of the South. Even the respected British historian Eric Hobsbawm did so when he defined the twentieth century as the "short century," a century that began in 1914 with World War I and ended with the collapse of the Soviet empire in 1991.[2] This foreshortened view of what has also been called the "American Century" subscribes to a narrow concept of America that excludes the southern part of the Western Hemisphere. Furthermore, the narrow periodization of the "short century" excludes the years that were perhaps most critical to the shaping of American identities and U.S. foreign policies in the twentieth century.

With the War of 1898 (also referred to as the Spanish-American War, the Hispano-American War, the Spanish-Cuban-American War, the Spanish-Cuban War, and the Cuban War for Independence), the United States committed itself to intervention in Latin America, effectively terminating just over four centuries of Spanish colonial rule in that region, and launching a paradigm for U.S.-Latin American relations that would dominate the twentieth century. Such a move did not come without a fair amount of public and congressional debate, heightened by the explosion of the U.S.S. *Maine* in the harbor near Havana. Cuba's war for independence from Spain (which had been under way intermittently since the Ten Years' War from 1868 to 1878, but most recently since 1895) ended less than four months after the United States intervened in the war. Under the terms of the Treaty of Paris, signed on 10 December 1898, Spain ceded Cuba, Puerto Rico, Guam, and, for twenty million dollars, the Philippine Islands to the United States. In the acquisitorial mood which was sweeping the country, the United States had annexed Hawaii earlier that year, after years of debate.[3] Shortly thereafter, Filipinos, who had been fighting their own battles for independence from Spain, reoriented their efforts, and in February 1899, the Philippine-American War (what was formerly known as the "Philippine Insurrection") began.[4]

The War of 1898 initiated a new era in world history. In the context of growing imperial rivalries, its conclusion marked the end of Spanish colonial rule, which had been on the wane for quite some time, and the emergence of the United States, Japan, and to some extent Germany as major imperial powers to challenge Britain's dominance.[5] The War of 1898 and its aftermath inaugurated a period of profound change in the U.S. sense of itself and its role in the world, in U.S. relations with Latin America, and in regional cultures and identities within the United States, Latin America, Spain, Cuba, Puerto Rico, Hawaii, Guam, and the Philippines. Without an understanding of the war and these legacies, it is difficult to make sense of the rest of the "American Century."

The representation of history is a controversial and vital matter for public policymakers. The past coexists with the present and projects into the future. In an early critical essay, the poet T. S. Eliot noted that how we formulate or represent the past shapes our understanding and views of the present.[6] Likewise, the present informs our understanding of the past. It is perhaps for this reason that such ambiguity can be found in the historiography of the War of 1898. As the historian Louis A. Pérez, Jr. has pointed out elsewhere, the U.S. historiography on the war depicts the war as both a premeditated war of expansion and an accidental war, as inevitable and unnecessary, and as a reasoned plot by U.S. politicians and an irrational outcome of heated public opinion.[7] In part, such dramatically different interpretations of the war relate directly to each historian's vision of America—visions which often belie national myths and contradictory realities. The variations in nomenclatures for and interpretations of the War of 1898 symbolize the clash between the many sectors vying to assert their claims to their version of history.

The War of 1898 is a war that is charged with emotion for many people. It is a war that some in the United States would prefer to forget, to sever from this century and from U.S. history as though it had no importance. The one-hundred-year anniversary of the war passed with nary a blink from official Washington. Public institutions tipped their hats or ignored it altogether. The curator for the National Museum of American History's display case on "1848: New Border, New Nation," told me that her institution consciously chose not to have a major exhibit on the War of 1898. Even if they could get support for it, she noted, it would be impossible to mount a display without mentioning the "I" word, and talk of imperialism in the nation's capital would be political suicide for public institutions.[8] Miguel Bretos, of the Smithsonian Institution's Center for Latino Initiatives, confirmed that the topic was too politically charged and lamented that they had not been able to do more.[9] Even the Library of Congress, whose Hispanic Division organized several forums and a website on the war and graciously agreed to cosponsor the event that gave rise to some of the chapters in this volume, made it clear that there were explicit political limits to what might be discussed under its auspices.[10] The Anti-Imperialist League, for example, was considered to be too hot a subject to warrant a speaker, even though it claimed the support of over half a million contributors by May 1899, had delegates representing thirty states at a national conference held four months later, and included among its ranks prominent citizens such as Grover Cleveland, William Jennings Bryan, Samuel Clemens (Mark Twain), Thomas B. Reed, Carl Schurz, and David Starr Jordan.[11] Talk of anti-imperialism, it seems, would suggest that the United States had a history of imperialism.

Among the recognition that was given to aspects of the war, the National Portrait Gallery mounted a small exhibit, "Theodore Roosevelt: Icon of the American Century," which described the twenty-sixth president's "exploits as a Rough Rider in the Spanish-American War and as a cowboy in the Dakota Territory" as "indicative of his spirit of adventure and love of the outdoors."[12] The *Smithsonian Magazine* ran a brief article for the centennial on the blowing up of the battleship *Maine* and the ongoing controversies about the causes of the explosion.[13] In 1998 the U.S. Post Office released a commemorative stamp that boasted an image of the battleship and the slogan "Remember the Maine." Beyond vague recollections of an explosion in Havana harbor that purportedly justified the U.S. entry into a war against Spain, and a general conclusion that American moral and military superiority defeated a decadent enemy there, the U.S. public is painfully ignorant about the details of what actually happened. Where textbooks mention the war at all, it is often represented as a "splendid little war"—one whose victory was both rapid and painless.

Many historians have documented the reluctance of U.S. historiography to acknowledge U.S. imperialist actions of the past.[14] Edna Acosta Belén and Carlos Santiago posit that such narratives disturb the myth of the melting pot.[15] For some, these narratives sound a discordant note in the hymn of America's past, which begins with the establishment of the thirteen colonies and crescendos in chords of multicultural harmony. Such a song has little room for the blues of other groups, including the Native Americans and Latinos whose presence in America preceded the signing of the Declaration of Independence. In the current "culture wars" sweeping Washington, the tunes of such groups are perceived as "disuniting, divisive, and essentially un-American."[16]

Yet "their" history is also "our" history. It is a history that is necessary to our future as a nation, to our knowledge of ourselves and others, and to our understanding of the complex relationships between and within America, particularly with our Latin American neighbors and the growing Latino population within our borders. From the vantage point of the twenty-first century, it seems particularly appropriate to examine U.S. actions one century ago and to extend the century to be more inclusive of a broader American constituency. Latinos, who now number thirty-one million in the United States, will be this country's largest minority by 2005.[17] The battles to define ownership of American history will intensify, as borders between the Americas become more porous and Americans from both sides of the Río Grande seek to articulate a history which connects them more directly to their past.

The occasion of a one-hundred-year anniversary provides us with a useful excuse to step back and reflect on a century of American history. Such reflection, in the best of cases, offers us an opportunity to venture beyond ourselves, to encounter other viewpoints, and to apply the rigor and discipline necessary for respecting our differences and commonalities. This volume, building on a conference held at the Library of Congress, creates the space and provides some of the nourishment for this reflective journey.

The War of 1898 is about more than ships, soldiers, and the redefinition of territorial boundaries. It is an integral part of the twentieth century in part because debates about U.S. intervention in the Cuban-Spanish War and the subsequent suppression of the Philippine nationalists in their war against U.S. control of their islands foreshadow in striking ways later foreign policy debates of the twentieth century. In the United States, we have witnessed in recent decades the following motifs which prevailed in relation to the War of 1898: the construction of myths that portray U.S. intentions and actions overseas as strictly noble and humanitarian; the deliberate neglect of peace overtures; the deliberate misrepresentation of popular support for rebel causes; terrorist tactics against civilian populations; racism within the U.S. military and in U.S. policies toward other cultures; the sacrifice of long-term national interests for short-term economic and political gains; false accusations and rash actions that have provided the pretext for military engagements; military corruption and atrocities glossed over or only minimally punished; and repeated efforts to put into effect what McKinley called a policy of "benevolent assimilation."[18]

Current debates about the propriety of U.S. intervention overseas and questions of honor and manhood echo concerns raised one century ago. Government discourse that idealizes U.S. allies and demonizes the foes of the United States in order to mask economic or geo-strategic interests also taps into a strategy used during the War of 1898. Debates over national sovereignty and international human rights standards foreshadow discussions which continue to this day. In this volume, Sylvia L. Hilton describes the conflict between nineteenth-century Spanish progressives who supported the defense of certain unalienable rights over the jurisdiction established by "State, race, religion, and family," on the one hand, and Spanish nationalists, who privileged national sovereignty over concepts of universal human rights, on the other. Her articulation of nineteenth-century standards of international human rights laws regarding acceptable conditions for intervention offers welcome insights for current politicized discussions of the same topic.[19]

As in the War of 1898, twentieth-century U.S. governments have frequently manipulated the language of human rights to rally the public behind interventionist policies. In the period before the war, U.S. public opinion was persuaded to oppose Spanish human rights violations in Cuba, including Spain's brutal policies of *reconcentración* (forcible removal of rural populations to the cities), the arbitrary detention of political prisoners, and the censoring of the press. Then as now consensus was more easily built around the condemnation of the violations than around the appropriate responses to such violations. Where U.S. public opinion and the U.S. Congress supported Cuban independence, in the aftermath of the war, Cuban leaders—the "victims" on whose behalf the United States intervened—were suddenly excluded from participation in the peace negotiations. The facts that U.S. intervention postponed rather than promoted Cuban sovereignty and that some of the Spanish abuses so harshly criticized by the U.S. government were in turn practiced by the United States in its newly acquired territories should give pause to even the staunchest advocates of interventionism. Beneath such actions, the attitudes that continue to inform U.S. foreign policies today betray an arrogance and sense of superiority, often justified by noble rhetoric, whose roots run deep into the last century.

U.S. hegemony in the Western Hemisphere and the U.S. role as policeman overseas, enshrined in the Roosevelt Corollary, stems largely from the U.S. victory in 1898 and its new sense of self vis-à-vis the community of nations. In his annual message to Congress in 1904, Theodore Roosevelt, whose charge on San Juan Hill in the war catapulted him into the presidency, announced that in cases of "chronic wrongdoing, or an impotence which results in a general loosening of the ties of civilized society," particularly in the Western Hemisphere, the United States might be forced to act as "an international police power."[20] In the following two decades, U.S. armed forces intervened twenty-one times in Latin America; by the end of the century they had engaged in nearly twice that many unilateral interventions in the region.[21]

The War of 1898 was a war of images and provides us with an early example of what one scholar has called "modern ideological warfare." It was the first war to be presented on film, generally of staged reenactments of the battles fought.[22] These images provided the fodder for the "yellow journalism" wars between William Randolph Hearst's *New York Journal* and Joseph Pulitzer's *The World*, and sparked debates about the role of the press, public opinion, Congress, and the president that continue to be kindled whenever the United States considers intervening overseas.

The War of 1898 set in place a critical role for nongovernmental organizations in affecting U.S. foreign policy. The international human rights movement today has its roots in a tradition of dissent related to the issues debated in the wake of the War of 1898.[23] The Anti-Imperialist League, born from a public protest meeting of citizens at Faneuil Hall in Boston on 15 June 1898, was itself an extension of earlier anti-imperialist stances taken in the United States's own independence war against British imperial rule, in the U.S. war with Mexico in the middle of the nineteenth century, in the abolitionist movement and during the Civil War,[24] and in the subsequent opposition to U.S. efforts to annex Cuba, the Sandwich Islands (including Hawaii), and Santo Domingo (the Dominican Republic). Yet such individual efforts, until after the War of 1898, were relatively few and spread thinly throughout the United States (and Europe and Latin America). As Jim Zwick illustrates in this volume, the anti-imperialist tradition in the United States was consolidated in the formation of the Anti-Imperialist League, whose activists provided continuity in subsequent organizations launched in the first decades of this century.

The War of 1898 is significant in part because it set in motion a series of questions relating to democratic values and behavior at home and abroad. Such questions launched the Anti-Imperialist League and continue to define our sense of American identity today. Was U.S. expansion overseas a logical extension of the notion of the manifest destiny which had propelled the United States into Mexican territory only fifty years earlier?[25] Was the United States, as Assistant Secretary of State John Bassett Moore suggested in 1912, merely "following a habit that had characterized our entire national existence"?[26] Or was U.S. intervention in the war in 1898 a departure from the U.S. heritage, marking what one scholar has called the "birth of imperialism"?[27] If so, could it be justified by moral and ethical imperatives aimed at aiding a less fortunate neighbor, staunching the abuses of Spanish tyranny, and saving Cuban souls from Catholic religious orthodoxy?[28]

Since its first major military intervention in Latin America one hundred years ago, the United States has had to deal with an inherent paradox of promoting American "democratic values" abroad, while often violating those same standards. The United States has tried to have it both ways—it claims to want democracy, but it wants to control the outcomes of its interventions. Thus, it intervenes to promote democracy abroad, but then turns a deaf ear and a blind eye to (or worse, persecutes) those whose ideas are perceived as incompatible with U.S. interests. The imposition of the Platt Amendment in the wake of the war is symbolic of this paradox. Under this amendment, which was appended to the Cuban Constitution and incorporated into a permanent treaty in 1903, Cuba was effectively made a protectorate state of the United States.[29] In the name of promoting democracy, the amendment denied Cuba the right to enter into contracts with foreign powers or to contract public debt and granted the United States the right to intervene in Cuba as it saw fit.[30] Underlying this act was an assumption that the United States alone could determine who was capable of self-government and who was not.

U.S. democracy one hundred years ago was undergoing a crisis at home, characterized by the questioning of the privileges of those who had political and economic power. American society was divided on many fronts—by region, class, gender, and race and ethnicity. Tensions between the North and the South continued to be heated in the wake of the Civil War and Reconstruction. Manifest destiny had justified the extension of U.S. territory clear to the Pacific Ocean in an expansion that entailed the forcible removal of indigenous peoples and Hispanics and the conquest of more than one-half of Mexico's national territory. After decades of confrontations with indigenous peoples in the path of western expansion, the U.S. Supreme Court had alienated many Native Americans when it ruled in *Elk v. Wilkins* (1884) that the Indians were not eligible to be citizens endowed with commensurate legal rights.[31] By the late 1880s, the Indians had been reduced to a population of some three hundred thousand individuals divided among 119 reservations, 50 of which were completely subject to presidential will.[32] Following their congregation on reservations, many Indians turned from armed resistance to cultural resistance. From 1869 until the 1890s, the cult of the Ghost Dance swept the West. The dance showcased dream visionaries who prophesied "the imminent return of the dead . . . , the ousting of the whites, and the restoration of Indian lands, food supplies, and way of life."[33] On 29 December 1890, U.S. soldiers opened fire on 146 Sioux men, women, and children at Wounded Knee, South Dakota, concluding the last major "battle" against the Indians.[34]

Disparities between the rich and the poor reached an all-time high during the Gilded Age. In 1890, the top 1 percent of the population received the same total income as that of the lowest half and owned more property than that owned by the remaining 99 percent of the population.[35] In Chicago's infamous Haymarket Square riots against police brutality in 1886, a bomb exploded, a wave of arrests were enacted against anarchists and alleged anarcho-syndicalists, and four anarchists were killed. Reporting on the riots, the Cuban patriot José Martí, an astute observer and interpreter of U.S. realities, wrote of a growing class-based divide that was creating two Americas in the heart of the United States. He observed, "The nation is terrified by the increased organization among the lower classes, by the sudden agreement among the working masses. . . . It is frightened of the impending separation of the country's population into the same two classes of privileged and discontented that cause so much ferment in European society."[36]

With industrialization and urbanization, the position of women (and with it, the nature of gender relations) in American society was also changing. Particularly following the depression of 1893, women entered industry, business, and professions in large numbers, mostly as domestic servants and in low-paying industrial jobs.[37] In 1890 the census showed that more than 4 million women were in the workforce. By the end of that decade, the figure had risen to 5.3 million.[38] Progressive women, particularly among the anarchists and socialists, were advocating for social and economic equality, and questioning traditional gender roles and relations. "Bicycle-riding, bloomer-wearing, college-educated, job-holding New Women," Kristin Hoganson argues, had put American manhood in a state of crisis.[39] Women were seeking to lay claim to the rights, guarantees, and economic opportunities that were an inherent part of full citizenship.

Yet the late 1890s was a period of relatively little progress for women. After the measure for women's suffrage was first introduced in 1868 and achieved a modicum of popularity, particularly in the West, support for the suffragists hit a low point in the years from 1896 to 1910. During that time, legislators in six state referendums (held three times in Oregon, and once each in Washington, South Dakota, and New Hampshire) opposed the measure to give women the vote. Women's efforts to gain the vote would not prove successful until the passage of the Nineteenth Amendment in 1920. At the close of the nineteenth century, the U.S. populace continued to hold widespread views that relegated women to the "private" sphere and men to "public" endeavors.[40]

African Americans, like Native Americans and women, were also experiencing setbacks in their quest for fuller participation. Following the Civil War, the Reconstruction era had ushered in a period of enfranchisement supported by federal laws that prohibited outright racial discrimination. From 1890 until 1908, however, every state of the former Confederacy enacted legislation that effectively disenfranchised blacks.[41] Some states required voters to be able to read and interpret the Constitution (a prerequisite that was unevenly applied to the disadvantage of blacks); others imposed stiff property requirements or polling taxes.[42] When blacks tried to overcome Jim Crow laws that segregated society and curtailed their civil rights, extra-official mechanisms were implemented to ensure their subordination. From 1889 to 1899, an annual average of 187.5 lynchings took place in the U.S. South.[43]

The presence of large numbers of immigrants raised further questions about who would be eligible to partake of the benefits of U.S. democracy. More than 9 million immigrants entered the United States in the last decades of the nineteenth century, bringing the U.S. population to nearly 76 million people. Until 1895 most of these immigrants were from northern or western Europe, but in the final five years of the nineteenth century, the majority of the immigrants were from southern or eastern Europe. The presence of these newcomers prompted new exclusionary policies and laws favoring immigration from northern and western Europe. (Until that time, the Chinese Exclusion Act passed by Congress in 1882 and extended indefinitely in 1902 was the only major legislation to restrict immigration from a specific geographic region.)

On the surface, the War of 1898 seemed to bring the country together. The war distracted the country from many of the domestic political, economic, and social battles raging at the time. It provided a national purpose that subsumed regional differences. North and South set aside their grievances for the first time since the Civil War and fought side by side in military combat. East and West united in common cause. A series of six cartoons by Frederick B. Opper, "The Spanish War Has Ended All Our Other Wars," published in the *New York Herald* (5 June 1898), illustrates this pervasive spirit of unity in satirical fashion. Opper's cartoons show the patriotic unification of capitalists and workers, teamsters and bicyclists, gold and free-silver advocates, ball players and umpires, tenement-house dwellers, and theater-goers.

Yet the war also exposed the fault lines in U.S. democracy, particularly in its application overseas. Contested ideas about class, race and ethnicity, and gender that had shaped domestic policy agendas influenced U.S. policies abroad. In Cuba, for example, U.S. policymakers sought to exclude the heavily Afro-Cuban military forces (*mambises*), who had been struggling to gain independence from Spain for half a century, in favor of a more deferential, upper-class, white, elite government. U.S. soldiers displaced Cubans from the front lines. U.S. officers forbade the Cuban rebel forces from entering the eastern capital of Santiago de Cuba and kept them out of the peace talks there. U.S. government authorities later excluded Cubans (to say nothing of the inhabitants of the other Spanish colonies) from the negotiations of the peace treaty in Paris that ended the war, and from later ceremonies transferring control of the island to the United States.[44] In practice, Cubans of all backgrounds were excluded from a more equitable relationship with the United States.

The War of 1898 put U.S. democracy on trial, especially in the eyes of the rest of the Western Hemisphere. Many Spanish American writers during the eighteenth-century revolution of the United States and the nineteenth-century revolutions in Latin America, looked to the United States and France as the models of revolutionary achievement, personal liberty, equal opportunity, and democratic governance. In the last speech he would give before his death, the Argentine statesman and intellectual Domingo Sarmiento addressed a group in Asunción, Paraguay. He noted, "It was in [the United States] that I studied the reasons for that nation's extraordinary development, and the bases of its liberties, in order to apply them to our lands. Thus the two extremes of America are linked in a single thought, and are moved by the hope that all the rest will soon follow in this great movement."[45]

This admiration for U.S. freedoms, tempered in midcentury during the U.S. war against Mexico, gave way by the end of the nineteenth century to concerns that the United States was more interested in safeguarding its accomplishments than in upholding democratic ideals. In 1884 the Cuban patriot José Martí warned, "The nation which has been the home of liberty must not—God forbid!—become the dragon on which conquest mounts, nor the new tomb of mankind, in the manner of those despotic or corrupt nations which have degraded or dominated the world."[46]

By the end of the nineteenth century, a new struggle—this time between Spanish America and Anglo-Saxon America—emerged in the battle for American identity. After the first international conference of American states was held in Washington in 1889, which led to the creation of the Pan-American Union the following year, Martí judged the United States to be "a nation that is beginning to regard liberty as its sole privilege, and [to] invoke it to deprive other nations of theirs."[47] In its own defense, argued Martí, Latin America must engage in a quest for a national and continental identity that set it apart from the imperial powers. Martí's "Nuestra América" (1891) gave voice to the urgent need to create this new identity. In that seminal essay, he called on Latin America to forge its own path—inspired but not dominated by U.S. democratic principles and models.

One cannot help but note a certain disappointment among the Latin American intellectuals in the war and postwar periods regarding U.S. notions of democracy. In his essay "Ariel" (1900), the Uruguayan José Enrique Rodó cautioned Latin American youths, enamored of U.S. economic and military prowess, to maintain their own spiritual identity. Soon thereafter Rubén Darío admonished in his poem "To Roosevelt" (1905) that Latin America would not easily succumb to domination by its neighbor to the north:

> Our América . . . lives.
> And dreams. And loves, and is the daughter of the Sun.
> Be careful. . . .
> You must become, by God's own will,
> the deadly Rifleman and the dreadful Hunter
> before you can clutch us in your iron claws.[48]

The War of 1898 was pivotal in the reconstruction and reconfiguring of the notion of America. It provided Latin Americans with cause to rethink their relationship with both Spain and their neighbor to the north.[49] Ironically, the war provided an occasion for Latin Americans to begin a process of reconciliation with their mother country. Latin America's new national elites needed to simultaneously control their own ethnically mixed populations and find international allies who would back their efforts. They now saw in Spain a potential ally against U.S. hegemonic aspirations. As the Spanish philosopher José Gaos has noted, "Spain . . . was the last Hispano-American nation that needed to gain independence—from itself and from the empire under which both Spanish America and peninsular Spain suffered."[50] Spain's liberation from its imperial practices, Gaos argues, achieved only after the U.S. victory in the War of 1898, allowed Spain to move toward a new relationship of reconciliation with its former colonies.[51]

The battles to define America and the relationship between the various entities contained in the Americas continue. As globalization, migration, war, and displacement create societies that are increasingly multicultural, the question "Whose America?" continues to be relevant. At the end of 1999, in a speech at the third international congress of Filosofía y Cultura del Caribe in Bahía Blanca, Argentina, the Mexican intellectual Leopoldo Zea underscored a shift that has occurred since the last century. He noted, "At the end of this century and this millennium, we can no longer speak of two Americas, ours as Latin and that of the north as Saxon, in a dialectic confrontation. We must speak of the America which extends from Alaska to Tierra del Fuego. . . . What was previously separated by history is now integrated by it."[52]

This volume examines the War of 1898 and the debates about American and national identities from a variety of geographic and thematic perspectives. It includes essays presented by four of the current authors (Lester D. Langley, Sylvia L. Hilton, Louis A. Pérez, Jr., and Francisco A. Scarano) at a conference, "Challenges to Peace in the Americas, 1898–1998: Lessons from the Past, Visions for the Future," held at the Library of Congress in October 1998.* The primary goal of the conference was to bring together academics and policymakers to reflect upon the context and impact of U.S. military intervention in the Caribbean in 1898, the subsequent development of international and regional conflict resolution mechanisms, and the current status of U.S.-Latin American relations. This volume includes sections on the historical underpinnings of the war, the war itself, and the legacies of the war. It also includes five new essays which address various aspects of domestic opposition to U.S. bellicose policies in Latin America, the gendered dimensions of U.S. congressional debates over the appropriate U.S. role in Cuba, the role of political cartoons in codifying images of Latin America, and the multiple divisions of the Cuban nation and their visions for the future of Cuba.

*The remaining conference papers (by Julio Ramos, Lars Schoultz, Douglas Farah, Margaret E. Crahan, Edgar J. Dosman, Michael Shifter, and John Cavanagh) deal with the evolution of U.S. foreign policies toward Latin America and the development of international human rights standards in the twentieth century; they will be published in a subsequent volume by Praeger.

The essays in this volume address various aspects of the different U.S. experiences and experiments in hemispheric intervention (diplomatic, economic, and cultural, as well as military) and the diverse responses to and legacies of such intervention. They examine the ways in which various nations have been marked by the events of the last century, beginning particularly with the events culminating in the War of 1898. Taken together, these essays begin to suggest the complexities involved in the formation of national identities, the pivotal role that the war played in exacerbating some tensions and suppressing others, at least temporarily, and the ongoing concerns over the ownership of America and its history. Collectively, they lead us to rethink our conceptualizations of the complex web of relations between, across, and within nations. They form the backbone of an approach to history that seeks out the local inflections of transnational phenomena.

The War of 1898, like any war, is steeped in controversy, in part because of the different perspectives presented by each contender for power. Yet while mythic national visions certainly existed or were invented to help cohere a national consciousness, the essays in this volume break down these monoliths. While traditional historiography can be divided into works that explore the causes, consequences, and conduct of the war, these essays are marked by the ways in which they signal the impact of the war and debates about the war not only on the formation of national consciousness in the United States, but in each of the locations affected by the war, especially Spain, Cuba, Puerto Rico, and the Philippines.[53]

Part 1 of the book lays out the historical underpinnings of the War of 1898 and provides the context for U.S. military intervention in the Caribbean at the turn of the last century. Lester D. Langley discusses the development of a hemisphere that contained two Americas, forged by centuries of historical contact and defined primarily by their differences. He begins by discussing the evolution of the notion of America and the Americas. He traces the ways in which culture and politics have shaped the meanings of American identity (which alternately included and excluded Latin America) since the 1770s. At the same time, Langley alludes to the struggles for power between regions within the United States (New England, the Middle Atlantic states, the lower Mississippi Valley) over the direction of U.S. foreign policy, and he suggests that the U.S. rejection of a hemispheric partnership responded more to regional attitudes and domestic concerns than to federal expansionist ambitions. He cautions that while the present trend appears to be moving toward economic and political integration, the historical record reminds us not to lose sight of the local factors. His essay sets the stage for the remaining essays, each of which addresses in some way the conflicting identities of multiple communities involved directly or tangentially in the contest to control and define America at the end of the nineteenth century.

The essays in Part 2 of this volume analyze the debates, discourse, and images about the war from a variety of geographic locations and perspectives. Sylvia L. Hilton presents a perspective of the war from the vantage point of Spain, which was fighting to hold on to the last remnants of its colonial empire in America. In the aftermath of defeat, the war became known simply as "*el desastre*," the disaster. It marked the definitive end of Spanish colonialism in the New World and spawned a collective angst and analysis of Spanish national character depicted in the writings of an entire generation, the so-called Generation of '98, and their successors, who pondered the nature of Spanish national character, honor, and identity.[54]

In her chapter, Hilton analyzes the ways in which Spanish political discourse opposing U.S. intervention was part of a destabilizing rhetoric in the domestic struggles to reconstitute or fashion the Spanish nation. She elucidates the appropriations of the Monroe Doctrine, which served as an "international cultural icon" whose meaning varied within and across several cultural systems, and she underscores the rhetorical usefulness of the Monroe Doctrine within the context of Spanish domestic policies. Hilton argues convincingly that in the political climate of the day, the defense of Spanish conciliatory positions discredited a government which was already under attack. Her analysis of both the domestic debates in Spain over the U.S. intervention in the colonial crises from 1895 to 1898, and the widely divergent interpretations of U.S. intervention, international human rights standards, and the Monroe Doctrine at the time reveals the shifting rationales given in Spain and Europe regarding U.S. intervention in Spain's overseas colonies.

Lillian Guerra's chapter then analyzes the conflicting nationalisms expressed in the politics of the Cuban exile community and that of the Cuban nationals struggling for independence on the island. Guerra underscores the ways in which each group sought to define and control the image of the Cuban revolution before, during, and after the war. Cuban émigré leaders interpreted the war, envisioned the nature of the nation-state, and related to the United States from a particular ideological and geographic site which was contingent upon their location in the American landscape. Guerra provides a nuanced analysis of the divisions among Cubans on the island and on the mainland, and their legacies for contemporary debates about the nature of Cuban society, conflicting identities and nationalisms, and U.S.-Cuban relations. She shows how the PRC (Partido Revolucionario Cubano) émigré's views of nation were what she calls "imperialist nationalist," based on Latin American liberal ideologies that favored foreign investment, the plantation model, and the mythic ideal of a white, culturally homogeneous, and politically conservative America. Following the death of José Martí, the intellectual most responsible for an inclusive project for Cuban independence, the PRC recast its function and that of the revolution to appeal to the U.S. public, dismissing the demands of blacks and working-class émigrés alike in order to represent the aspirations of the Cubans as identical to those represented by U.S. myths of social progress and inclusive democracy. Ideologies about race, ethnicity, and class (and although not fully explored here by Guerra, gender) shaped the émigré's visions of self and Cuba, and the projection of that self in the images conveyed to win over the U.S. public to the Cuban cause.[55] This projection responded to Spanish racial ideologies in that the PRC sought to contest Spanish representations of the revolutionary forces as "ignorant Negroes" and engaged in its own campaign of anti-Spanish and anti-Catholic propaganda. Not incidentally, Guerra suggests that the PRC shared considerable responsibility (with the U.S. media industry and yellow journalists) for packaging the Cuban revolution to suit its own needs.

In her chapter on political cartoons and the War of 1898, Virginia M. Bouvier analyzes the visual discourse provided in U.S. political cartoons published in one prominent New York newspaper in the critical period just prior to U.S. intervention and during the war itself. Her essay documents the ways in which images reflected and shaped evolving concepts of national identity as the United States gained a sense of self-importance in the course of the war. The cartoons reveal the schisms within the body politic over going to war, and how once the decision was made to declare war on Spain (retroactively, it might be noted, to precede Spain's own formal declaration of war), the war was transformed, literally and figuratively, into a source of national unity. In tandem with U.S. imperial actions, cartoons also largely excluded the inhabitants of the intervened colonial societies. When the Spanish colonial subjects were represented at all, they were portrayed as unreasonable, childish, ungrateful, and culturally or politically inferior to their U.S. counterparts. Such representations ultimately justified the marginalization of colonial subjects from the conduct of their own national affairs. These insidious images have persisted and provide unwritten scripts that reinforce attitudes of U.S. superiority underlying current inter-American relations. Following the war, the cartoons also provided an avenue for critiquing U.S. imperialist policies and expressed concerns over the integration of these racially different "others" into the American nation.

Shifting to the halls of the U.S. Congress, Kristin Hoganson provides another prism through which to view domestic debates about U.S. national character and national interests. Hoganson argues that gendered discourse defined the Spanish-American and Philippine-American conflicts in terms of honor and manhood, frames which made entering the war an imperative of manhood and a defining element of national identity. This public articulation of the imperatives of honor effectively marginalized both women (who had not yet gained the vote) and male anti-imperialists alike from the nation, and solidified, at least temporarily, white male hegemony in a moment when notions of manhood were perceived to be under attack.

In Part 3 of this volume, the authors analyze case studies of the legacies of the war as it related to Cuba, Puerto Rico, the Philippines, and the United States. Louis A. Pérez, Jr. argues that although Cuba succeeded in gaining independence from Spain, postwar conditions, particularly the severe dislocations, massive devastation, and the magnitude of material impoverishment of the island made Cuban society particularly vulnerable to a vast transfer of U.S. cultural mores, market-driven values, and representational forms. Cuban separatists, he argues, were particularly ill equipped to define the terms of the nationhood for which they had fought.

In the following chapter, Francisco A. Scarano argues for the need to analyze the case of Puerto Rico in relation to the history of the United States and U.S. expansionism. U.S. intervention in (or, as Scarano argues, possession of) Puerto Rico in 1898 continues to define the shape of the island's political, economic, and cultural relationships with the mainland. Scarano notes that Puerto Rico's experience of 1898 both prefigured and anticipated the consequences of similar interventions in other Latin American nations. Local collaboration was critical in establishing the contours of the ensuing relationship, which was marked by the island's complete, if constitutionally ambiguous, incorporation into the U.S. sphere. The depth of nationalist sentiment in Puerto Rico and the extent to which the United States continues to "possess" that island despite repeated efforts by the Puerto Rican people to define a new relationship with the United States came to a head at the opening of the twenty-first century, when the United States determined that it would continue to hold naval exercises on the island of Vieques despite years of protest on the part of the island's inhabitants.[56]

We then turn to the war in the Philippines and the domestic ideological battles to define America's identity and its future role in the world which U.S. engagement there provoked. In the final chapter, Jim Zwick analyzes the factors affecting the emergence, formation, influence, strategies, and eventual demise of the Anti-Imperialist League and other social actors who opposed U.S. imperialist policies overseas. He argues that the Anti-Imperialist League warrants special recognition as the first of a succession of anti-imperialist, noninterventionist, and solidarity groups that were formed in the twentieth century. Such groups are in the twenty-first century an integral and increasingly recognized part of the fabric of American society. Zwick's work effectively reweaves the American social fabric in a way that reveals the multiple threads represented by nongovernmental organizations trying to affect the policymaking process a century ago. His provocative essay reveals an America divided by the struggle to design foreign policies consistent with democratic ideals.

Taken together, these essays suggest a wide range of themes that merit further investigation, including questions of national identity; the roots, continuities, and changes in human rights advocacy; the long-range impact of interventions; the role of nationalism and sovereignty in war and resistance; the roles of images, gender, race and ethnicity, and class in the formation of foreign policies; and questions of representation and legitimacy.

The essays invite consideration of cross-national approaches and perspectives, are sure to prompt new research in this growing field, and contribute to a broader understanding of the significance of the war for subsequent U.S. policy debates.

NOTES

1. Quoted in Seymour Hersh, *The Price of Power* (New York: Summit, 1983), 263.
2. Eric Hobsbawm, with Antonio Polito, *On the Edge of the New Century* (New York: New Press, 2000).
3. In 1893 American businessmen overthrew Hawaii's sovereign, Queen Lilioukalani, and U.S. troops were sent in. In 1993 President Bill Clinton signed into law a joint resolution (PL 103–150), which apologized for U.S. actions in Hawaii one century earlier. For a discussion of the struggles over Hawaiian sovereignty, see Deborah Wei and Rachael Kamel, *Resistance in Paradise: Rethinking 100 Years of U.S. Involvement in the Caribbean and the Pacific* (Philadelphia: American Friends Service Committee in cooperation with Office of Curriculum Support, School District of Philadelphia, 1998), 131–58.
4. In March 1998, under pressure from historians and activists, Library of Congress officials announced they would change the official classification of the "Philippine Insurrection" to the "Philippine-American War" and the "Philippine Revolution." See Jim Zwick, "Library of Congress Recognizes Philippine Revolution and Philippine-American War," *Sentenaryo/Centennial*, online at http://www. bondocksnet.com/sctexts/loc_cats.html [Accessed 12 July 2000].
5. Angel Smith and Emma Dávila-Cox, *The Crisis of 1898: Colonial Redistribution and Nationalist Mobilization* (New York: St. Martin's Press, 1999), 1.
6. Quoted in Edward W. Said, *Culture and Imperialism* (New York: Vintage Books, 1994), 4.
7. Louis A. Pérez, Jr., *The War of 1898: The United States and Cuba in History and Historiography* (Chapel Hill: University of North Carolina Press, 1998), ix–x.
8. Interview with the author, 8 September 1998.
9. Phone interview with the author, 11 July 2000.
10. To view the website of the Hispanic Division of the Library of Congress website, see "The World of 1898: The Spanish-American War," at http://lcweb.loc.gov/rr/hispanic/1898/ [Accessed 13 July 2000].
11. Fred Harvey Harrington, "The Anti-Imperialist Movement in the United States, 1898–1900," *Mississippi Valley Historical Review* 22 (1935): 211, 223.
12. Smithsonian National Portrait Gallery, "Theodore Roosevelt: Icon of the American Century," at http://www.npg.si.edu/exh/roosevelt/trintro2.htm [Accessed 13 July 2000].
13. Tom Miller, "Remember the Maine," abstract online at *Smithsonian Magazine* (February 1998), http://www.smithsonianmag.si.edu/smithsonian/issues98/feb98/maine.html [Accessed 12 July 2000].
14. Amy Kaplan and Donald Pease, eds., *Cultures of U.S. Imperialism* (Durham, N.C.: Duke University Press, 1993); and Pérez, *War of 1898* provide numerous examples.

15. Edna Acosta-Belén and Carlos E. Santiago, "Merging Borders: The Remapping of America," *The Latino Review of Books* 1, no. 1 (spring 1995), 5.

16. Acosta-Belén and Santiago, "Merging Borders," 5.

17. Brook Larmer, "Latin U.S.A.: How Young Hispanics Are Changing America," 4 July 1999, TBH Online, http://www.tbhonline.com/cns/9907/990704latin_usa.htm [Accessed 3 July 2000].

18. See Howard Zinn's introductory remarks with regard to the Philippines in Daniel B. Schirmer, *Republic or Empire: American Resistance to the Philippine War* (Cambridge: Schenkman Publishing Company, 1972).

19. See Margaret E. Crahan, "The Evolution of International Human Rights Standards and Organizations: Their Impact on Conflict Resolution," in Virginia M. Bouvier, ed., *The Globalization of U.S.-Latin American Relations: Democracy, Intervention, and Human Rights* (Westport, Ct.: Praeger, 2001).

20. *Congressional Record*, 58th Congress, 3rd session, p. 19.

21. See Lars Schoultz, "Evolving Concepts of Intervention: Promoting Democracy," and Carrie A. Foster, "Confronting Economic Imperialism, 1915–1930," in Bouvier, *Globalization of U.S.-Latin American Relations.*

22. More than one hundred of these films are held in the Library of Congress Motion Picture, Broadcasting and Recorded Sound Division. Some sixty-eight motion pictures are available online through the American Memory project of the Library of Congress. See "The Spanish-American War in Motion Pictures," at http://memory.loc.gov/ammem/sawhtml/sawhome.html [Accessed 12 July 2000].

23. See Carrie A. Foster, *The Women and the Warriors* (Syracuse, N.Y.: Syracuse University Press, 1995); Schirmer, *Republic or Empire*, 7; and Jim Zwick, "The Anti-Imperialist Movement, 1898–1921," this volume.

24. For examples of domestic opposition to the Mexican-American War, slavery, the Civil War, and earlier U.S. attempts to annex Cuba, the Sandwich Islands (including Hawaii), and Santo Domingo (Dominican Republic), see Philip S. Foner and Richard C. Winchester, *The Anti-Imperialist Reader, Vol. I: From the Mexican War to the Election of 1900* (New York: Holmes & Meier Publishers, 1984); and Schirmer, *Republic or Empire*, 7.

25. See discussions in Albert K. Weinberg, *Manifest Destiny: A Study of Nationalist Expansionism in American History* (Chicago: Quadrangle, 1935; reprint, 1963); Julius W. Pratt, "Manifest Destiny and the American Century," *Current History* 29, no. 172 (1955): 331–36; and John Fiske, "Manifest Destiny," *Harper's New Monthly Magazine* 70 (1885): 578–90.

26. Quoted in Philip Foner, *The Spanish-Cuban-American War and the Birth of Imperialism, 1895–1902* (New York: Monthly Review Press, 1972), viii.

27. Ibid.

28. James Henry Brownlee, ed., *War-Time Echoes: Patriotic Poems, Heroic and Pathetic, Humorous and Dialectic, of the Spanish-American War* (New York: Werner, 1898), ix.

29. See Louis A. Pérez, Jr., *Cuba between Empires, 1878–1902* (Pittsburgh, Pa.: University of Pittsburgh Press, 1983); and his *Cuba under the Platt Amendment* (Pittsburgh, Pa.: University of Pittsburgh Press, 1986).

30. See Wilfrid Hardy Callcott, *The Caribbean Policy of the United States*, 1890–1920 (New York: Octagon Books, 1966), 180.

31. The opposite strategy was enacted in Canada. See Roger L. Nichols, *Indians*

in the United States and Canada: A Comparative History (Lincoln: University of Nebraska Press, 1998), 226.

32. Deborah Shnookal and Mirta Muñiz, *José Martí Reader: Writings on the Americas* (New York: Ocean Press, 1999), 53–55. A classic text on the situation of the American Indians at the end of the nineteenth century is Helen Hunt Jackson, *A Century of Dishonor: A Sketch of the United States Government's Dealings with Some of the Tribes* (New York: Harper & Brothers, 1881).

33. "Ghost Dance," *Encyclopædia Britannica Online*, at <http://www.search.eb.com/bol/topic?idxref=138190> [Accessed 10 July 2000].

34. Eric Foner and John A. Garraty, eds., *The Reader's Companion to American History* (n.p.: Houghton Mifflin, 1991), online at http://www.historychannel.com/perl/print_book.pl?ID=35845 [Accessed 6 July 2000].

35. Eric Foner, *The Story of American Freedom* (New York: W. W. Norton & Company, 1998), 117.

36. José Martí [Buenos Aires, 1888], in Shnookal and Muñiz, *José Martí Reader*, 87.

37. Foner, *Story of American Freedom*, 109.

38. Eleanor Flexner, *Century of Struggle: The Women's Rights Movement in the United States* (New York: Athencum, 1971), 230.

39. Kristin L. Hoganson, *Fighting for American Manhood: How Gender Politics Provoked the Spanish-American and Philippine-American Wars* (New Haven: Yale University Press, 1998), 12.

40. Mary Ryan, *Womanhood in America: From Colonial Times to the Present* (New York: Harper and Row, 1975).

41. "United States, history of," *Encyclopaedia Britannica Online*, at http://www.eb.com:180/bol/topic?eu=121261&sctn=10 [Accessed 24 June 2000].

42. For a discussion of the relationship between segregationist legislation and political disenfranchisement in the South, see C. Vann Woodward, *The Strange Career of Jim Crow* (New York: Oxford University Press, 1955); and Joel Williamson, *The Crucible of Race: Black-White Relations in the American South since Emancipation* (New York: Oxford University Press, 1984).

43. "United States, history of," *Encyclopaedia Britannica Online*, at http://www.eb.com:180/bol/topic?eu=121261&sctn=10 [Accessed 24 June 2000].

44. On U.S. relations with the Cuban Liberation Army and the conflicting accounts of Cuban participation in the war, see Pérez, *War of 1898*, esp. 81–107.

45. Domingo Sarmiento [Asunción, 30 May 1887], *Discursos populares* (Buenos Aires, 1927), 245–46; cited in José de Onís, *The United States as Seen by Spanish American Writers, 1776–1890* (New York: Hispanic Institute in the United States, 1952), 196.

46. José Martí, *Obras completas* (hereafter *OC*), 74 vols., ed. Gonzalo de Quesada y Miranda (Havana, 1936–1953), 16: 187; cited in Onís, *United States as Seen by Spanish American Writers*, 197.)

47. Martí, *OC*, 21:50; cited in ibid., 197–98.

48. Rubén Darío, "A Roosevelt," in Stephen Tapscott, ed., *Twentieth-Century Latin American Poetry: A Bilingual Anthology* (Austin: University of Texas Press, 1996): 38–39.

49. See Aurea Matilde Fernández Muñiz, "España y Cuba: ruptura y continuidad en el 98," *Casa de las Américas*, no. 211 (April–June 1998): 78–83.

50. Quoted in Leopoldo Zea, "1898, Latinoamérica y la reconciliación iberoamericana," *Cuadernos americanos* [Mexico], no. 74 (March–April 1999): 13.

51. Recent centennial congresses have examined the ongoing effects of the war on the relationship between Spain, Latin America, and the Caribbean. The theme of the sixth international congress of the Sociedad Latinoamericana de Estudios Sobre América Latina y el Caribe (*SOLAR*), which met in Toluca, Mexico, 16–19 November 1998 was "Primer centenario de la reconciliación ibero-americana, 1898–1998." See the conference papers published in *Cuadernos americanos* [Mexico], no. 74 (March–April 1999).

52. "En este fin de siglo y de milenio no podemos ya hablar de dos Américas, la nuestra como latina y la del norte como sajona en dialéctico enfrentamiento. Debemos hablar de la América que va desde Alaska hasta la Tierra de Fuego. . . . Lo que la historia antes separaba, ahora lo integra." [Trans. mine.] Leopoldo Zea, "Identidad continental multirracial y multicultural," *Cuadernos americanos* [Mexico] 2, no. 80 (March–April 2000): 15.

53. This volume does not, unfortunately, include a chapter on Guam. For background on Guam, one of the Mariana Islands ceded to the United States, see Robert Rogers, *Destiny's Landfall: A History of Guam* (Honolulu: University of Hawaii Press, 1995); Pedro C. Sanchez, *Guahan Guam: The History of Our Island* (Agaña, Guam: Sanchez Publishing House, 1988); and Wei and Kamel, *Resistance in Paradise*, 109–30.

54. For an interesting assessment of the disjuncture between Cuban colonial realities and Spanish intellectuals of the time, see Enrico Mario Santí, "Cuba, Spain, and '98: Narcissism, Melancholy, and the Crisis of Historical Memory," *Cuban Studies* 28 (Pittsburgh, Pa.: University of Pittsburgh Press, 1999).

55. See Guerra, this volume; Joseph Smith, "The American Image of the Cuban Insurgents in 1898," *Zeitschrift feur Anglistik und Amerikanistik* 40, no. 4 (1992): 319; and Francesco Federico Falco, "La representación de Cuba Libre durante la 'última guerra de independencia,' " *Cuba Contemporánea* 19 (February 1919): 120–48.

56. Robert Rabin, Archivo Histórico de Vieques, "Vieques: Five Centuries of Struggles and Resistance," online at http://www.vieques-island.com/rabin.html [Accessed 8 July 2000].

PART I

HISTORICAL UNDERPINNINGS OF FOREIGN INTERVENTION

1

The Two Americas

Lester D. Langley

"America" is a protean word continually redefined by politics and culture. For lexicographers and most geographers, of course, "America" and "Americas" may always mean the Western Hemisphere. In English, however, "America" is commonly understood to stand for the United States and "American" to refer to a resident of the United States; "pro-" and "anti-American" are taken to refer to sentiments about the United States. A Costa Rican or a Brazilian may not wince when a visitor from the United States casually uses "American" to refer only to a person from the United States, but the Mexican or Chilean may take offense, preferring "North American" or perhaps *estadounidense* ("United Statesian"), and our Canadian neighbors will insist that they are also North Americans but definitely not Americans. In 1800 the learned used "America" and "Americans" as hemispheric references. By 1900 North and Latin American cultural and political elites identified two Americas to denote sharply different and often conflicting cultural preferences. In our times, they still do.[1]

One of the earliest definitions of the Two Americas came in the revolutionary age of the Americas (1770s–1820s). As the revolutionary movements in South America were ending in the early 1820s, U.S. leaders were expressing dismay about Latin America's prospects for self-governance and suspicions about closer political ties with the new Spanish American republics. Edward Everett expressed a sentiment fairly common among his contemporaries when he wrote in the prestigious *North American Review*, "We have no concern with South America; we have no sympathy, we can have no well founded political sympathy with them. We are sprung from different stocks."[2]

Thomas Jefferson, who in the 1780s and 1790s had been more optimistic about the revolutionary promise in the Americas, penned a more confusing definition of "America" in his final years. In a decade when U.S. leaders were purposefully articulating a unifying political language for the nation while simultaneously assessing the meaning of Spanish-American independence, Jefferson incorporated the new republics of Spanish America in his definition of "America," but he was doubtful about their political future. "History," he asserted, "furnishes no example of a priest-ridden people maintaining a free civil government." Yet that prospect was for Jefferson preferable to continued European rule over the continent. He noted, "But in whatever governments they end, they will be American governments, no longer to be involved in the never-ceasing broils of Europe. . . . America has a hemisphere to itself."[3]

To the south would lie republics, Jefferson believed, but they would be weak republics and thus no threat to the United States. Like many of his contemporaries, he was particularly critical of the Venezuelan Simón Bolívar, Spanish America's most famous revolutionary leader, who called for a defensive confederation of Spain's former colonies and who warned his contemporaries about U.S. expansion in the Western Hemisphere. President James Monroe's message of December 1823, though committing the United States to Latin American independence (except, of course, in the strategically important Caribbean, where the Haitian revolution of 1791–1804 had terrified a generation of North and Latin American leaders), did not reassure the skeptical Bolívar. Bolívar's reasoning was a montage of cultural biases and political acumen. Commenting on the proposal for a continental federation, Bolívar noted that the inclusion of Haiti and the United States would be "ill-advised." Great Britain with its naval might, he reflected in the early 1820s, had the power to prevent a European *reconquista* of Spanish America but would try to "lay down the law to us." The United States acted only out of self-interest.[4]

The birth of independent Spanish American republics in the 1820s and the parallel articulation of a distinctive U.S. policy in the Western Hemisphere in the 1820s led to a continuing debate about the Americas embodied in Monroeism, which implied U.S. domination of Latin America, and Bolivarism, which suggested an alternative vision of an alliance of sovereign nations. Both views have persisted down to the present day, yet each is a distortion of the thinking of President James Monroe and his contemporaries and Bolívar. Monroe and especially his secretary of state, John Quincy Adams (Monroe's successor as president), were less concerned about laying out a blueprint for future U.S. expansion in the hemisphere than in responding to the challenges of such trans-Appalachian political upstarts as Andrew Jackson, who called for a more nationalistic foreign policy as a way of securing the nation's southern and southwestern borders and retained throughout his life a deep suspicion of Spanish intrigue in the old Southwest and hostility to Latin American culture. Bolívar did have a continental vision, but his plan for hemispheric unity (expressed in his call for a congress that convened in Panama and then because of the fever plaguing the isthmus moved to Mexico City in 1826) did not include the United States or any of the non-Spanish territories in the Americas because Bolívar believed that only the former Spanish colonies could fashion a strong defensive alliance to shield them from a Spanish reconquest. As the British threat waned, Bolívar's suspicions of U.S. goals in the hemisphere deepened: The North American republic, he wrote in 1829, as the Andrew Jackson administration was pressing Mexico to sell Texas to the United States, "seemed destined by Providence to plague America with torments in the name of freedom."[5]

In the United States, political considerations militated against any strong commitment to the notion of a united hemisphere. From 1810 to the early 1820s, the disintegrating Spanish empire created a crisis with both domestic and international dimensions for the first generation of U.S. political leaders, who were struggling to articulate and then fashion more viable bonds of unity between the states, regions, and citizens within the new United States. In New England or the Middle Atlantic states, few people had experienced the apprehensions felt by residents of the South about the Spanish presence in the lower Mississippi Valley or the Floridas. In this context, then, the contemporary debates within the United States over the precise posture toward the newly emerging Spanish-American states in the 1820s were not simply a matter of the United States rejecting a Latin American offer of hemispheric partnership because of U.S. expansionist ambitions on the North American continent. President John Quincy Adams saw in Bolívar's plan and Spanish-American unity a parallel to the form or at least the spirit of unionism that had taken root in the United States. The American Revolution had culminated in the creation of a federal republic; so, too, had the wars of independence everywhere in mainland Latin America except for Brazil, which became independent in 1889.[6]

But it was doubtful that such a common experience among very different peoples could provide a basis for stronger hemispheric ties between "federated" republics. Just as the promise of neighborhood in the Americas gained strength with Adams and some of his contemporaries, their political challengers were expressing very different views. The peoples of the trans-Appalachian states, who identified with Andrew Jackson (one of Adams's political adversaries), saw the strengthening of the federal government and federal power as menacing to their interests. More important, they had a different view about hemispheric unity than their eastern contemporaries. Though some trans-Appalachian peoples settled as invited migrants in Mexican Texas, the relationship between Mexico and the United States continually worsened, particularly after Texas won its independence from Mexico in 1836, and culminated in war after Texas was admitted into the union nine years later.[7]

The belief that the federal government might win greater public support by responding to expansionist urges helps us to understand U.S. continentalism in the nineteenth century and the relationship of the Two Americas. Within a decade after the U.S. victory over Mexico in 1848, several Latin American governments expressed understandable concerns about the "North American" peril. In 1856 Latin American delegates at a continental congress meeting in Santiago, Chile signed a treaty of mutual assistance, mostly out of fear of filibustering expeditions (particularly that of William Walker and his band, who ruled Nicaragua in the mid-1850s with the tacit blessing of prominent U.S. politicians) and U.S. expansion in the hemisphere. In the early 1880s, Secretary of State James G. Blaine, stressing the common interest of hemispheric nations in quelling intrahemispheric wars and in limiting European (principally British) economic influence, called for a Panamerican conference in which commercial rather than political issues would dominate. With much fanfare, the first in the modern series of inter-American conferences got under way in Washington, D.C., in 1889.[8]

The meeting was not a convening of equals, as the subsequent record of the United States in the hemisphere demonstrated. On the eve of the "Imperial Age" in the history of the Americas—an era of unparalleled U.S. economic, military, and even cultural penetration of Latin America and the Caribbean—the differences in the Two Americas were still striking. Theodore Roosevelt, architect of the new U.S. imperial order, equated America with the United States, which by the 1890s had surpassed the European nations in its industrial might. As president (1901–9), Roosevelt provoked a generation of Latin Americans with his 1904 statement that the United States must be the "policeman" of the Western Hemisphere. The other America, "Our America," was that described in the unforgettable prose of José Martí, who more than any other Cuban (or Latin American) of his generation articulated the Latin response to U.S. pretensions and its arrogant dismissal of Latin American capabilities for governance, sometimes expressed in racist caricatures. Writing in the early 1890s, Martí clearly anticipated the danger Latin Americans confronted in Roosevelt's "America." Although the threat seemed to escalate after the U.S. victory over Spain in 1898, Martí naively believed that the "scorn of our formidable neighbor who does not know us is Our America's greatest danger. And since the day of the visit is near, it is imperative that our neighbor know us, and soon, so that it will not scorn us. Through ignorance it might even come to lay its hands on us. Once it does know us, it will remove its hands out of respect."[9]

More interested in political and ideological goals than in the character of the Caribbean economies where his revolutionary message seemed most appropriate, Martí was the classic example of the Latin American revolutionary whose energies (and life) were expended in a cause that for some seemed more relevant to the revolutionary age in the Americas than the late-nineteenth-century era of economic transformation and social discord. His justification of the Cuban struggle for independence invoked arguments similar to those made by Latin (and British) American revolutionaries more than a century before. "Spain is inferior to Cuba in her aptitude for modern work and free government," he wrote, "and finds it necessary to shut off the island . . . from the productivity of great nations, in order to maintain, by violently oppressing a useful American nation, the only market for Spanish industries and the revenue with which Cuba is paying Spain's debts upon the continent and maintaining in leisure and power the favored and unproductive classes."[10]

His phrases echoed sentiments expressed by a generation of British and Spanish American revolutionaries of an earlier age in the Americas. Yet Martí also spoke to the contemporary condition of people of color and lauded the rights of urban and country laborers throughout the Americas. In this sense, his definition of America incorporated the rural tenant or unemployed industrial laborer or Indian or African American or immigrant of the United States. And, it should be noted, Roosevelt's articulation of North American materialist values and his call for order and progress appealed to a generation of Latin American political leaders who shared the U.S. president's social and racial prejudices. Martí became the intellectual mentor of a generation of Latin American writers, essayists, and poets, and the quintessential revolutionary yet praised throughout the continent, but he was never able to persuade the leaders of "Our America" (particularly the Argentines, Chileans, and even the racially mixed Brazilians) that the cause of Cuba was their cause. U.S. military and industrial might impressed South America's political elites, but such sentiments often reinforced their beliefs about differences. As the Peruvian Francisco García Calderón wrote in 1913, "There are two Americas. In the north . . . is a powerful industrial republic. . . . In the south are twenty leisurely states of unequal civilisation, troubled by anarchy and the colour problem. The prestige of the United States, their imperialism, and their wealth, have cast a shade over the less orderly Latin republics of the south. The title of America seems to be applied solely to the great imperial democracy of the north."[11]

García's comment implied that Latin America (Martí's "Our America") was undeserving of the title of America. Some of his contemporaries (the Uruguayan José Enrique Rodó or the Argentine Manuel Ugarte) were more sharply critical of U.S. material culture despite their occasional acknowledgment of this nation's technological accomplishments. In spite of the obvious disparities between the two Americas—what became known as "Greater America"—the search for a common history gained strength in the aftermath of World War I and reached its zenith in the 1930s and especially in the 1940s, when the U.S. government enthusiastically promoted hemispheric unity as a strategic necessity in waging global war. In a widely discussed essay, a distinguished historian of Spanish borderlands history, Herbert Eugene Bolton, called for more appreciation of the Spanish background of U.S. history in order to understand the history of "Greater America." Bolton's critics pointed out that his concerns lay not so much with the entire hemisphere but with North America's colonial experience. In 1939 the Mexican Edmundo O'Gorman, in an evaluation widely publicized among historians, politely chastised Bolton for his preoccupation with material development and seeming indifference to "spiritual" differences. O'Gorman thus expressed what many Latin American scholars have long contended: the peoples of the Americas may share a continent but they do not share similar beliefs about the meaning of America.[12]

The political and economic experience of the Americas in World War II and especially in the Cold War did not fundamentally alter O'Gorman's judgment that a single American culture was but a myth. Yet in 2000, the notion of One not Two Americas, particularly if the perspective is economic, has gained new adherents. The hemispheric economic future, certainly in North America, promises integration, not diversity. By one reckoning, those who argued for a Latin America modeled on free-market economic principles appear to be vindicated by the economic statistics of the post–Cold War era. Presumably, modernization through economic and political development has at least made possible a quality of life and corresponding individual liberties in Latin America only dimly imagined in the late nineteenth century. Perhaps the most impressive validation of this long-range trend has been Latin America's widespread rejection of authoritarian and military governments and the continent's return to civilian rule and the peaceful transfer of power in the last two decades of the twentieth century.[13]

But the present condition of the Americas does not uniformly conform to the prognoses made in the early 1960s, when the United States supported the Alliance for Progress—an ambitious program dedicated to Latin America's political, economic, and social transformation through peaceful means. The environmental costs of a half-century of development and the distortions accompanying the globalization of hemispheric economies prompt a reconsideration of the development models of the postwar generation.[14] Certainly, with the end of the Cold War, the prospects for hemispheric unity should be heartening. At the two Summits of the Americas held in the 1990s, hemispheric leaders touted their commitment to democracy, human rights, economic integration, eradication of poverty and discrimination, and sustainable development.[15]

Some of these promises echo those made under the auspices of the Alliance for Progress in the 1960s, which failed to materialize in the wake of increased tensions between the United States and Cuba and the resurgence of military governments in Latin America. Will the invigorated hemispheric economies of our time now fulfill the promises of the Alliance for the next generation? Will such trade agreements as NAFTA (North American Free

Trade Agreement) fundamentally transform the three very disparate political entities of Canada, the United States, and Mexico?[16]

Perhaps. But before we subscribe to such reassuring notions about the inevitability of an economic superstructure that facilitates hemispheric economic integration and the presumed convergence of social values, we should consider the historical record. The Western Hemisphere is no longer a combination of powerful and weak national or regional economies but a complex web of transnational, regional, and local economies where the power of the state (even the powerful states) to control or even manage this economic superstructure has diminished. More disturbingly, despite the reality that these may be the best of times in the Americas, national governments throughout the Americas (even in the relatively more prosperous United States and Canada) are at the turn of the twenty-first century confronted with a reality as relevant today as it was a century ago—the widening gulf between those in the upper and lower tiers of society.[17]

Do the prospects for hemispheric economic unity and the parallel sobering comments about deepening social chasms between the "haves" and "have-nots" in every nation in the hemisphere validate the claim of a "common history" of the Americas? I think not. We may be taking the wrong approach when we look for similarities because we are more than likely to find more diversity than similarity in the history of the Americas, especially if the focus is the nation-state. While we must necessarily take into account the role of government and the nation-state and the dynamics of a global economy if we are to explain the history of the Americas since the mid–eighteenth century, we must not lose sight of local factors. Elsewhere, I have suggested that the wars of independence in the Americas could better be understood by giving greater attention to particular dynamics of these wars than to the transatlantic political and ideological issues that divided metropole and colony.[18]

A close examination of the local character of the hemispheric economy gives us a very different perspective. A few examples may suffice to illustrate the importance of looking at certain factors up close. The impact of the North American Free Trade Agreement on the national economy of the United States is negligible, but its influence alters dramatically when the focus shifts to the U.S. and Mexican state border economies and especially to local metropolitan economies. The U.S.-Dominican relationship since the mid-1960s provides another case study of the U.S. role in Latin American political and economic development. Once we consider such myriad but interrelated factors as Dominican migration to the United States, Dominican urbanization, and the transformation of the Dominican countryside over the past three decades, we must necessarily ask broader questions about the nature of that development. Specifically, we cannot understand U.S.-Dominican relations (and, by implication, U.S.-Latin American relations) as simply the imposition of U.S. military and economic power on hapless Dominicans. We must look beyond political and economic configurations to cultural relationships.

A reconsideration of modern revolution in the Americas, particularly in those countries that have endured U.S. military intervention, should help us to understand why it is possible to identify both pro- and anti-American sentiments not only in the same Latin American country but often in the same person! Often, these contradictory feelings can be found in those Latin American countries and people who have suffered most from U.S. intervention. Their anti-Americanism can usually be explained as an understandably hostile reaction to what is perceived as a denial of self-determination. But the Latin American who objects (sometimes violently) to U.S. government policies in the hemisphere may applaud many of the cultural preferences or political values he or she identifies with the people of the United States.[19]

Unarguably, the history of the Western Hemisphere and its peoples is an integral part of global history and culture, but the governments, economies, cultures, and societies of the Two Americas do relate differently to one another than to the rest of the world, and they always have. I am not suggesting that the Americas have a "common history" but that belonging to a common hemisphere has made a difference. Fundamental political, economic, social, and cultural patterns acquire their most persuasive meaning in a hemispheric context. From the age of revolution and the formation of newly independent states until the present, these linkages in the Americas have been ideological (the "idea" of the Western Hemisphere as something distinct from the Old World) as well as material. Among the first U.S. emissaries to the Spanish-American revolutions were Yankee traders who ferried copies of the Declaration of Independence and George Washington's Farewell Address along with the wares they were peddling. In our times, the cultural and commercial exchanges continue. The concept of a hemisphere with a past and especially a future distinct from the rest of the world took hold and continues unto this day.

In a curious but understandable way, the fact that the encounter between several hemispheric nations and cultures has often been conflictive rather than harmonious reinforces the contention that the Americas have a history unlike that of any region of comparable size and diversity in the world. The nations and peoples of the Americas are linked together in obvious ways, such as formal economic and political agreements, but also through informal cultural exchanges and human encounters. Americanization is a global phenomenon, but in the Western Hemisphere its cultural power resonates in often curious ways. Cuba has been the most defiantly anti-American state in the Americas since the late 1950s, but North American culture has exercised a profound influence in shaping Cubans' sense of identity.[20]

Issues that have historically divided hemispheric peoples have also united them. Citizens of the Western Hemisphere may dispute the meaning of revolution but express common professions about the right of self-determination and sovereignty; their political leaders are divided over the degree of state intervention in the national economy but share beliefs that regional or hemispheric economic agreements will better shield their national economies from the uncertainties of global economic and political currents. Modernization has failed to bring about a convergence of social and cultural values in the Americas, as some sociologists were predicting in the 1950s and 1960s, but middle classes throughout the hemisphere have begun to express a common apprehension over the fragmentation of contemporary society and the estrangement of political systems from the citizenry.

The Western Hemisphere in our times exhibits all the promises and the uncertainties and contradictions identified a century ago or even two centuries ago. Thomas Jefferson would be able to comprehend our age; so, too, would José Martí. They would understand the contradictory but interrelated histories of nations and peoples who occupy the same hemisphere and who are linked together in ways their often combative governments can no longer deny. Recognizing and nurturing those binding ties may hold out the best promise that the Two Americas may one day become One not only in thought but in deed.

NOTES

1. Writing at the height of the Cold War in the early 1960s, the distinguished Colombian historian and diplomat Germán Arciniegas identified not Two but Four Americas—Indo-Spanish America, Portuguese America, English America, and Anglo-French America. He noted that "when the colonists of the north became independent and their philosophers gathered in Philadelphia to draw up the constitution of Jefferson and Adams, they did not think of giving the new state a name of its own, and thus the United States is the only country in the world that does not have one. To say United States is like saying federation, republic, or monarchy." Germán Arciniegas, "The Four Americas," in Lewis Hanke, ed., *Do the Americas Have a Common History? A Critique of the Bolton Thesis* (New York: Alfred A. Knopf, 1964): 235–49, esp. 237–38.

2. Quoted in Lester D. Langley, *The Americas in the Age of Revolution, 1750–1850* (New Haven: Yale University Press, 1996), 240. In a recent study, *Beneath the United States: A History of U.S. Policy toward Latin America* (Cambridge: Harvard University Press, 1998), Lars Schoultz effectively shows how the negative historical images of Latin America and Latin Americans—essentially, that Latin America is backward and its peoples inferior—have shaped U.S. policy toward the region. See also Fredrick B. Pike, *The United States and Latin America: Myths and Stereotypes of Civilization and Nature* (Austin: University of Texas Press, 1992); and Leopoldo Zea, *The Role of the Americas in History*, ed. Amy A. Oliver, trans. Sonja Karsen (Savage, Md.: Rowman & Littlefield, 1992).

3. Quoted in Arthur P. Whitaker, *The Western Hemisphere Idea: Its Rise and Decline* (Ithaca: Cornell University Press, 1954), 28, 29. The Mexican philosopher Leopoldo Zea expresses a parallel sentiment from the Latin American perspective.

"The idea of finding yourself on the fringe of history . . . is felt by Americans both of Anglo-Saxon and of Latin descent. However, it is in the latter that this idea acquires greater impact and almost tragic consequences [because] . . . [a]long with Spain [and] Portugal . . . [Latin Americans] ha[ve] been placed on the fringe of a new culture . . . , on the fringe of history" (Zea, *Role of the Americas in History*, 8–9).

4. Quoted in ibid., 158.

5. Quoted in ibid. Haiti and the United States did receive invitations to the Panama conference, principally because the Central Americans believed they should participate. Bolívar had another reason for wishing to exclude the first two independent states of the hemisphere in his proposed confederation: "North Americans and the Haitians are foreigners to us, if only because they are heterogeneous in character." Harold Bierck, ed., *Selected Writings of Bolívar*, Vicente Lecuna, comp., Lewis Bertrand, trans., 2 vols. (New York: Banco de Venezuela, 1951), 2: 507–8; see also 543.

6. See the classic study by Arthur P. Whitaker, *The United States and the Independence of Latin America, 1800–1830* (1941; reprint New York: W. W. Norton, 1964); and John J. Johnson, *A Hemisphere Apart: The Foundations of United States Policy toward Latin America* (Baltimore: Johns Hopkins University Press, 1990). For a contrasting assessment, see Alonso Aguilar, *Pan-Americanism from Monroe to the Present: A View from the Other Side*, trans. Asa Zatz (1964; reprint, New York: Monthly Review, 1968).

7. James E. Lewis, *The American Union and the Problem of Neighborhood: The United States and the Collapse of the Spanish Empire, 1783–1829* (Chapel Hill: University of North Carolina Press, 1998).

8. For contrasting assessments of U.S.-Latin American relations in the late nineteenth century, see Walter LaFeber, *The New Empire: An Interpretation of American Expansion, 1860–1898* (1963; reprint, Ithaca: Cornell University Press, 1998); and David M. Pletcher, *The Diplomacy of Trade and Investment: American Economic Expansion in the Hemisphere, 1865–1900* (Columbia: University of Missouri Press, 1998).

9. "Our America," in *La Revista Ilustrada* (New York), 10 January 1891, reprinted in José Martí, *Our America: Writings on Latin America and the Struggle for Cuban Independence*, ed. Philip S. Foner, trans. Elinor Randall, Juan de Onís, and Roslyn H. Foner (New York: Monthly Review Press, 1977).

10. José Martí, Letter to the *New York Herald*, 2 May 1895, quoted in ibid., 427. Foner speculates that the letter was not published.

11. Francisco García Calderón, *Latin America: Its Rise and Progress* (London: T. Fisher Unwin, 1913), 15. On Martí, see Enrico Mario Santí, " 'Our America,' the Gilded Age, and the Crisis of Latinamericanism," in Jeffrey Belnap and Raúl Fernández, eds., *José Martí's "Our America": From National to Hemispheric Cultural Studies* (Durham: Duke University Press, 1998), 179–90. In the 1920s, the Peruvian Víctor Raúl Haya de la Torre articulated another definition of America—Indoamerica.

12. Herbert E. Bolton, "The Epic of Greater America," in Hanke, *Do the Americas Have a Common History?* 67–100. This essay was based on Bolton's 1932 American Historical Association presidential address. See also Edmundo O'Gorman, "Do the Americas Have a Common History," in ibid., 103–18; and Russell M. Magnaghi, *Herbert E. Bolton and the Historiography of the Americas* (Westport, Ct.: Greenwood Publishing, 1998).

Beginning college students, Bolton believed, should take introductory courses in European history and America (or the History of the Americas, as it was commonly known), followed by national courses in French or English history and U.S. or Mexican history. It was a wildly impractical idea, of course, but on the eve of World War II, one of Bolton's contemporaries, Samuel Guy Inman, noting that the center of Anglo and Latin civilization had moved across the Atlantic, called for a return to the original meaning of America, "the whole mighty land from the North Pole to the South . . . where democracy is unanimously accepted as the ideal." See Inman, *Latin America: Its Place in World Life* (1937; reprint, New York: Harcourt, Brace, and Co., 1942, 4.

13. See Albert Fishlow and James Jones, eds., *The United States and the Americas: A Twenty-First Century View* (New York: W. W. Norton, 1999); and Mark Peceny, "The Inter-American System as a Liberal 'Pacific Union'?" *Latin American Research Review* 29, no. 3 (1994): 188–201.

14. In a perceptive article, Peter Smith assesses the relevance of modernization theory to the social science agenda of post–Cold War Latin America. See "The Changing Agenda for Social Science Research on Latin America," in Peter Smith, ed., *Latin America in Comparative Perspective: New Approaches to Methods and Analysis* (Boulder, Co.: Westview Press, 1995), 1–29. For a devastating critique of modernization theory, see Arturo Escobar, *Encountering Development: The Making and Unmaking of the Third World* (Princeton: Princeton University Press, 1995).

15. For the declaration of the Second Summit at Santiago, Chile, in 1998, see Fishlow and Jones, *United States and the Americas*, 207–213.

16. For a pessimistic view about the prospects for hemispheric unity, see Lawrence Harrison, *The Pan-American Dream: Do Latin America's Cultural Values Discourage True Partnership with the United States and Canada?* (New York: Basic Books, 1997).

17. The literature on this topic is voluminous, but the reader might begin with the following: Jorge G. Castañeda, *Utopia Unarmed: The Latin American Left after the Cold War* (New York: Alfred A. Knopf, 1993); Urie Bronfenbrenner et al., *The State of Americans* (New York: The Free Press, 1996); and Nancy Birdsall, Nora Lustig, and Lesley O'Connell, "The United States and the Social Challenge in Latin America: The New Agenda Needs New Instruments," in Fishlow and Jones, *United States and the Americas*, 79–108.

18. See Langley, *The Americas in the Age of Revolution.*

19. On the impact of NAFTA at the national and local levels, see Sidney Weintraub, *NAFTA at Three: A Progress Report* (Washington, D.C.: Center for Strategic and International Studies, 1997). On the "love-hate" attitudes of Latin Americans toward the United States, see Carlos Rángel, *The Latin Americans—Their Love-Hate Relationship with the United States* (1976; reprint New York: Harcourt Brace Jovanovich, 1977); and Lester D. Langley, *America and the Americas: The United States in the Western Hemisphere* (Athens: University of Georgia Press, 1988).

20. Louis A. Pérez, Jr., *On Becoming Cuban: Identity, Nationality, and Culture* (Chapel Hill: University of North Carolina Press, 1999).

PART II

THE WAR OF 1898

2

U.S. Intervention and Monroeism: Spanish Perspectives on the American Role in the Colonial Crisis of 1895–98

Sylvia L. Hilton

LABRA ON INTERNATIONAL LAW, INTERVENTION, AND THE UNITED STATES

Rafael María de Labra, a moderate, soft-spoken republican who was an active advocate of democratic policies in late-nineteenth-century Spain, may represent, as one of the more clear-eyed admirers of the United States, Spanish recognition of American contributions to the development of international law.[1] The well-read Labra appreciated American influence in such areas as "the reform of the colonial regime, the principle of non-intervention, freedom of the seas, the broadening of the circle of nations, international arbitration, more precise definition of the duties of neutral countries, the inviolability of private property in wartime, the effectiveness of non-written international law."[2]

In Labra's view, the nineteenth-century progressive trend was toward two main goals: "to take certain interests away from the exclusive jurisdiction of particular States," and "to require that nations meet certain internal political conditions, in order to be able to act, with a perfect right, in the international concert."[3] These goals required international law to focus on defining the concept of nation, on promoting a superior organism that would represent the society of nations, and on providing for the defense of the natural inalienable rights of human beings, over and above the narrow boundaries of state, race, religion, and family.[4] Labra himself gave priority to this last trend, saying "neither is a State like a herd, nor is the nation an end in itself, but a means to sustain and enlarge the human personality"; a position that led him to justify the right of intervention.[5]

He was well aware of the controversy surrounding such notions. The idea that human rights might take precedence over national sovereignty to the extent of justifying foreign intervention in a country was fraught with myriad moral, legal, and practical risks. Summarizing the views of notable European theoreticians, he concluded that most of them stood in a murky middle ground, vaguely accepting the principle of intervention but offering many obstacles to its practical execution. Late-nineteenth-century nationalists looked askance at the right of intervention, which they saw as seriously undermining national sovereignty. Labra, however, supported it unequivocally "in the name of humanity and the peace of the world," but only on condition that there be "guarantees . . . to prevent it degenerating in abuse of the weak and unjustifiable violence of the powerful." He noted, "The society of nations can and must intervene in the internal life of each one of its members." He carefully added, "Such intervention must not benefit the exclusive interests of the intervening nations and it must be carried out by their common action and to benefit the entire world."[6] American intervention in Cuba, though justified on precisely the humanitarian grounds defended by Labra, met none of these conditions.

SPANISH VIEWS OF U.S. INTERVENTION

While progovernment public discourse within Spain tended to play down U.S. intervention, a majority of other Spanish political groups and newspapers exploited all the real and imagined instances of U.S. interference in the colonial conflict as a means of criticizing the incumbent governments, and even (in the case of Carlists and republicans) the Alphonsine regime itself.[7] Thus, whatever the legal and moral merits of each grievance, most public discussion of U.S. attitudes and policies was designed for domestic consumption in the struggle for power within Spain. Unable to accede to power through the peaceful working of the electoral process, which was tightly controlled by the government, agitation to bring about political change by violent means was undoubtedly the main aim of opposition newspapers, whether of far-right traditionalists and Carlists, the various republican parties, or socialists and other left-leaning groups. Even the different liberal or conservative coalitions that had real aspirations to power within the Restoration system cultivated similar destabilizing rhetoric. Thus, the primary purpose of the political discourse of opposition groups was to emphasize the incompetence and weakness of the Spanish government in the face of treacherous colonial insurrection and U.S. intromission in a bid to whip up sufficient patriotic ire to trigger a popular revolution and/or a military coup.[8]

Spanish perspectives on American intervention touched several different chords.[9] Most of the commonly repeated themes were predictable and understandable. Intervention was seen as: (1) the logical, inevitable result of the criminal ineptitude and servility of the Spanish government and/or the Alphonsine monarchical regime, which encouraged U.S. audacity; (2) the consequence of Spain's diplomatic isolation, itself a dangerous result of government incompetence, which led to the inhibition of the European powers when they might otherwise have intervened more effectively to check U.S. freedom of action; (3) the long-foreseen culmination of a well-documented, historical U.S. political and strategic interest in acquiring Cuba; (4) the expression of U.S. economic growth and commercial expansionism, which had become increasingly apparent in the Caribbean and elsewhere in Latin America since the 1870s, and now greedily sought new investment opportunities and markets for U.S. surpluses; (5) the confirmation of the long-held belief in the impossibility of an independent Cuba, not only because of U.S. interest in annexation and Cuban economic dependency, but because of intractable racial and social tensions within Cuba itself; (6) the product of popular and congressional jingoism in the United States, fanned by a rabidly irresponsible "yellow" press, which basely exploited the cultural prejudices of anti-Spanish Anglo-Saxonism; (7) the deliberate abortion of the successful new Cuban autonomous regime, which would have revitalized Spain's sovereignty over her Caribbean possessions, a prospect that the United States found unacceptable; (8) the brutal affirmation of American material and military strength; (9) unwarranted intromission in the internal affairs of a friendly nation, and gross, willful, and repeated violations of justice and U.S. obligations as a neutral state under international law; and as (10) a manifestation of aggressive Monroeism, which aspired to rid the Americas of all European colonialism and establish U.S. hegemony.

Under the general category of U.S. violations of international law, the list of specific Spanish grievances was very long and provided endless grist to the rhetorical mill churning out patriotic and partisan venom. The long-feared U.S. military intervention, it must be understood, was only the last phase of what was seen as a purposeful policy of constant intromission which took many forms. A full study of such grievances, all of which have been adequately documented and analyzed in the existing historiography, cannot be contemplated here. Quotations from two very different ideological sectors will suffice to illustrate the tone and the main thrust of Spanish criticism of U.S. interference and, more importantly, the function of such criticism in Spanish politics. In the summer of 1896, Carlist representative in the legislature Juan Vázquez de Mella, responding to suggestions that it was imprudent to talk of U.S. intervention, inveighed:

> According to the government . . . it is inopportune for us to talk about the United States; but it is not inopportune for the U.S. Congress to discuss at length whether or not to recognize Cuban insurgent belligerency, and what is worse, hurling insults,

calumnies and outrages against Spain, such as have never been uttered in any other parliamentary chambers. . . . I want you to tell me if we are going to continue to act as we have been doing towards the United States, if the servile complaisance shown so far is going to continue. Do you think that Spanish dignity suffers no detriment, discredit or affront in the "Alliance" affair, in the payment of the Mora indemnity, in those constant satisfactions given to the U.S. government, in matters such as the "Competitor," unprocessed tobacco, and others? Is it not an indisputable fact . . . that filibustering expeditions are constantly leaving U.S. coasts for Cuba? Is it not true, gentlemen, that from the United States come arms, men, and all the things necessary for war? Is it not true that the operational base of the Cuban filibustering army, to call it something, is in the United States? Well then, is the government going to maintain this truly punishable passiveness?[10]

For its part, the progressive republican daily *El País*, making one of its many calls for the revolutionary overthrow of the monarchy, raged in a May 1897 editorial entitled "Behind the Capitol":

Yes, behind, beggarly, hypocritical, weak, hobbling wretchedly, sunk in the most dreadful discredit, abdicating its own dignity; that is the graceful situation of the government that rules Spain's destiny. . . . The neo-monarchy has been a crime, a disgrace, and that carries a price; the expiation is beginning. The Capitol in Washington drags the Spanish monarchy behind it, like a dog . . . the Cuban reforms have been dictated and imposed by the Yankee Senate, the intervention of the United States in Cuba is no longer confined within the U.S. Congress; it invades the island, with personal interventions, it regulates and decrees, Spain has no government. . . . The Capitol commands, and it does so despising what is contemptible. . . . and the conservative government looks on impassively. . . . But you, the people, cravenly shorn and sold like a flock of sheep, cannon fodder and wretched mass, what are you waiting for? Your sacrifices, your ruin, your immense love of national honour, have served only to take the monarchy to the Capitol. Behind is the Tarpeian rock. Cast off that miserable rag that dishonours you, or die with it in disgrace and ignominy.[11]

In September, the caustic destabilizing campaign continued unabated in the pages of *El País*:

Now Mr. Woodford is here. There he is, ready to present us with a flood of indemnity accounts and to ask us for goodness knows how many extravagances. . . . In the first place, in view of the ease with which our government gave the millions of the Mora indemnity, he will insist on a few thousand for the widow of the filibustering dentist Ruiz; then he will present a list of American citizens, more or less authentic and more or less *mambises* [black insurgents], that will add a few more million pesos, and when that matter is settled, he will ask for a tariff reform, so that everything taken to Cuban markets will be American products, and everything exported from Cuba will go to American markets. . . . For this we have been suffering the vile insults of a handful of pork dealers, raised to the category of legislators, with less justification perhaps than the Roman emperor had when he made his horse a senator.[12]

Similar condemnations of U.S. intromission were voiced from widely different political and ideological positions, varying the tone and the relative emphasis within their diverse interpretive combinations.[13] Without disputing the justice and legitimate indignation of such protests, the essential rhetorical point of all this insistent disparagement of the United States was that conciliatory responses to U.S. pressure discredited the Spanish government even more. Only the federalist republicans, led by their high-minded founder and main ideologue Francisco Pí y Margall, struggled desperately to maintain the notion of U.S. intervention as a blow for humanity and for the liberation of oppressed peoples.[14]

INTERVENTION AS MONROEISM

One of the more common, and at first glance not entirely logical, threads of Spanish public discourse was the perception of U.S. intervention as a function of the Monroe Doctrine. The overwhelming majority of Spanish commentators endorsed this interpretation.[15] It may be added that Spanish newspapers often carried summaries and extracts of articles published in a vast array of European periodical publications that held similar views. There is some indication that this surprised contemporary U.S. journalists. They, of course, were aware that President McKinley hardly mentioned the Monroe Doctrine during his election campaign, and once in office, did not often allude to it regarding U.S. policies in Latin America. Most interestingly, considering the fact that the war of 1898 may symbolically represent the beginning of U.S. "imperialism," the "great American dogma" was also absent from official justifications of U.S. policy in 1895–98.[16]

Held in thrall to their own primary sources, most U.S. historians of McKinley or the War of 1898 have missed or ignored the Monroeist theme entirely, following Dexter Perkins's 1955 version, which dismissed critical allusions to Monroeism as the effect of the "general hostility" and "prejudice" of "cynical" and "jealous" Europeans.[17] Only relatively recently have U.S. scholars attempted to see the global picture.[18] One need not accept the idea that all U.S. armed interventions can only be understood as manifestations of "imperialism" in order to recognize the usefulness and necessity of trying to seek a "larger meaning" in the events of 1898.[19] Historians and policymakers undoubtedly need to explore "the mind sets of leaders and people across national borders," as well as security and trade issues, in order to fully understand the forces behind international cooperation and conflict.[20] The presence of the Monroe Doctrine in non–U.S. public discourse of 1895–98 may be examined as a case study for the concepts of cultural internationalism and imperialism, inasmuch as this doctrine can be seen as an example of an international cultural icon, a symbol that was shared (and recreated) within and across several cultural systems.

For the greater part of the nineteenth century, and despite logical misgivings, Spanish political leaders considered the Monroe Doctrine almost as a guarantee for Spain's continuing possession of her American provinces. This "guarantee" had not been requested, may well have been unwanted, and was often criticized and ridiculed, but in the last analysis, it did serve on occasion as protection against early Latin American revolutionary aims, against the colonial ambitions of other European powers, and against Cuban separatism. It was therefore of some diplomatic value to Spain.[21]

At the same time, other more laudatory views existed among Spanish democrats. For Labra, champion of the abolition of slavery and of Cuban autonomy, Monroe's original message was a praiseworthy gesture in defense of the sovereignty of nations and of democratic principles, and a stance against despotic European monarchical interventionism in the fledgling Spanish American republics.[22] He thought that many European politicians and publicists, disinclined to look favorably on the United States, often deliberately interpreted the doctrine in alarmist terms in order to foment popular anti-Americanism for domestic purposes in their own countries,[23] an observation that will be relevant for the analysis of Spanish political discourse in the crisis of 1895–98.

As the nineteenth century wore on, however, successive U.S. presidents' interpretive extensions to the Monroe Doctrine gave increasing concern to Spanish leaders, who were uneasy about repeated U.S. manifestations of interest in acquiring Cuba, large U.S. investments in the island, and the growing commercial dependence of Cuban sugar on the U.S. market. Consequently in 1895, as the Cuban separatist war flared up, Spanish fears of U.S. interference quickly latched onto the perceived Monroeist threat. Emilio Castelar, the old-guard republican who had helped to stabilize the Restoration regime, criticized the United States for "thinking of extending their political tutelage over the whole New World, interpreting the Monroe doctrine Yankee-style."[24] *La Vanguardia*, a liberal Catalonian newspaper, criticized the way American political leaders exploited the propagandistic value of this most American of symbols, deceiving "the less enlightened sector of public opinion in the United States, who believe that the famous Monroe Doctrine (America for the Americans) is applicable to the Cuban insurrection, simply because it is invoked and recalled in every conflict or problem that arises between any Americans at all and any Europeans at all, whoever they might be."[25]

In late 1895, the Western world rippled in protest at the interpretation given to the Monroe Doctrine by President Cleveland and his secretary of state, Richard Olney, in justification of U.S. intervention in the Anglo-Venezuelan boundary dispute. Their contention that the Monroe Doctrine gave the United States the right to intervene in virtually any conflict between a European power and an American nation was flatly rejected by the British prime minister, Lord Salisbury. Most European and many Latin American commentators were equally dismissive—when not downright derisive—of this claim. According to Labra, "The theory formulated . . . by President Cleveland . . . and . . . Mr. Olney . . . was universally interpreted as the manifestation of an inadmissible international law and as the intolerable claim of the Washington government to the superior direction of all American affairs. I affirm that there is not a single periodical, a single journal of any repute among the experts in the science of International Law that has supported the most recent American theories."[26] The majority of Spanish newspapers tended to agree with this reaction. Thus, the conservative *La Epoca* declared, "The invocation of the Monroe doctrine, in order to interfere in everything affecting the relations between an American power and a European one, implies an absorption of America by the United States and a challenge to European influence that deserve a serious corrective."[27]

Nonetheless, legal and theoretical disputations aside, it was fear at the prospect of American intervention in Spain's own colonial conflict that was the major practical consideration determining Spanish rejection of the validity of this "new" Monroeism. Spanish possessions in the Caribbean were obviously threatened by Cleveland's unexpected stance which, at such a sensitive time, reaffirmed the long-standing U.S. desire to free the Western Hemisphere from all European colonialism.[28]

Spanish conservatives, however, understandably thought it prudent at first to avoid any linkage between British Guiana and Cuba, and they consequently muted any suggestions that the two conflicts were comparable or that the newly defined doctrine might apply to Cuba.[29] Clinging to traditional, if reluctant, Spanish tolerance of the Monroe Doctrine, *La Epoca* insisted: "That President's declaration contained a categorical exception in favour of the European nations which at that time still retained colonies in the New World, and that was the case of Spain."[30] Similarly, right up to the eve of the War of 1898, newspapers of diverse political leanings published explanations of the historical circumstances surrounding the formulation of Monroe's message, in support of its value as an American "guarantee" of colonies existing in 1823.[31]

Not all observers were equally discreet, however. Liberal and left-leaning journalists, always alert to chances to turn news items into means of discomforting the government, were quick to point out the relation between the two cases—both conflicts involved American territories and European colonialism—and to discuss the possible implications of "new" Monroeism for the Spanish crisis. *El Liberal* and *La Vanguardia*, while insisting that the doctrine was not legally applicable to Cuba, warned of the heightened danger for Spanish possessions in the Caribbean.[32] A British newspaper debate, which was continuing its tendentious attempt to trace a Monroeist link between British Guiana and Cuba, was amply summarized in *El Liberal*.[33] Another liberal newspaper published a long article praising Edward J. Phelps, U.S. minister in London during Cleveland's first administration. Phelps, in a speech offered at the Brooklyn Institute of Arts and Sciences, expressed his fear that "this new Monroe doctrine . . . has brought us to the brink of war with England and is bringing us closer, I can see, to a war with Spain."[34]

For their part, republicans were hopelessly divided, although all but the unconditional supporters of federalist Pí y Margall pointedly signed a manifesto protesting "against the slightest intention or the merest suggestion of any foreign power that might impair the indisputable sovereignty of the Spanish nation."[35] Emilio Castelar, a longtime admirer of the United States, hurled vitriolic condemnation at the "new" Monroeism. Clearly linking the Anglo-Venezuelan case and the Spanish-Cuban crisis, he regretted the "entrance on the scene of the United States, which is attempting, by absurd and Machiavellian interpretations of Monroe's dogma, to claim for itself an innate arbitratorship to resolve quarrels between American powers and European powers, on top of a pontificate enriched with excommunications and anathemas which they allow themselves, with patent insolence and no right at all, regarding our method of combating internal insurrections."[36]

The following year his scorn was boundless. He wrote,

> Many believe that the Americans impose Monroe's program at the point of the sword. No such thing! They don't care a fig about it. They do not call the worn out program law, right, jurisprudence or anything like that, because of the religious respect all Anglo-Saxons have for the literal meaning of their legal codes. They call it doctrine, the Monroe doctrine. Why do they call it doctrine? To interpret it depending on the occasion, the circumstance, the interest. So they are interested in preventing the French from opening a canal through Panama? Well, they invoke the Monroe doctrine. They want to build a canal through Nicaragua themselves? Well, seeing that they do not have enough money, they give half of the canal to the English in violation of the Monroe doctrine. So much for obeying Monroe. That phrase is no more than what they call a platform; what we call a wild card.[37]

The more cautious Labra, who was well informed about American writings on international law and about trends of public opinion in the United States, pondered in the summer of 1896:

> I do not deny that in the United States . . . there are many theorists . . . who do not interpret the Monroe doctrine in the perturbing sense that I have mentioned; but I cannot deny . . . that . . . the dominant tendency, that which constitutes the general sentiment of the nation, is the extension of the 1823 doctrine to a great continental exclusivism and the absorption of all America by the spirit, the interests, the government and the representation of the United States. . . . This tendency has become very patent as a result of the Venezuela affair; it is becoming more so taking the Cuban problem as a pretext, although the aspects it will have in that regard will not be exactly the same, however great the insistence and however obvious the inclinations of the American Republic.[38]

This last prediction that the two cases would not receive the same treatment would be borne out in fact, but his later attempt to point this out would be drowned in the cacophony of less subtle accusations.

Nonetheless, a few republican voices expressed a different view, still sustaining the idealistic democratic notion that Monroe's original message contained principles of the highest value.[39] Early in the crisis, *La Justicia*, the mouthpiece of the opportunistic Nicolás Salmerón, defined the Monroe Doctrine in mythical terms which, moreover, hinted at underlying sympathy for Cuban independence: "It is no less than the recognition of the independence and autonomy of all political organisms . . . it is the negation of all authority and sovereignty imposed from outside; it is the affirmation of the substantivity of all social aggregates to live and exercise self-determination that is enclosed in those four words . . . 'America for the Americans.' "[40]

The most arresting comments at this stage, however, came from the federalist republican weekly *El Nuevo Régimen*, written almost entirely by Francisco Pí y Margall. Although essentially agreeing with the predominant opinion that Cleveland and Olney had altered the original meaning of Monroe's message, and that it was not applicable to the Anglo-Venezuelan case, this newspaper suggested not only that it could be invoked to justify intervention in the Spanish-Cuban conflict but, dissenting radically from other views, that such an application might not be a bad thing.[41] If Cleveland were sincere in his defense of the proper meaning of the principle "America for the Americans," he should support all American independence movements. But Pí saw a contradiction between Cleveland's energetic determination in the Anglo-Venezuelan case and his hesitancy regarding the Cuban war and was disconcerted by this perceived duplicity.[42]

For his part, William McKinley had firmly endorsed Cleveland's message to the Congress of December 1895 on the Anglo-Venezuelan dispute,[43] and his own electoral platform of 1896 included a strong defense of the Monroe Doctrine, consistent with long-standing republican tradition, and moreover, mentioning the Cuban problem in the same paragraph.[44] Even the tariff bill that bore his name made him "a legitimate heir to Monroe."[45] From the start, then, McKinley was perceived in Spain as "the incarnation of the Monroe doctrine."[46]

McKinley's first attempt to obtain Senate approval for the annexation of Hawaii in 1897 triggered warnings that this was connected with Monroeist expansionism. One Carlist newspaper averred: "They, the *Yankees*, are annexing the Hawaiian Islands, and want to annex Cuba and Puerto Rico and the whole of what was Spanish America, disguising their ambition under Monroe's maxim, 'America for the Americans.' "[47] The presidential message to Congress in December 1897 was the occasion for another flurry of worried editorials stressing McKinley's Monroeism. The conservative *La Epoca* judged that the message included "not a few declarations favourable to

Spain stated with clarity and firmness; but there are also others that involve the affirmation of the Monroe doctrine, which limit the rights of our country and leave pending the motives of conflict that the Message tends to postpone for the present. . . . We should be clearly warned that Mr. McKinley admits and continues the Monroe doctrine, since he affirms with no hesitation the right of the United States to intervene in Cuba's destiny."[48] Similar forebodings, linking McKinley's threat of intervention and Monroeism, could be found in other Spanish newspapers representing a broad range of ideological positions.[49]

Surprisingly, despite mounting tension, traditional liberal views of the doctrine did not disappear entirely from the Spanish press in 1898. At the end of March, the moderate *El Globo*, committed to the defense of the regime and obviously attempting to pour calming oil, commented approvingly on the opinion of a prestigious American theorist of international law, professor John Bassett Moore, who interpreted conservatively that the Monroe Doctrine was, in short, "a doctrine of defense and not of aggression."[50] The progressive republican weekly *Las Dominicales del Libre Pensamiento* published three long contributions by Luis V. Varela, a lawyer writing from Buenos Aires, who, while expressing serious doubts concerning McKinley's understanding of the doctrine, eulogized the idealistic version of the 1823 message.[51]

By now, however, this was decidedly a minority point of view. Throughout the early months of 1898, growing fears of U.S. interventionism prompted numerous articles condemning the threat posed by "new" Monroeism for Spanish possessions in the Caribbean. Negation of the legitimacy of the doctrine took several forms: the simple denial of its validity as a norm of international law; contempt born of its history of arbitrary applications in specific cases; sarcastic scorn of a "dogma" that symbolized the hypocritical and barbaric arrogance of U.S. culture in general; hurt indignation against a claim that ignored the historical and cultural bonds between Spain and America; or outright dismissal of the doctrine as mere camouflage for selfish capitalist expansionism.[52]

Developing its "patriotic" destabilizing strategy, *El País* painted the danger in terms of criticism of the Spanish government, saying: "it puts us in the awful position of humiliating ourselves in the face of the impositions of those who profess and practise the doctrines of Monroe."[53] Similarly counting on visceral popular reactions to demonized Monroeism, accusations of government incompetence came from the far Carlist right. *El Correo Español* warned: "unfortunately [our government] will not reach an understanding with the 'Yankees,' arrogant with their maxim 'America for the Americans,' and war will come."[54] The convergence of such widely disparate political sectors in essentially the same rhetorical tactics was striking, to say the least.

The outbreak of war forced proponents of official versions to abandon the long-held view of the Monroe Doctrine as "guarantee," and the Spanish minister for overseas possessions Segismundo Moret found it expedient, in a speech to the Senate, to claim that the war had come "because American policy, with the Monroe doctrine, has been waiting for years now for the moment when the island of Cuba might fall into its hands."[55] Evidently, the "hidden" meaning of this assertion was that a well-publicized threat of such long standing gave a sense of historical inevitability to the current crisis, thus diminishing the culpability of the present government.

Even the federalists, struggling painfully between their immense admiration for the "Great Republic" and irrefutable signs that a new phase was beginning in U.S. foreign policy, reluctantly came to the conclusion that "the broadening of the Monroe Doctrine has come to the aid of the Cuban rebels. . . . [T]oday it is maintained that America is for the Americans, and the European intruder must be thrown out. This policy has begun by throwing us out."[56] Labra, in his scrupulous way, made one attempt to go against the current, pointing out that McKinley had not, in fact, used the Monroe Doctrine to justify intervention. He thought that this showed some talent on the president's part. McKinley, he decided, wished to avoid any repetition of the virulent European protests against Cleveland's "Monroeist" intervention of 1895, and astutely chose instead to base his justifications ostensibly on modern theories regarding the right of intervention.[57] However, in the end, like most other Spanish observers, he was too forcefully struck by the underlying Monroeist theme. Contemplating the international significance of the U.S. intervention in the Spanish crisis, he judged: "I really believe that what is happening now in Cuba is of immense international importance. The American government is unscrupulously developing the Monroe policy in its third interpretation, to the detriment of Latin American independence, in contempt of Europe, and in grave violation of International Law that no longer consents to conquests or universal empires or exclusivisms of religion, race or continent."[58]

INTERVENTION AND MONROEISM FROM INTERNATIONAL PERSPECTIVES

Such evaluations show quite clearly that, apart from the perception of the war as a national disaster, contemporary Spaniards were well aware of the multilayered international interest in U.S. intervention in Spain's colonial crisis and the significance for world affairs of seeing that intervention as a function of the Monroe Doctrine.[59]

In the first place, widespread European indignation at the "new" Monroeism of 1895 invited Spanish commentators to speculate about the possibility of obtaining European support to prevent similar interference in Cuba. The foreseeable application of the newly defined doctrine to all European dependencies in America, the Spanish press henceforth insistently warned, tended toward the expulsion of Europe from the Americas.

Therefore, the European powers ought to take up the Spanish cause in their own self-interest.[60] In the summer of 1896, the Spanish government itself, seeking European aid, prepared an official note warning that the expansive Monroe Doctrine endangered all colonial and maritime interests. U.S. ambassador Taylor's quick response could have left no doubt regarding the American position. The United States would not tolerate European interference in American affairs, and any attempt to mobilize the great powers in Spain's behalf, instead of helping matters, might in fact precipitate U.S. intervention.[61]

Nonetheless, during the latter months of 1897 and most of 1898, a ubiquitous theme in the Spanish press was the hope of European solidarity with the Spanish cause, primarily as a self-serving reaction against Monroeism, but also as a kind of intervention that would be compatible with international law and ethics.[62] Moreover, echoing Austrian and German proposals that Europe should form a union to defend common economic interests and oppose Monroeism, the idea of a European counterweight to the Monroe Doctrine was formulated: a kind of "Europe for Europeans," a notion "that would consist of totally preventing the United States from undertaking the slightest intromission in European affairs."[63]

Significantly, in consonance with hopes of British aid to maintain Spanish sovereignty in Cuba (which would increase the likelihood of obtaining general European support), the Spanish press had shown some sympathy toward Britain early in the Anglo-American crisis of 1895, not only criticizing Cleveland's stance, but also praising the cool English self-control and expressing hopes of a peaceful solution.[64] However, this mildly pro-British attitude soon gave way to charges that, for selfish reasons, the powerful Great Britain strengthened the "new" Monroe Doctrine by giving it implicit recognition. European sources were often cited to corroborate this impression, which would become steadily stronger as Spanish observers began to perceive the effects of the new Anglo-American friendship on U.S. attitudes toward Cuba. In the light of British inhibition (others said encouragement) regarding U.S. interventionism, Spanish suspicions and criticism linking Monroeism and Anglo-Saxonism became more frequent.[65] An editorial in *El Progreso* explained, "The absorbing character of the Anglo-Saxon race, the ideals that inspire it and the aspirations that encourage it found complete expression and a definite and clear purpose in Monroe's formula."[66] Fears that the United States and Britain might establish an alliance based on the acceptance of "new" Monroeism inspired accusations that Anglo-Saxon imperialists despised and threatened other "races," particularly the Hispanic "race."

Thus, the Monroe Doctrine became inextricably identified, in the minds and rhetoric of its detractors, with a threat that greatly transcended the immediate problem of the Cuban conflict and pointed at "Latin" cultural and "racial" worth and survival. This was a useful rhetorical weapon for

Spanish politicians (all except federalists and socialists) bent on cultivating an opposing creed of Hispanic or Latin superiority and domination.[67] Such discourse was aided by the growth in Latin America of pan-Hispanic sentiments that reflected both defensive nationalist reactions against U.S. expansionism and the ascendancy of ruling elites with strong conservative, Catholic, racist, and Hispanophile opinions, whose official attitudes in 1895–98 tended to be pro-Spanish, despite widespread popular sympathy for the Cuban cause.[68] Naturally then, Spanish commentators of all ideological persuasions discussed U.S. interference in the Spanish-Cuban war in terms of its possible repercussions for Latin Americans, whose ambivalence towards the doctrine was often exploited in editorials containing lugubrious warnings about hegemonism and the tutelary designs of the United States in the Americas. "The Monroe doctrine," said the conservative *La Epoca*, "like the god Janus, has two faces, of which, if one expressed sympathy and affection, the other expresses arrogance and domination."[69] *El Nuevo País* reproduced an article by Rubén Darío published in Buenos Aires, defending the Spanish cause and lamenting Latin American inconsistency regarding "Monroe's boastful *slang*," vehemently denounced by Darío.[70] For its part, *El Correo Español*, which was skeptical about any European aid, thought that "Spain's natural ally against the United States, whose absorbing tendencies are not new, . . . is not in Europe, but in America itself . . . the peoples who belong to our race, . . . those nations, in sum, have been the first to see that the Monroe doctrine is a truly vile trick to enslave them, because the *Yankees* do not want America to be for the Americans, as that doctrine teaches, but for the United States."[71]

Labra, too, in his reflections on the international context of the war, regretted that the Spanish government did not try to seek Latin American aid. He thought, quite correctly, that one of the serious general defects of Spanish diplomacy was its lack of a clear, globally conceived Latin American policy.[72] Not easily moved to strong language, he spoke in the Senate about the "repugnant tone and manner" of U.S. policy towards weak Latin American nations, which he thought was becoming exaggerated in the case of Cuba.[73]

Nonetheless, few Spaniards showed any real sympathy for legitimate Latin American concerns. Indeed, the majority of Spanish denunciations of Monroeism revealed an unrelenting imperialist perspective. Seemingly unaware of any ideological incongruities, even most republicans dreamed of an imperial Spanish republic that would preside over a Latin hegemony to counter Monroeism. Thus, *El País* could rant, "a republican Spain . . . would be the bond of union among all the Iberian nations of both continents, and the absorbing, selfish, utilitarian Monroe Doctrine, behind which Yankee ambition hides, would be substituted by the more logical and more positive principle of the hegemony of the Latin race in America, which could easily become the hegemony of the Latin race in the whole world."[74]

The fundamental problem with this discourse, however, was the coexistence of different, essentially incompatible versions. On the one hand, notions of Spanish (-Portuguese)-Latin American union were based on cultural and "racial" ties, while a much-touted Spanish-French (-Portuguese) union represented a flagrantly European colonialist stance. Evidently, Spanish commentators scarcely considered that, if Latin American republics looked on U.S. hemispheric policy with growing suspicion, attempts to promote European colonialist solidarity with Spain must have seemed equally discouraging.

In the end, three fundamental messages of interest to the international community emerged from the perceived role of Monroeism in U.S. interventionism of 1895–98. First, for democrats it meant a U.S. rupture with traditions and values associated with the revolutionary American model, and the betrayal of the so-called original spirit of Monroe's message, an interpretation that had resulted from its appropriation and mythification by anti-imperialists and others, both in the United States and throughout the Western world. Thus, this intervention signaled the death knell of idealistic Monroeism.[75] Second, the emergence of the United States as a great power, much encouraged in its "imperialist" tendencies by the Anglo-American rapprochement, was widely associated with the tandem threats of Anglo-Saxonism and expansive Monroeism. Third, the long history of arbitrary applications of the doctrine, as well as the manifest incompatibility between declared motivations for intervention and results thereof, also increased fears of a new ascendancy of arbitrariness and force over international law and order.[76]

CONCLUSIONS

Spanish public discourse on U.S. policy in 1895–98 clearly shows that political leaders and journalists (in Spain and other Western countries) considered Monroeism as one of the major motivations of American intervention. The fact that U.S. publicists and policymakers did not ostensibly base their attitudes and decisions regarding Cuba on the doctrine was almost universally ignored. Attention to this significant difference of perception affords a chance to venture several interpretive suggestions.

In the first place, Spaniards, like many other realistic Europeans and Latin Americans, took the long view, clearly discerning patterns and connections, and making reasonable conjectures based on historical and empirical evidence. Their interpretations need not be dismissed as cynical and prejudiced, or as less generous, merely because they compared declared motives and purposes with actions and consequences.

A second interpretive approach stems from the fact that the Spanish political class, formed by a small, educated elite, was much given to historicism when discussing current affairs. Thus, historical reconstructions, full of value judgments, were habitually used in the service of political agendas and ideology. The majority of editorials and speeches referring to the origins and evolution of the Monroe Doctrine illustrate this tendency, and any analysis must therefore consider their rhetorical usefulness in the context of Spanish domestic politics.

Supporters of the government, for example, at first attempted to calm patriotic belligerency by pointing out the Monroe Doctrine's value as a "guarantee" of existing Spanish possessions, but later, as war loomed nearer, recalled that it was a long-standing threat, in an attempt to show intent and inevitability, in accusation of the United States and exoneration of the incumbent government.

Diverse opposition groups (Carlists and republicans most notoriously but not exclusively) instrumentalized widespread anti-Americanism in an inflammatory discourse aimed primarily at destabilizing the government at home and, if possible, the monarchical regime itself. Thus, one of the most well-known American symbols was cast as a shorthand synonym of selfish capitalist expansionism; of political hegemonism backed by the brute force of military superiority; and of barbaric, arrogant Anglo-Saxonism bent on destroying the Spanish, the Latin, the Hispanic or the Iberian "race" and culture. However, the many variations on these themes reveal ideological contradictions that weakened the persuasive power of such rhetoric. This rhetorical strategy thus failed to change Spanish domestic politics, but it undoubtedly reinforced negative images of the United States and the Monroe Doctrine.

The careful Labra did attempt to point out that the Monroe Doctrine had not been invoked by the American government, but then abandoned this tack, no doubt persuaded, as others must have been, that such literal nitpicking could not counter the prevalent view that this intervention was indeed one more instance of adulterated Monroeism. Consequently, he and a few other democrats, together with Spanish federalists, while accepting that view, insistently argued that this had nothing to do with Monroe's original message which, for them, symbolized universal democratic ideals connected with the freedom of peoples, such as international anticolonialist solidarity in defense of the right of national self-determination and the principle of nonintervention. This discourse, then, emphasized the sense of betrayal and loss, the sense of a U.S. rupture with glorious traditions, and the sense of changes that spelled future uncertainties and dangers, both for the integrity of American democracy and for world affairs.

One thread of this concern stressed the association of the Monroe Doctrine with arbitrariness and the threat this posed to international law and order. In 1895–96, Latin American and British suggestions that an international conference might define and give recognition to the Monroe Doctrine fell on deaf ears, as did the idea of U.S. congressional definition and approval. This failure was compounded by the results of U.S. intervention in the Spanish colonial crisis, weakening still further the idealistic construct of the doctrine, which had been functioning as an icon of cultural internationalism. The cultural imperialism implicit in U.S. insistence on unilaterally controlling the definition and use of the Monroe Doctrine not only frustrated foreign attempts to participate in its construction, ignoring its value as an American symbol for promoting universal democratic principles and international cooperation, but even worse, resulted in the consolidation after 1898 of negative evaluations.[77]

In sum, the Monroe Doctrine figured so prominently in Spanish public discourse of 1895–98, not because Cleveland or McKinley actually invoked it in connection with the Spanish crisis, but because the Monroe Doctrine was a symbol intricately associated with Western images (positive and negative) of the United States, and with political ideologies and agendas at the Spanish domestic level and at several different international levels. The rhetorical uses to which the doctrine was put in Spanish political discourse show that the United States had all but lost its power to control the meaning of the "great American dogma" for better or worse.

NOTES

1. Rafael María de Labra, "De la representación e influencia de los Estados Unidos de América en el Derecho Internacional," 1 April 1877, repr. in his *Discursos políticos, académicos y forenses*, 2ª serie (Madrid: Imprenta de Marcelino Burgase, 1886), 168–215. See also Rafael María de Labra, "El principio de intervención," 5 April 1881, in his *Discursos políticos, académicos y forenses*, 1ª serie (Madrid: Imprenta de Aurelio J. Alaria, 1884), 135–64; and his *La crisis colonial de España (1868 a 1898). Estudios de política palpitante, y Discursos parlamentarios* (Madrid: Tip. de Alfredo Alonso, 1901), passim. On Labra, see Elena Hernández Sandoica, "Rafael María de Labra y Cadrana (1841–1919): una biografía política," *Revista de Indias* [Madrid] 54: 200 (1994): 107–36; and M. Dolores Domingo, "Rafael María de Labra ante la cuestión de Cuba, 1898," *Anuario de Estudios Americanos* [Sevilla] 55, no. 1 (1998): 153–64.

2. Labra, "De la representación," 215. The 1871 treaty of Washington and the 1872 Geneva arbitration merited special praise (210) as an "immense triumph" in the "application of principles of international law not recognized in special treaties, but that rest on reason and the culture of the times." See also Labra, "El principio de intervención," 148. In 1895–98, U.S. intervention in Cuba would often be criticized (not least by Labra himself) as a contravention of the jurisprudence established in 1871–72; see for example in Lluhí, "Conflicto con los Estados Unidos," *El Progreso*, 4 April 1898.

3. Labra, "El principio de intervención," 149.

4. Labra, *La crisis colonial*, 640–648. Also his *La política exterior de España* (Madrid: Tip. de Alfredo Alonso, 1910), 28.

5. Labra, "El principio de intervención," 152–54.

6. Ibid., 154, 156.

7. Most Spaniards were loyal to the queen regent María Cristina and her young

son, Alfonso XIII, who represented liberal constitutionalism. Since the beginning of the century, Carlists had supported a line of pretenders to the Spanish throne, represented from 1863 to 1909 by Carlos María de los Dolores de Borbón y Austria Este. Carlism was associated with Catholic and monarchical traditionalism and had strong followings in the Basque provinces as well as in Navarre, Catalonia, Valencia, and Aragon.

8. See S. L. Hilton, "The United States through Spanish Republican Eyes in the Colonial Crisis of 1895–98," in Sylvia L. Hilton and Steve J. S. Ickringill, eds., *European Perceptions of the Spanish-American War of 1898* (New York: Peter Lang, 1999), 53–70.

9. This essay is based on extensive reading of Spanish newspapers and other contemporary sources of public discourse. Hereafter, the following abbreviations will be used: *DC, Diario de Cádiz; ECE, El Correo Español; EG, El Globo; EL, El Liberal; E(N)Pa, El (Nuevo) País; ENR, El Nuevo Régimen; EPr, El Progreso; EPu, El Pueblo; ES, El Socialista; LC, La Correspondencia; LDLP, Las Dominicales del Libre Pensamiento; LE, La Epoca; LEM, La España Moderna; LJ, La Justicia; LV, La Vanguardia.*

10. Juan Vázquez de Mella, "Las causas de la guerra de Cuba y el anuncio de la guerra con los Estados Unidos," 8 July 1896, in his *Discursos parlamentarios*, 2 vols. (Madrid: Imprenta del Asilo de Huérfanos del Sagrado Corazón, 1927–28), 1:246–48. See also his "La responsabilidad de la catástrofe colonial," 6 and 7 May 1898, in ibid., 2:227–28.

11. "Detrás del Capitolio," *EPa*, 29 May 1897.

12. "La política. A moro muerto . . . ," *EPa*, 3 September 1897.

13. Traditional Spanish historiography has tended to reflect these same views, but more recent scholarship offers new perspectives, which are both broader in scope and less pessimistic and judgmental in tone. See S. L. Hilton, "Democracy Beats the 'Disaster' Complex: Spanish Interpretations of the Colonial Crisis of 1895–98," *Magazine of History* (OAH) 12, no. 3 (1998): 11–17.

14. See S. L. Hilton, "Los Estados Unidos como modelo: los federalistas españoles y el mito americano durante la crisis colonial de 1895–98," *Ibero-Americana Pragensia* [Prague] 32 (1998): 11–29. With a very different agenda, the Basque Nationalist leader Sabino Arana tried to telegraph McKinley in September 1898 to congratulate him for Cuban independence. Calling U.S. intervention an example of magnanimity and devotion to justice and liberty unparalleled in history, his main point was that if Europe followed this example, the Basque nation, too, would be free.

15. Space limitations preclude full documentary and historiographical data here. For greater detail, see S. L. Hilton, "La 'nueva' Doctrina Monroe de 1895 y sus implicaciones para el Caribe español: algunas interpretaciones coetáneas españolas," *Anuario de Estudios Americanos* [Sevilla] 55, no. 1 (1998): 125–51.

16. The Monroe Doctrine was not, however, absent from McKinley's thought. See S. L. Hilton and S. J. S. Ickringill, " 'Its Fiat Is Law'?: McKinley's Strange Silence on the 'Great American Dogma' in 1898," in Groupe de Recherche et d'Etudes Nord-Américaines, ed., *Mythes et Représentations aux États-Unis: Normes et Autorité* (Aix-en-Provence: Université de Provence, 1997), 109–27, or a revised version, " 'Americana en letra y espíritu': la Doctrina Monroe y el Presidente McKinley en 1898," *Cuadernos de Historia Contemporánea* [Madrid] 20 (1998): 205–19.

17. Dexter Perkins, *A History of the Monroe Doctrine* (Boston: Little, Brown & Co., 1955), 196–201.

18. See for example Edward P. Crapol, "Coming to Terms with Empire: The Historiography of Late-Nineteenth-Century American Foreign Relations," *Diplomatic History* 16 (1992): 573–97; Joseph A. Fry, "Imperialism, American Style, 1890–1916," in Gordon Martel, ed., *American Foreign Relations Reconsidered, 1890–1993* (London-New York: Routledge, 1994), 52–70.

19. See Louis A. Pérez, Jr., "1898 and Beyond: Historiographical Variations on War and Empire," *Pacific Historical Review* 65, no. 2 (1996): 313–15.

20. See Akira Iriye, "Culture and International History," in Michael J. Hogan and Thomas G. Paterson, eds., *Explaining the History of American Foreign Relations* (Cambridge: Cambridge University Press, 1991): 214–25.

21. R. M. de Labra, *Aspecto internacional de la cuestión de Cuba* (Madrid: Tip. de Alfredo Alonso, 1900), especially 167–83, gives a lucid analysis of this subject. See also his *La crisis colonial*, 658–64.

22. Labra, "De la representación," especially 190–95, and "El principio de intervención," 144.

23. Labra, "De la representación," 194–95. Although recognizing in another work that important interpretive extensions had been introduced by later U.S. governments, Labra still revered "the high moral significance and juridical value of the transcendental protest of 1823." See his *Aspecto internacional*, 76, 235.

24. Emilio Castelar, "La insurrección cubana y los periódicos extranjeros," *DC*, 8 September 1895, in Manuel Baraja, *La guerra de independencia cubana a través de 'Diario de Cádiz,' 1895–1898* (Cádiz: El Autor, 1979): 233–35. See also an early allusion in *DC*, 18 March 1895 (1979): 169.

25. "La actitud de los Estados Unidos con relación a España y Cuba," *LV*, 11 October 1895.

26. R. M. de Labra, "La cuestión de Cuba," 10 May 1898 (1901): 432–33.

27. "Los Estados Unidos e Inglaterra," *LE*, 18 October 1895.

28. Ernest R. May, *Imperial Democracy: The Emergence of America as a Great Power* (New York: Harper & Row, 1961): 85–86, offers an original interpretive speculation, not discussed by other authors, about the motives behind the 17 December 1895 message to Congress, when he suggests that "Cleveland may even have delivered the message partly as a warning to European powers that might ally with Spain."

29. "Inglaterra y los Estados Unidos," *LE*, 8 December 1895, however, noted the attempt of *The Standard* to link the two cases. Also "Europa y los Estados Unidos," *LE*, 16 November 1896. Later historiography has reinforced this view, as few works have made any connection or comparison between the two cases. See S. J. S. Ickringill and S. L. Hilton, "Cleveland and the Anglo-Venezuelan Dispute in 1895: A Prelude to McKinley's Intervention in the Spanish-Cuban War," in *Antes del 'Desastre': Orígenes y antecedentes de la crisis del '98*, ed. Juan Pablo Fusi and Antonio Niño (Madrid: Universidad Complutense, Departamento de Historia Contemporánea, 1996): 337–58.

30. "España en América," *LE*, 18 October 1895. "Notas de última hora," *LE*, 24 December 1895, published without comment the parts of Olney's July note that might apply to Cuba.

31. See for example, "Enseñanzas de la Historia," *LJ*, 20 July 1895; "La beligerancia de los insurrectos cubanos," *EL*, 18 October 1895; Emilio Castelar, "Crónica

internacional," *LEM*, January 1898, repr. in E. Castelar, *Crónica internacional*, ed. Dámaso de Lario (Madrid: Editora Nacional, 1982), 398; "Justificación de Weyler," *LDLP*, 13 January 1898.

32. "Con y contra España," *LV*, 10 October 1895; "Los precedentes," *EL*, 1 November 1895; "La política de los Estados Unidos," *LV*, 10 November 1895; "Carta de Nueva York," *EL*, 12 December 1895; "Inglaterra y los Estados Unidos," *EL*, 19 December 1895; "Carta de Washington. Venezuela y Monroe," *EL*, 2 January 1896.

33. "España y los Estados Unidos—La prensa inglesa," *EL*, 25 December 1896. See also "Cosas yankees," *LJ*, 24 December 1896. Joseph E. Wisan, *The Cuban Crisis as Reflected in the New York Press (1895–1898)* (1934; repr. New York: Octagon Books, 1977), 244, mentions Spanish displeasure at Cleveland's 1896 message to Congress, saying "The *Journal* reported Madrid as fearful that the message foreshadowed a dangerous extension of the Monroe Doctrine": a reaction that Wisan neglects to discuss.

34. *Cronista de Tenerife*, 25 May 1896, repr. in José R. Fernández et al., *La prensa burguesa* (Santa Cruz de Tenerife: Centro de Cultura Popular Canaria, 1986), 75–77.

35. Quoted in Melchor Fernández Almagro, *Historia política de la España contemporánea* (Madrid: Pegaso, 1959), 2:293.

36. E. Castelar, "Crónica internacional," *LEM*, February 1896 (1982): 338.

37. E. Castelar, "La acción diplomática," *EL*, 17 January 1897.

38. R. M. de Labra, "La cuestión de Cuba en 1896," 30 June–4 July 1896, [1901], p. 194–96.

39. Even Castelar's long-standing admiration for Monroe's message of 1823 surfaced briefly, despite his earlier condemnation of 'new' Monroeism, in "Declaraciones del Sr. Castelar," *EL*, 23 December 1896.

40. "Para los españoles," *LJ*, 24 October 1895. Only a few months later, in "¡Solos!" *LJ*, 1 February 1896, this newspaper reversed its earlier stance, so as to better criticize the government's foreign policy, thus: "It may be that some of the government officials of inferior rank that the Restoration uses in times of difficulty, have taken seriously the so-called Monroe doctrine, which is not a doctrine at all, nor strictly speaking was it an intellectual invention of Monroe's, nor indeed is it more than a disjointed collection of incoherent affirmations."

41. "Rumores," *ENR*, 26 October 1895. See also "Extranjero. Venezuela," *ENR*, 28 December 1895; "América y Europa," *ENR*, 4 January 1896; "Peligros," *ENR*, 9 May 1896.

42. "Cleveland," *ENR*, 21 December 1895: "This two-faced policy that we observe in Cleveland is not, to tell the truth, agreeable to us." That this analysis was not far off the mark and, in fact, was belatedly perceived by Olney himself, is suggested by May, *Imperial Democracy*, 90, and well documented by Gerald G. Eggert, *Richard Olney: Evolution of a Statesman* (University Park: Pennsylvania State University Press, 1974): 266.

43. See Lewis Gould, *The Spanish-American War and President McKinley* (Lawrence; University of Kansas Press, 1982), 11.

44. See K. H. Porter and B. Johnson, comps., *National Party Platforms, 1840–1960* (Urbana: University of Illinois Press, 1961), 108.

45. "Contingencias posibles," *EL*, 5 November 1896.

46. "Estados Unidos," *EPa*, 10 November 1896. Also "MacKinley," *ENR*, 7 November 1896.

47. "Contrastes," *ECE*, 10 December 1897.

48. "El mensaje de Mac-Kinley. Lo dulce y lo amargo," *LE*, 7 December 1897.

49. For example "El Mensaje de Mac-Kinley," *EPr*, 9 December 1897; "Contrastes," *ECE*, 10 December 1897; "El mensaje de MacKinley. La intervención," *ENR*, 11 December 1897.

50. "La América del Norte. Recuerdos oportunos," *EG*, 25 March 1898. See John B. Moore, *The Monroe Doctrine: Its Origin and Meaning* (New York: The Evening Post Publishing Co., 1895), and "The Monroe Doctrine," *Political Science Quarterly* 11 (March 1896): 1–29. Moore was not only a scholar but actively involved in foreign policymaking. His influence was doubtless a key factor in McKinley's decision to abstain from invoking the doctrine in 1898.

51. L. V. Varela, "El fondo de la cuestión," *LDLP*, 19 May 1898; "España y Estados Unidos. Monroe y Mac Kinley," *LDLP*, 26 May 1898; and "España y Estados Unidos. Monroe y MacKinley. Las dos doctrinas," *LDLP*, 2 June 1898.

52. "Unica solución," *LDLP*, 16 April 1898, for example, asked: "How does the Northern republican Union even dare to invoke the Monroe doctrine against a Spain that held in her heart the greater part of the American heart?" while "Una opinión sobre la guerra," *EG*, 5 May 1898, reviled "the Monroe doctrine as a principle of industrial exploitation abroad."

53. "Política incolora," *EPa*, 7 February 1898.

54. "España y los Estados Unidos. El paso de las potencias," *ECE*, 9 April 1898.

55. "El discurso del señor Moret," *EG*, 7 May 1898.

56. "Don Federico Rubio," *ENR*, 12 November 1898. See also "Una consulta," *ENR*, 23 July 1898.

57. R. M. de Labra, "La cuestión de Cuba," 10 May 1898, speech in the Senate, in his *La crisis colonial*, 406–7, 423.

58. R. M. de Labra, "Los problemas de Ultramar en 1898," in *La crisis colonial*, 318–19.

59. A measure of such contemporary interest in these aspects can be seen from the following: Marqués de Olivart, "Le différend entre l'Espagne et les Etats-Unis au sujet de la question cubaine," *Revue Générale de Droit International Public* 4 (1897): 577–620; 5 (1898): 358–422, 499–555; 7 (1900): 541–629; 9 (1902): 161–202; A. Desjardins, "La guerre hispano-américaine et le droit des gens," *Revue de Deux Mondes* 147 (1898): 518–49; Felix Stoerck, "Amerikanisches Völkerrecht," *Deutsche Revue* 23:2 (1898): 366–75, transl. into Spanish as "El derecho internacional americano: estudio doctrinal y crítico," *Revista de los Tribunales* [Madrid] 1898; José de Vargas Machuca, *Cuba y los Estados Unidos: Estudio vulgar acerca de las cuestiones pendientes con el gobierno de la Unión Federal bajo el punto de vista del derecho positivo americano* (Madrid: F. Fé, 1898); Ricardo Becerra, *Cuestión palpitante: un poco de historia a propósito de la independencia de Cuba y Puerto Rico, y la Doctrina Monroe y la intervención norteamericana en Cuba* (Caracas: Tip. Moderna, 1898); Louis Érasme LeFur, *Etude sur la guerre hispano-américaine de 1898, envisagée au point de vue du droit international public* (Paris: A. Pedone, 1899); John B. Moore, "International Law in the War with Spain," *Review of Reviews* 19 (1899): 563–68; Elie Lebraud, *La guerre hispano-américaine et le droit des gens* (Paris: A.

Rousseau, 1904); Elbert Jay Benton, *International Law and the Diplomacy of the Spanish-American War* (Baltimore: Johns Hopkins University Press, 1908).

60. See for example, "Los Estados Unidos e Inglaterra," *LE*, 18 October 1895; "La alianza europea," *EPa*, 20 October 1895; "La cuestión de Venezuela," *LE*, 24 October 1895; "España en América," *EPa*, 25 October 1895; "Europa y la doctrina de Monroe," *LE*, 25 October 1895; "La doctrina de Monroe," *LJ*, 20 December 1895; "Inglaterra y los Estados Unidos," *LE*, 22 December 1895; "Peligros," *ENR*, 9 May 1896; "Estado de la cuestión," *EL*, 26 December 1896.

61. On the diplomatic context, see John L. Offner, *An Unwanted War: The Diplomacy of the United States and Spain over Cuba, 1895–1898* (Chapel Hill: University of North Carolina Press, 1992), 17–36; Rosario de la Torre, "1895–1898: Inglaterra y la búsqueda de un compromiso internacional para frenar la intervención norteamericana en Cuba," *Hispania* [Madrid] 57:196 (1997): 515–49; and Javier Rubio, *El gobierno español en busca de una garantía internacional sobre Cuba en vísperas de 1898* (Madrid: Comisión Española de Historia de las Relaciones Internacionales, 1998). For further historiographical and coetaneous views on European responses generally, see the introduction to Hilton and Ickringill, *European Perceptions*, 9–33, and the individual essays on Austrian, British, Dutch, French, German, Italian, Northern Irish, Portuguese, Russian, and Spanish perspectives.

62. For example, "Las islas Hawaii," *ENR*, 19 June 1897, 2/2; "España y la triple alianza," *EPa*, 30 September 1897; "La bandera de la revolución. Unión con Francia y Rusia," *EPa*, 5 October 1897, is revealing in that its preference for a French alliance, while based on colonialist solidarity against Monroeism, also entertains the notion that it would aid the advent of a republic in Spain; "Europa contra los Estados Unidos," *EPr*, 26 November 1897; "Más sobre el Mensaje," *EPa*, 9 December 1897; "Extracto de la prensa. *La Correspondencia Militar*," *EPr*, 10 December 1897; "Bajo tutela," *EPr*, 12 December 1897; "La cuestión de Cuba," *EPa*, 8 January 1898, trusted in "the aid of some powers, greatly interested in seeing that the Monroe doctrine does not prevail in America, against all laws of history and justice"; Lluhí, "Conflicto con los Estados Unidos," *EPr*, 4 April 1898; "La prensa suiza. Europa no debe aceptar la doctrina de Monroe," *EG*, 18 April 1898; "Los yankees contra Francia," *EPa*, 1 May 1898; "Jactancia de los yanquis," *EPr*, 16 May 1898; "Hungría. España y las grandes potencias," *ECE*, 30 May 1898; "La Doctrina de Monroe," *ENPa*, 16 October 1898.

63. "La intervención de Europa," *EG*, 25 July 1898. Also "Con el mazo dando," *EG*, 11 October 1898.

64. "El conflicto de Venezuela," *LJ*, 14 December 1896, said: "the British showed the good sense that characterizes them, setting aside issues of pride." Paradoxically, the defense of Spanish "pride" would be one of this newspaper's ostensible priorities in 1898.

65. "El arbitraje anglo-americano," *LJ*, 14 November 1896; "El conflicto angloamericano," *LV*, 15 November 1896; "Europa y los Estados Unidos," *LE*, 16 November 1896; "Inglaterra y los Estados Unidos," *LE*, 17 November 1896; "La diplomacia de los Estados Unidos," *EL*, 6 December 1896; "Ni arrogancia ni flaqueza," *EL*, 20 December 1896; "Notas parisienses. La opinión ante el conflicto," *EG*, 1 May 1898; "Inglaterra y los Estados Unidos," *EPa*, 2 June 1898; "Inglaterra y los Estados Unidos," *ECE*, 11 August 1898; "Un artículo de Castelar," *EG*, 28 October 1898.

66. "Crónicas americanas," *EPr*, 6 November 1897.

67. The myriad themes inextricably meshed in the Hispanic/Latin vs. Anglo-Saxon dichotomy (and works thereon) cannot be even suggested here. See, for example, Fredrick B. Pike, *Hispanismo, 1898–1936: Spanish Conservatives and Liberals and Their Relations with Spanish America* (Notre Dame and London: University of Notre Dame, 1971), 1–72; Lily Litvak, *Latinos y anglosajones: orígenes de una polémica* (Barcelona: Puvill Editor, 1980).

68. See for example C. Gómez Palacios, *La raza latina: la guerra de España con los Estados Unidos ante el Derecho de España y América* (Buenos Aires: El Correo Español, 1898). Useful recent studies of Latin American attitudes include Sergio Vilaboy, "La revolución independentista de Cuba y la Guerra de 1898 desde la perspectiva de América Latina," *Contrastes. Revista de Historia Moderna* [Murcia] 7–8 (1991–93): 65–83; Mónica Quijada, "Latinos y anglosajones. El 98 en el fin de siglo sudamericano," *Hispania* [Madrid] 57:2:196 (1997): 589–609; Francisco Corral, "El 98 en Paraguay: Rafael Barret," and Ignacio García, "La colonia española en Buenos Aires y la Guerra de Cuba," both in Manuel Alcántara, ed., *América Latina, realidades y perspectivas* (Salamanca: Ediciones Universidad de Salamanca, 1997): 74–103 and 190–218; José L. Abellán et al., *El 98 iberoamericano* (Madrid: Editorial Pablo Iglesias, 1998); Walter L. Bernecker, ed., *1898: su significado para Centroamérica y el Caribe. ¿Cesura, cambio, continuidad?* (Frankfurt: Vervuert, 1998); Salvador Morales, "Visión mexicana del 98," Agustín Sánchez, "La crisis del 98 y las relaciones hispanomexicanas," and Sara Ortelli, "La colonia española de México frente al conflicto del 98," *Cuadernos Hispanoamericanos* [Madrid] 577–78 (1998): 23–43, 45–58, and 73–85; and the interesting sequel studied by Ascensión Martínez Riaza, "Otros escenarios del 98. Estados Unidos y España, árbitros en el conflicto Perú-Chile (1898–1901)," in M. José Alvarez et al., eds., *Fin de Siglo: crisis y nuevos principios* (León: Universidad de Léon, 1999), 259–67.

69. "España en América," *LE*, 24 October 1895. Apart from sources already cited, see also, "La cuestión de Venezuela," *EPa*, 25 October 1895; "El mensaje presidencial," *LV*, 20 December 1895; "La cuestión anglo-americana," *LE*, 21 December 1895; "Venezuela y los Estados Unidos," *EPa*, 22 December 1895; "Carta de Londres," *LE*, 6 January 1896; "El americanismo contra Europa," *LV*, 23 January 1896; "América para los norteamericanos," *EPa*, 20 January 1897; "Aislamiento," *EPr*, 26 December 1897.

70. R. Darío, "El triunfo de Calibán. Contra los yankis," *ENPa*, 21 August 1898.

71. "Aún es tiempo," *ECE*, 19 March 1898.

72. R. M. de Labra, *Aspecto internacional*, 73–97.

73. R. M. de Labra, "La cuestión de Cuba," 10 May 1898 (1901): 425–26.

74. "España en América," *EPa*, 25 October 1895. See also "La Unión Ibero Americana," *EPa*, 3 November 1896.

75. See for example, articles by L. V. Varela in *LDLP*, 26 May 1898 (pointing out that Latin Americans themselves had promoted erroneous constructions of Monroe's message), and *LDLP*, 2 June 1898; R. M. de Labra, "Los problemas de Ultramar en 1898," in *La crisis colonial*, 417, 423–25; "La gaceta de Voss. Artículo sensato," *EPa*, 3 February 1899; and on federalist reactions S. L. Hilton, "Los Estados Unidos como modelo," 11–29.

76. For these themes, see Labra, *Aspecto internacional*, especially 99 and 229–30; "Las colonias españolas después del Tratado de París," *Boletín de la Sociedad Geo-*

gráfica [Madrid] 42 (1900); "La cuestión de Cuba," 10 May 1898, in *La crisis colonial*, 417–33 and 727–30; and his *El Derecho Internacional en España* (Madrid: Imp. de los Hijos de M. G. Hernández, 1905). Heavy sarcasm stressing arbitrariness is patent in "El protocolo. La paz con los Estados Unidos," *EPa*, 14 August 1898: "The Yankees throw us out of America in the name of the Monroe doctrine, and at once forget the Monroe doctrine in order to set their foot on our possessions in Oceania."

77. David F. Trask, *The War with Spain in 1898* (New York: Macmillan, 1981), 486, also argues that "expansion proved costly in legal and moral as well as practical terms."

3

Contradictory Identities, Conflicted Nations: Cuban Émigrés in the United States and the Last War for Independence (1895–98)

Lillian Guerra

On 25 May 1895, the Cuban general J. M. Aguirre wrote a secret letter to a fellow inmate and revolutionary conspirator from his cell in the Spanish fort of La Cabaña in Havana. Part lamentation and part analysis, Aguirre's letter speculated on what the recent death of José Martí, a key organizer of the Cuban Revolution of 1895, would mean to the cohesiveness of the war effort. Prior to joining the rebel army scarcely a month before, Martí had spent years recruiting thousands of Cuban émigrés to the rebel cause. Like Martí (a fifteen-year resident of New York City), most émigrés had settled in the United States after Cuba's first war for independence (1868–78). Driven into exile for their separatist views or by reason of economic necessity (or both), many built new lives for themselves as professionals, small businessmen, and skilled workers in New York, Key West, and Tampa. Despite the social diversity and geographic dispersion of their communities, Martí had forged links among émigrés abroad by organizing them into a network of revolutionary clubs under the mantle of the Partido Revolucionario Cubano (PRC), headquartered in New York. He also successfully pledged the support of these clubs to key military leaders of earlier independence wars.

The most important of these leaders, unlike the majority of their civilian counterparts, had left Cuba to settle in the republics of Central America and the Caribbean rather than the United States. As founder and president of the PRC since 1892, Martí had embarked on an extensive political pilgrimage to meet with and unite émigré clubs in the United States and other countries behind the military leadership and insurgent campaign being organized on the island. Yet, while Martí's efforts had yielded a broad base of support and secure funds for the revolution by 1895, the two phalanges that would eventually make it up—the military organization on the island and civilian clubs abroad—required ideological and logistical coordination if they were to function as a united front during war. As Aguirre pointed out, it was precisely the dualistic framework of the revolutionary movement that Martí had established that—without Martí—could prove the greatest liability to Cuban independence. He wrote, "He who is here does not command the one who is over there nor the one who is over there command the one who is here. This one fights and that one helps. That one sends men, arms, munitions and this one employs them. [. . . But] over there, there is peace, over here, war."[1] Indeed, the radically different contexts from which the civilian and military wings of the Revolution not only experienced the war, but formulated its objectives, proved critical to its direction in the years to come.

Martí had divided the labor of representing the Revolution abroad from that of actually carrying it out between two distinct columns, one comprised of civilian émigrés, the other of armed rebels. Thus, circumstances converged with strategy to create two distinct fronts to Cuba's 1895 War: (1) a diplomatic front overseen by PRC leaders in New York; and (2) a military front overseen by army officers and members of the Government of the Republic-in-Arms, a provisional body of elected officials that received the PRC's diplomatic correspondence and prepared legal codes for the administration of liberated zones. After Martí's death, however, PRC leaders in New York quickly consolidated their power as the authoritative voice of the Revolution before the world. Acting independently of many émigré clubs and increasingly, of army officers in Cuba, PRC leaders actively suppressed the more radical, socially transformative nationalism espoused by top rebel officers, the mass of popular-class soldiers, and their social counterparts in the United States. They did so by centralizing control over the image of the Revolution and by articulating a much more politically conservative project for the Cuban "nation" within the United States. Largely underestimated by historians of this period, the social dimensions of the U.S. context within which Cuban émigré leaders interpreted the war greatly informed the nature of the nation-state that the latter imagined would result. The lessons and beliefs PRC leaders derived from this context also affected the decisions they would make once U.S. intervention ensured the confluence of Cuba's destiny with the economic and political forces of U.S. imperialism.[2]

Driven by men who did not share Martí's passion for keeping the United States out of the war, the PRC responded to Martí's death by focusing its strategies on exactly the opposite goal: that of bringing the United States into the war. Ultimately, the project of "nation" put forth by PRC leaders showed itself to be compatible with not only U.S. intervention in 1898, but with the promotion of U.S. imperialist objectives more broadly. Utterly blinded by ambition and an unshakable faith in their own convictions, these émigrés perceived no contradiction between the goal of Cuban political sovereignty and the means they devised for ensuring that goal. By fanning the flames of U.S. expansionism and endorsing the values of individual expansionists (great and small), PRC leaders and their émigré supporters encouraged the public and U.S. officials to identify with the cause of Cuban rebels by identifying these rebels as cultural and political extensions of themselves. PRC leaders saw no contradiction between imagining a "nation" defined in terms of its political, economic, and social intimacy with a foreign power because they themselves had for so long lived within the borders of that power. Far from constrained or jeopardized by the proclivities of U.S. capitalist-driven culture, their personal success as businessmen and professionals seemed to confirm the ability of U.S. power to liberate and modernize not just individuals like themselves, but the society from which they hailed and which they one day hoped to lead as the future "nation" of Cuba.

Arguably, PRC leaders invoked the tenets of a unique émigré nationalism whose constant referencing of U.S. interests and social values made it "imperialist" long before U.S. imperialism asserted itself on Cuba's war-ravaged shores. Born of their own cultural assimilation to U.S. social and political norms, these émigrés saw an ideological kinship between their own project of liberating Cuba from the corrupt barbarity of Spanish rule and the recent U.S. history of liberating the West and South from a similar history of economic backwardness and cultural stagnation. Thus, the nationalism these Cubans expressed was from the beginning dependent on the United States for its ideological legitimation; achieving modernity through gradual social change and rapid, foreign-financed technological improvement were two of its primary goals. PRC leaders rooted both of these goals in an idealized, illusory interpretation of U.S. society and what they imagined would be a gratefully compliant, future Cuban public.

Seeking to explain why former PRC leaders later emerged as key facilitators of U.S. imperialism in the wake of 1898 (especially in their approbation of the Platt Amendment and the validation of its economic repercussions), some historians have hinged their arguments on depictions of key figures in the PRC as traitors to the nationalist cause. In doing so, these historians fail to explain how many of the same men whom Martí had once condemned as "annexationists" in the late 1880s could so quickly have become his closest associates prior to the war and his subsequent death in 1895.[3] Still others contend that PRC leaders maliciously disguised their "real" intentions at the beginning of the war in the shadow of Martí and later behind the legacy of his rhetoric. Further, they argue, Tomás Estrada Palma (Martí's successor at the helm of the PRC) never veered from a course toward U.S. annexation and saw his dream only partially fulfilled in 1898.[4]

This chapter argues for a more complicated interpretation, one which begins by recognizing what Martí himself may have realized: namely, that the same émigrés whose passion for linking Cuba's destiny with the United States he once understood as "annexationist" were in fact, operating out of what they felt was genuine nationalism. This, more than anything, made them viable partners in the battle for independence from Spain, not just in Martí's eyes but more importantly, in their own. Specifically, this chapter contends that the actions and expressions of PRC leaders represented a unique vision of "nation" that was not "annexationist" but, as explained above, "imperialist nationalist." Stressing foreign investment and reliance on a more industrial, corporate plantation model for Cuba's sugar-centered economy, these Cubans believed the Revolution needed to be founded on the tenets of turn-of-the-century Latin American liberalism.

Championed in the 1890s by political elites in countries as diverse as Brazil, Colombia, and Guatemala, this liberal ideology emphasized social advancement and the achievement of modernity on a par with the United States through the building of modern infrastructure, a growing agro-export trade, education, an accelerated program of social improvement (usually through white immigration), and an appreciation for the values of manual labor in the lower classes.[5] Notably, while capital amassed within the country and technological improvements were financed through foreign investment, this labor was to be done by the lower classes for others. Benefits would first accrue to elites, then to the state, and finally to society as a whole as resources and opportunities began to trickle down to the lower classes themselves. Yet imperialist nationalist leaders of the PRC did not find inspiration in Latin American liberalism alone. They found the most critical components of their vision for Cuba in the mythical ideal of a mostly white, culturally homogeneous, and politically conservative "America" that to their eyes already existed in the United States.

Having lived for as many as twenty years in a country that imagined itself the pinnacle of "modernity" and "civilization," PRC leaders projected their "imperialist nationalist" vision of the nation for which they believed the Revolution was being fought through their policies and their rationalizations of those policies. Tomás Estrada Palma, Gonzalo de Quesada, Benjamín Guerra, and other top PRC heads who had become U.S. citizens during their exile did not expect to make Cuba a part of the United States as much as they expected to recast Cuba as a smaller version of the United States. This "Americanized" Cuba would, nonetheless, remain eminently Cuban—or at least as "Cuban" as they were. Focused outwardly, on the liberation of a society they had not seen in years, they viewed that society through the prism of their own immigrant experience in another, radically different society. In other words, PRC leaders and those generally wealthy émigrés who supported them reflected an internally contradictory sense of identity. Expressions of this experience sought to counter American cultural prejudices and racial fears toward Cubans and Cuban independence by actively engaging U.S. models of culture and conduct. That many revolutionaries—including prominent military officers such as Antonio Maceo or Máximo Gómez—did not hold the same values or compulsion to follow a U.S.-designed liberal road map to modernity as a means of self- and "national" validation did not matter to these émigrés. Steeped in the urban milieu of bourgeois New York society, their own sense of *Cubanidad* was an amalgam of nostalgia, ambition, liberal ideology, and unshakable faith in the United States. For them, the nation not only extended forth from an imperialist nationalist identity; its future depended on it.

In the following pages, we will first explore the process by which PRC leaders sought to centralize control over the images and ideological orientation of the Revolution. Recasting the organization's function within a framework of action and discourse that would appeal to the U.S. public, PRC leaders increasingly dismissed the demands of black and working-class émigrés and denied the need of revolutionaries in Cuba to use guerrilla tactics in order to bring about a successful conclusion to the war. We begin by examining how PRC leaders interpreted the organization's function and elaborated the imperialist nationalist image of nation within a discourse of civilization and modernity meant to appeal more to the U.S. public than to the armed revolutionaries in Cuba themselves. As we shall see, the PRC did not have in mind a vague or ambiguous sense of what it wanted to achieve. In fact, the PRC's certainty about its goals was, at least from the perspective of other revolutionaries, precisely the problem.

DOMESTICATING *CUBA LIBRE* IN THE UNITED STATES: PRC LEADERS AND THE CIVILIZED REVOLUTION

The articulation of imperialist nationalism to the center of the revolutionary project over time owed a great deal to the distinctions of role and purpose to which civilian and military leaders agreed from the outset of the war in 1895. On the other hand, part of the problem had to do with Martí. Between 1891 and 1895, Martí had effectively integrated the predominantly working-class interests of Cuban émigrés into the PRC's nationalist outlook and concerns. Gathering worker-affiliated newspapermen such as Ramón Rivero and the Afro-Cuban Guillermo Sorondo of Florida's cigar-making communities to the center of the Revolution, Martí had formulated the program of the PRC outside of the sphere of New York's sugar-planting and professional elites and in direct consultation with delegates from Tampa and Key West's poorer, patriotic clubs. Although Martí, like Estrada Palma, held most of the reins of control over the PRC network in his hands during the last months of his life (as undisputed president and plenipotentiary delegate of the diplomatic legation), he had demonstrated a history and a style of taking traditionally marginal elements like Cuban workers and blacks into account. After his death, Estrada Palma could not seem to be bothered with such elements, let alone be actively engaged in the articulation of their views.

Thus, while Martí may have been less than democratic in his willingness to oversee the control and direction of the PRC, the very means by which he did so—often by making personal trips to hotbeds of discontent in order to serve as peacemaker—made him a trustworthy patron in the eyes of Florida's and New York's working-class émigrés. By contrast, under the leadership of Tomás Estrada Palma, the PRC became increasingly oriented to the class interests and needs of the resident planting and business elite that had directed conspiratorial insurgencies before or had openly sponsored projects for U.S. annexation. Estrada Palma's amenability to elite interests, while comparable to Martí's, was not balanced by sensitivity to popular-class needs or opinions. As we shall discover, part of the reason lay in the fact that the PRC correctly perceived wealthy Cuban émigrés as having greater influence than their poorer counterparts with the U.S. congressional and executive branches. Estrada Palma's PRC saw U.S. support as vital to the cause of independence whereas Martí's PRC had seen it as dangerous. The difference would prove critical in more ways than one.

After the PRC formally recognized Martí's death in July 1895, the Revolution as the PRC perceived and presented it took a decidedly conservative turn. Former foes of Martí such as Enrique Trujillo, who had considered the Revolution too radical under Martí's direction and the influence of Florida's "militants," would subsequently declare their solidarity with the PRC's new leadership.[6] Formally known under Martí's editorial watch for its discussions of race, class, and Cuban identity, *Patria* quickly dispensed with social themes altogether under the new editorial direction of Enrique José Varona—except of course, whenever the opportunity to minimize black participation in the Revolution presented itself.[7] In response to these developments, radical black émigrés like Rafael Serra (who had worked closely with Martí in La Liga, a night school and reading circle for mostly Afro-Cuban workers) founded a newspaper fully focused on the racial and socially oriented aspects of the independence project that Martí had sponsored and that the Revolution officially endorsed.

Edited by Serra, *La Doctrina de Martí* recruited and received the public support of such progressive middle-class and working-class patriots of Tampa, Ibor City, and Key West as Eligio and Nestor Carbonell, Antonio Palacios, Rosendo Rivero, and Emiliana Brava. As these patriots attested in their letters to the PRC leadership, Serra characterized Martí as "a radical revolutionary" and promoted the tenets of revolutionary nationalism on the basis of the incontrovertible legitimacy that Martí's name inspired among the Revolution's forces.[8] Even more importantly, he openly criticized the emerging social conservatism of those who would confuse "war" with "revolution" by carrying out the former without furthering the latter: "There are those who believe that to revolutionize is to *remedy* a system, or to add or take something away, . . . when this is nothing more than to *evolutionize.* Revolution pulls the tree out by its roots, and plants new seeds. . . . The tree of colonialism in Cuba must be attacked at its roots. We must revolutionize."[9] Significantly, however, Serra did not so much refer in his critiques to the attitudes of the PRC under Estrada Palma's leadership—Serra regarded Estrada Palma as a personal friend and confidante until at least 1902.[10] Rather, he referred to the small, but extremely powerful group of wealthy exiles who threatened to turn the PRC ever more firmly toward their interests alone. Despite the growing discontent of such individuals like Serra and others, it seemed that nothing could stop the transformation of the PRC into the instrument of financial and diplomatic power that imperialist nationalists needed to subvert the views of more radical revolutionaries by gaining external support for their own imperialist nationalist project and leadership from the United States.

Yet, however appealing the tendency to view Estrada Palma as a sellout to conservatives at best and an annexationist at worst, such a view tends to obscure what were otherwise important ideological differences between the post-Martí PRC leadership and the aristocratic proponents of Spanish autonomy or U.S. annexation whom the PRC—both before and after Martí—counted as "allies." The latter, led by Enrique Trujillo, Hector de Saavedra, and Enrique José Varona, were by and large organized into the Sociedad de Estudios de la Jurídica y Economía (Society of Legal Studies and Economy; hereafter, SEJE), an émigré version of Havana's influential Sociedad Económica de Amigos del País (Economic Society of Friends of the Country). Although the disappearance of Martí's populism and the rise of even more "centrist" elements in the PRC brought about a thawing of relations and patriotic promises from Trujillo and the like, there is no doubt that tremendous hostility and suspicions of PRC "radicalism" continued among members of the SEJE. In the winter of 1896–97, such feelings exploded onto the public arena in New York when de Saavedra took it upon himself to denounce the PRC's leadership before a meeting of the SEJE. Although no details of de Saavedra's charges were ever published, so shocking were his allegations (and the Society's apparent endorsement of them) that the PRC advisory council in New York was forced to call for a formal vote of confidence on behalf of Estrada Palma.

According to Eduardo Yero, a member of the PRC's advisory council, the editors of *Patria* only reluctantly agreed to publish the vote, one in which all émigré revolutionary clubs in the United States and elsewhere participated. Amazingly, Yero found himself forced to write a defense of the PRC in *La Doctrina de Martí, Patria*'s radical (and highly critical) rival. Despite its role as the PRC's official party organ, Yero charged, *Patria* had become an unofficial *vocero* (voicebox) for the SEJE.[11] A few weeks later, the SEJE came under such heavy criticism for betraying the Cuban cause of social unity for the sake of independence that it was forced to dissolve. In the end, the image of a united revolutionary front of émigrés before the public and in the midst of war superseded any political misgivings that conservatives might have had.[12] Reflecting on the matter, Hector de Saavedra privately explained the source of his and others' frustrations as lying with the PRC's long-standing willingness to court black and working-class interests. Although Martí, the primary ringleader of such strategies had vanished, current PRC leaders were reluctant to do away with the connections Martí had established to these radical and apparently, uppity groups. One of these leaders noted,

> There is a tremendous internal struggle here. The Society of Legal Studies had to disband out of patriotism, for not providing fodder to the chatterings of a certain "democratic black" element that here calls us "the intellectuals." They are making a tremendous war on Varona to strip him of his position at *Patria* to which your friend Yero aspires. In short, there is an Advisory Council, dogged by two blacks, Serra and Figuero, and various cigar-workers with Yero in the lead that dominate [Estrada] Palma through terror and make or pretend to establish the doctrine that they, those of the rabble, are the only ones with the right to direct things in Cuba. With imagine what future end![13]

In light of such racist and elitist attitudes, Estrada Palma's pedigree as a middle-class reformer emerges in sharper relief. Clearly, his commitment to a heavily liberal, market-driven, and foreign-subsidized future for Cuba made his inclusion of marginal elements into the PRC as pragmatic and paternalistic in inspiration as similar actions carried out by Martí might have been. However, if by comparison, Martí was a populist who entertained a more socially revolutionary and anti-imperialist nationalist vision along the lines of Máximo Gómez and Antonio Maceo, Estrada Palma was a moderate whose centrism can only be appreciated in full view of the rabid conservativism of wealthy émigrés.

As a moderate, though, Estrada Palma defined his tenure at the PRC helm in paternal and increasingly authoritarian terms—possibly as a way of offsetting his more conservative critics. Estrada Palma viewed the PRC's primary objective to be U.S. recognition of Cuban belligerency rights or independence (a feat that would have facilitated the shipping of arms to the field and increased the Revolution's legitimacy abroad). However, the PRC never managed to sway New York's congressional or senatorial delegates in favor of either. This may well speak to the power of New York's émigré conservatives and the SEJE: many members held property and commercial interests in Cuba or, as lawyers, represented Americans who did. As a result, they pressed first the Cleveland and then the McKinley administrations for restraint. Only in the context of a full-scale U.S. military intervention were

Northeastern corporate interests and their representatives in Congress prepared to consider seriously any alternative to Spanish rule.[14]

However, if those in the SEJE camp viewed Estrada Palma as too radical, working-class émigrés and their supporters in New York and Florida saw him as not radical enough. Thus, on the heels of the Government-in-Arms' confirmation of Estrada Palma as president of the diplomatic legation following Martí's death, members of Florida's revolutionary community expressed discomfort with the reorganization of PRC statutes. The new statutes allowed Estrada Palma to hold both the presidency of the PRC and the office of supreme delegate for the clubs in his hands. Not surprisingly, in March 1896 they appealed to the man known as Martí's closest friend, Gonzalo de Quesada, as a possible alternative candidate. Although de Quesada dared not accept the nomination of the clubs to run against Estrada Palma, he did admit that Estrada Palma was well aware of the support de Quesada had among grass-roots supporters for the position of delegate. He also insinuated that if Estrada Palma announced his own candidacy, it would be to squelch the advance of any potential rival.[15] Only one month later, de Quesada's belief was confirmed: the Government-in-Arms and PRC leadership rewrote the statutes of the PRC so that whomever was appointed president of the diplomatic legation by the Government-in-Arms would *automatically* become the supreme delegate of the network of revolutionary clubs. No vote by the clubs on the matter was required. The move effectively centralized power and made Estrada Palma no longer responsible to the working-class and progressive grass-root organizations that had been responsible for formulating the PRC's program with Martí in the first place.[16]

Incredible as it seems, such expressions of authoritarianism were the products of men who considered themselves lovers of liberty and democracy. The middle-class professionals at the head of the PRC did not see any contradiction between their brand of nationalism and revolutionary practice in their own elitist policymaking. As discussed below, there really was no contradiction: the nature of the imperialist form of nationalism they espoused was inextricably wedded to the ideals and standards of "modern civilization," a condition to which Cuba and most Cubans—or so they thought—could only still aspire. Attaining it would require of the Revolution and the emerging nation, patience, unswerving confidence in PRC leaders, and respect for social (and economic) order created along the lines of the American model of "civilization." For PRC leaders, inculcating the values and customs of modern civilization into the Cuban nation began with the war effort itself. They did this principally in two ways: first, by carrying out a publicity campaign in the United States meant to highlight their own perspective on Cuba's past and future; and second, by desperately trying to enforce "civilized" standards of conducting warfare with regard to property and the personal treatment of wealthy loyalists in Cuba among the Revolution's military cadres.

Many historians have identified the "yellow" press and specific newspaper moguls as principal players in the media campaign to popularize the Cuban war among the U.S. public and expansionist Washington officials. Although such efforts were undoubtedly central to building momentum for a U.S. intervention in 1898, research into the attitudes and activities of PRC leaders reveal an organized, concerted strategy to appeal to the ideological convictions of U.S. citizens and the interests of the business community—all for the benefit of the PRC's own imperialist nationalist vision of *Cuba Libre*. The PRC employed media specialists who toured the greater Northeast and cities as far west as Chicago to publicize the PRC's vision.[17] Key among these was Fidel Pierra, a Cuban-born businessman. Pierra had spent his teenage years learning English in the United States and faced extradition upon returning to Cuba during the first war for Cuban independence, known as the Ten Years' War (1868–78), when his activities as a Freemason and publisher of liberal newspapers marked him as a potential rebel to Spanish authorities. After escaping to New York City in 1872, Pierra had become a prominent member of Brooklyn's working- and middle-class émigré communities after establishing various mutual aid and "free-thinking" societies.[18] As a PRC agent under Estrada Palma's direction, Pierra's travels promoted the Cuban cause in New York, Rhode Island, Pennsylvania, Ohio, and Virginia in the first two years of the war alone.

Typically, Pierra would arrive by train in the host city, where he would be met by a delegation of prominent local citizens and politicians who escorted him to his hotel and frequently offered to pay his expenses—an offer Pierra always turned down in order to prevent the 1895 Revolution from bearing any resemblance to earlier Cuban and U.S.-sponsored filibustering ventures to annex Cuba to the United States.[19] During his stay, he would attend both large public gatherings and small, intimate meetings with the politically and socially powerful. Yet, the sheer range and number of citizens who flocked to his speeches (often amid fierce weather) reflected the extent to which Americans of various classes felt an affinity for the Cuban cause, a cause Pierra worked to associate with his audience's own national myths of social progress and an inclusive democracy. For instance, in Cleveland, Ohio, over three thousand people turned out to hear Pierra's address extolling the sacrifices and suffering of Cuba's virtuous elite men at the hands of greedy and cruel Spaniards; ten thousand ribbons advertising the event had been sold in advance. The Cuban American League of Cleveland, formed immediately thereafter, promised to generate more propaganda materials and to forward all proceeds to PRC headquarters in New York. Pierra also made sure to meet with reporters of all the local newspapers and gratefully declined offers by local men who promised to raise armed volunteer militias at the disposition of the Liberating Army.[20]

Pierra's success in generating solidarity for Cuba among Northern veterans of the U.S. Civil War and, possibly, former abolitionists only underscores the nature of PRC efforts to appeal to Americans' perceptions of themselves as models of social and political progress.[21] Like other PRC leaders, Pierra was convinced that the strategic and discursive unity of black and white Cubans was critical to winning the war. However, unity did not necessarily imply a mutual, overt commitment to the ideals of racial equality, but rather a mutual, covert recognition of the role that racial divisions had played in impeding the success of previous independence struggles, most especially the Ten Years' War.[22] Originally conceived by Martí, the PRC's official discourse with regard to race promoted the idea of racial tolerance but did so through the silencing of discussions on race and the role that race had played in the historical exploitation of one class of Cubans by another.

Thus, white Cubans' participation in the slave regime, their endorsement of racial hierarchy, and their general complicity in the marginalization of blacks before and after Spain abolished slavery in 1886 were glossed as historical evils whose destruction depended on the triumph of independence. The legacies of these evils, so Martí argued, had already been (or were in the process of being) expunged by black and white Cubans' mutual shedding of blood and personal sacrifice.[23] In any case, the Spanish were to blame for the hatred sown among Cubans in the past; to be a patriot required submission to the idea that the Spanish were the enemy and that the mantle of *Cubanidad* provided a refuge for all Cubans regardless of race—at least so long as Cubans agreed to speak of equal treatment on the basis of their qualifications for citizenship and *not* on the role race had played in conditioning their qualifications.[24]

It was on the basis of such views that Pierra articulated his message of solidarity with the Cuban cause to a U.S. audience which, he believed, shared a similar set of assumptions regarding race and white Northerners' own struggle in the recent Civil War. Pierra presumed that Northerners understood that the U.S. Civil War had been fought for national unity in the name of progress. By illustrating the Cuban revolutionary cause in similar terms, Pierra engaged the rationale that Americans had fought against the economic and cultural backwardness that had enslaved U.S. blacks and impeded modern industrial development in the U.S. South. Cuban rebels were not "other" to Americans themselves, but merely represented a variation on the core values and beliefs for which Americans stood. As an imperialist nationalist, it was natural that Pierra should present the case of Cuba in this way: after all, the ideal Cuban revolutionary in his mind was precisely that—an extension of and, perhaps, an improvement on the American identity.

Judging from the success of his appeals, Pierra's presumptions about his audience's sensibilities proved accurate. For example, the Philadelphia Brigade Association, a veterans' organization, mobilized a coalition of Protestant and Catholic ministers who joined in sending a petition to Congress in November 1895 that demanded immediate recognition of the Cuban republic. The next day, Governor Claude Matthews of Indiana, together with Estrada Palma, presided over a rally on behalf of Cuban independence.[25] While Pierra undoubtedly hoped to appeal to as broad and diverse an American public as possible, he never neglected to pay special attention to those who could not only make a political difference in Washington but also an economic one in Cuba once independence was achieved. Thus, despite his own acknowledgment that the majority of the one thousand supporters who turned out to hear him give a speech in Providence were middle- and working-class citizens, Pierra emphasized in reports to the PRC the presence of those belonging to "the better society," including the mayor and representatives of the local men's athletic club.[26] The PRC welcomed and courted the support of all Americans but especially appreciated those whose class status marked them as champions of the social and political project promoted by PRC leaders.

Like Pierra's speeches, PRC propaganda materials including English-language books such as *Free Cuba* by Rafael Merchán and *The History of the War* by Gonzalo de Quesada emphasized three themes that leaders believed would most appeal to American sensibilities: (1) the Spanish colonial administration's corruption and frequent embezzlement of island revenues; (2) the near absence of a public school system for the Cuban majority; and (3) Spain's persecution of rich revolutionaries who unselfishly sacrificed their titles of nobility and wealth for "freedom."[27] Indeed, when rendering specific testimony to Congress, PRC leaders depicted the rebel army as dominated by cultured, wealthy, and mostly white men too long victimized by Spanish barbarism. They adamantly downplayed the role of blacks among Cuban forces, insisting that blacks comprised no more than one-third of the army's enlisted ranks instead of the two-thirds that they probably did. Similarly, PRC leaders took every opportunity to celebrate the presence of former aristocrats in their officer corps and provisional government.[28] Presumably, most Americans would be comforted by the idea that PRC leaders saw blacks as marginal rather than central to the cause and perceive white Cubans (whom the PRC depicted as wealthy blue bloods) as at least as "white" as they. Moreover, in presenting their case for U.S. recognition of Cuban belligerency rights and/or independence before Washington's social elite, PRC agents strove to demonstrate their qualifications as future leaders of a Cuban nation cast in their own design through the cultural-class idiom of refined tastes and a keen fashion sense. Thus, in a memoir of his longtime association with émigré leaders Martí and Estrada Palma, American lawyer Horatio S. Rubens recalled the effect of Ricardo Díaz Albertini's appointment to the PRC's Washington office:

> Albertini was valuable; he had a social flair; . . . He was a fixture in fashionable circles in Europe and America, among people who shuddered delicately at "those disturbed conditions." . . . Many people, nevertheless, marveled that so polished a man of the

world would consort with "revolutionists." Albertini's clothes were from England, though; his shoes from Italy; his ties from France and made to a special specification of form. He danced beautifully; he dined with a manner. He knew knives and forks.[29]

By way of contrast, Rubens noted that Albertini's good taste served to eclipse that of his less worldly though equally pompous PRC colleague in Washington, Gonzalo de Quesada, whom he noted, "wore removable cuffs." As Pierra stated in a speech in Washington, the object of such efforts was to contest Spanish representations of the revolutionary forces as consisting of "only some ignorant Negroes, a few white people of the lowest class of society, some bandits and a few foreign adventurers."[30] Through men such as Albertini, the embodiment of European etiquette, and Pierra, of American sensibilities, the PRC showed the Cuban cause for what it "really" was: a struggle to promote a Euro-American-styled civilization led by white, elite Cubans in what had been until then a barbarically ruled and savage land.

Accordingly, Pierra and other PRC publicity "commissioners" sent a glamorous and appealing message to elite-class sectors of American society, making what Teddy Roosevelt's secretary of state, John Hay, would later call a "splendid little war" seem like the latest philanthropic cause of choice. For example, from 25 to 30 May 1896, Pierra held a lavish "Cuban-American Fair" for the war in Madison Square Garden, which he advertised under the motto "Cuba appreciates sympathy—she must have assistance."[31] The fair collected nineteen thousand dollars for the war effort but cost a whopping fourteen thousand dollars in expenses.[32] Indeed, the holding of celebratory dances, balls, and other such events by affiliated émigré clubs projected a sophisticated, cosmopolitan image of Cuba's society and cultural prospects that were in keeping with the liberal philosophies of PRC leaders. Often, the self-sacrificing white hero of Cuban independence took center stage in the form of José Martí. Pale, meticulously (if starkly) dressed, and thin enough that his robust intellect contrasted with the appearance of physical frailty, Martí had during his lifetime fulfilled the standard of Victorian-age masculinity so glorified in the romantic literature of the time. Subsequent to his death, Cuban émigrés came to recognize this as both inspiring and powerfully self-validating of their own worth as noncombatant representatives of the civilized ideal. Ignoring the fact that Martí's fulfillment of the heroic Victorian ideal of civilized man confronting the evils of barbarism had cost him his life, imperialist nationalist émigrés portrayed themselves as authentic embodiments of Martí's ideals. They, like Martí, were the "minds" behind the Revolution, its cerebral and cultural soul. Thus, the PRC club of Manhattan, "José Martí," organized an evening of music and English-language theater for an American audience, promising that one of the scenes of the dramatic production would include a bust of José Martí on the stage.[33]

Not surprisingly, elite émigré women played a critical role in the construction of an image of *Cuba Libre* (Free Cuba) founded on imperialist nationalist principles. Using the sacrifice of their own personal wealth as an analogous symbol of the property and wealth sacrificed by white, elite-class soldiers, rich ladies in West Tampa were moved to send a collection of diamond and other precious gem-encrusted jewelry to New York as a donation to PRC coffers.[34] Similarly, the statutes of the all-female club Disciples of Martí recalled the heroic principle of self-denial typified by the ideal Victorian male by requiring all its female members to be unmarried. Further, they prohibited members from dancing at the very parties the club arranged to raise funds for independence until that goal was achieved.[35] Celebrating the star quality of its central hero, the letterhead of the club carried a sketch of the face of José Martí heralded by the club's name and a halo of tiny, boldly printed hearts.[36]

Moreover, magazines like Raimundo Cabrera's *Cuba y América* frequently carried descriptions of such activities and photographs of women's clubs on their "society pages," a column redefined to include only social engagements strictly connected to the cause of *Cuba Libre.*[37] Elite women supporters of the Revolution in exile also contributed to the PRC's civilizing mission through the nature of their fundraising activities and the items they chose to send to soldiers in the field. Thus, Carmen Mantilla, now widely considered to be Martí's common-law wife during his exile in New York, reported in April 1895 that her own club, Hijas de Cuba, would be holding both a bazaar and a party under the patronage of New York émigré socialite Emilio Agramonte, with benefits to go to the PRC. She summed up the efficacy of such efforts in monetary terms: in one month alone, Hijas de Cuba had collected one thousand dollars.[38]

The PRC also reached beyond these informational speeches, fairs, and gala parties to raise funds and drum up support for self-styled, imperialist nationalist images of *Cuba Libre.* Consistently, PRC leaders contracted sympathetic agents among the U.S. press and on occasion, directly manipulated the war news by misreporting or leaking information. Traditionally, the process of "packaging" the Cuban Revolution of 1895 for American consumption has been seen as one-sided, dominated by the burgeoning U.S. media industry that not only sold newspapers but also catered to a broad spectrum of readers, which included workers, corporate moguls, and eager imperialist policymakers. In reality, though, this process was quite dialectical, involving the conscious efforts of PRC leaders to shape and represent the Revolution of 1895 in terms meaningful both to them as imperialist nationalists and to the very sectors whose economic interests and political connections they sought to exploit. Apparently, PRC courting of and reliance on American reporters to tell the Revolution's story from the leadership's perspective was well known and commonly accepted, even by secret revolutionary agents operating in Havana.[39] For example, the PRC patronized the trip of New

York war correspondent Franc R. E. Woodward to meet Maceo's troops in Cuba by providing him with letters of introduction for Martí, Gómez, and Maceo. Additionally, PRC leaders conferred on him the commissioned rank of captain in the Liberating Army.[40] Sylvester Scoval, of the *World*, accompanied an expedition of Cuban émigrés departing from Key West with arms for the Revolution in the spring of 1896.[41] So trusting was the relationship between PRC leaders and the press that American reporters were often recruited to scout out Spanish spies among fellow media correspondents on the war front and to warn the leadership of their identities.[42]

Far less commonly known among American contemporaries (and historians of the period alike) was the fact that Fidel Pierra secretly penned dozens of articles on Cuba's society, history, economic condition, war, and political future as a republic for such influential newspapers as *The Journal* (New York), *The New Republic, Peterson's Magazine, The Sun, The Shipping and Commercial List*, and the *Boston Herald*. As Pierra admitted, most of the articles were not signed by him "because it was preferable that they be presented as if they were the product of American pens so as to inspire greater confidence" among readers. So successful was Pierra at this political and discursive masquerade that he bragged to the PRC's second-in-command, Joaquín del Castillo, about a front-page piece he wrote on Spanish governor Valeriano Weyler's anti-insurgent policies for *The Journal*. According to Pierra, the article had been read as testimony of American public opinion before the U.S. Senate at the request of Senator Sherman in early 1896.[43]

These developments underscore the ideological orientation of PRC leaders toward the practices, beliefs, and institutions of the "modern" sectors of U.S. society. More importantly, they also reveal the lengths to which the PRC would go to ensure U.S. diplomatic recognition, mediation, or even military intervention on Cuba's behalf in as short a time as possible. The need for such a solution grew into a veritable obsession between the summer of 1895 and late 1897, as Estrada Palma, de Quesada, and other PRC agents scrambled to garner first congressional and then presidential support of Cuba's right to belligerency and/or independence. The results of their efforts—continuing hostility from the White House and faltering enthusiasm in Congress—fell far short of PRC expectations. The need to turn the tide diplomatically and end the war categorically was crucial to PRC leaders for two reasons: first, because of their commitment to maintaining the structures of a plantation society under the republic and, second, because liberal principles dictated that they attract foreign investment to the country in order to assure future growth. The longer the fighting dragged on, the further Cuba's economy and her few symbols of modernity (such as the railroad and telegraph system) were reduced to rubble by their own rebel forces and Spanish troops alike. Differences in the way that Cuba's civilian and military leaderships perceived this situation paved the way for the PRC's imperialist nationalists to seek outside allies in order to assert their dominance within the revolutionary enterprise of nation building.

To PRC leaders, attaining the goal of a viable nation-state required patience on the part of the lower classes, unswerving confidence in the PRC's own leadership, and a healthy dose of respect for the socioeconomic order from Cuban revolutionaries themselves. From New York, these émigrés believed that laying the groundwork for the inculcation of these values and customs into the future "nation" they desired had to begin with the war effort itself. Increasingly, they began to do this by trying to enforce "civilized" standards of conduct among revolutionaries in the field by criticizing the guerrilla nature of rebel warfare itself, especially in terms of its destruction of property and the brutal treatment of royalist elites in Cuba. Many military caudillos, especially the veterans of previous independence wars, held no such proclivities. For revolutionaries like Maceo and Gómez, Cuba's struggle was about ending oppression on multiple levels. Destroying the structures and mindset regarding the role of Cuba's popular classes in society was both the first step to ending colonialism and the first step toward independent nationhood. Not surprisingly, then, PRC efforts brought them into conflict with the Revolution's military cadres. By extension, they also brought the imperialist nationalist image of "nation" into conflict with the alternative social project and image of nation espoused by more radical military officers. Committed to opening up the economy to a wider number of Cuban, not foreign, participants, these officers hoped to make the education and the social condition of the popular classes a priority for the future state. Contrasting markedly with the vision of New York's elite émigrés, the "nation" for which they were fighting was steeped in the ideals of this alternative, revolutionary nationalism. Ultimately, ideological clashes over the nature of the "nation" for which revolutionaries were fighting on international and domestic fronts jeopardized the goal of independence itself during the war. Enduring conflicts between imperialist nationalist and revolutionary nationalist "nations" wrought before 1898 could only ensure the vulnerability of any alliance against U.S. imperialism in times of peace.

FINANCING FREEDOM, CONFRONTING COSTS: PRC LEADERS AND THE CUBAN MILITARY

Conflicts over the meaning of "revolution" and its implications for the prospect of nation building among civilian and military leaders were perhaps best illustrated in the divergent approach and attitude of each toward the strategies of warfare employed by the Liberating Army. In order to face the larger and better-equipped Spanish army, Cuban rebels relied on weapons—including machetes—often imported secretly from the United States to the war front. To buy arms, print *Patria* (the PRC's newspaper), subsidize the newspapers of other clubs, and provide stipends for PRC agents, revolutionaries in Cuba relied on the expropriation of supplies from island plantations and the acquisition of direct cash payments from planters. They did this by threatening planters with the destruction of their crops and sugar mills. Such cash payments, given in exchange for the Liberating Army's protection, were called a revolutionary "tax." Like plantation and town raids by rebel forces, this taxation strategy became a mainstay of their activities. Of course, many planters felt besieged on all sides and only reluctantly agreed to fill the liberators' war chests.[44] Máximo Gómez described a typical encounter with such a planter in this way:

> "Do not order the destruction of the sugar mill, because that is savage" the landowner began to shout, and I answered him: "Sure, then why don't you get those little Spanish soldiers out of your house [*Pues sáqueme Ud. los soldaditos españoles de su casa*] and pay for your reasonable share to the revolution, or go with your sugar mill back to Spain. What is in Cuba belongs to the Cubans." And the landowner then began to deal with the revolution, and [the revolution], being honorable, shall know how to respect and fulfill her contracts.[45]

Alternating subtle and direct means of coercion, revolutionaries in the field found the policy of extorting wealthy planters extremely effective in generating funds and often, in swelling their ranks with popular-class recruits. By relying on guerrilla strategies of plantation raids and town invasions, the Liberating Army articulated a world-turned-upside-down scheme for consolidating a radically different "nation," which naturally appealed to the many former slaves, plantation workers, and peasants who joined rebel officers. Many (if not most) elite-class white officers did not interpret their tactics in the same way.[46] However, the fact that key military leaders like Maceo and Gómez did recognize their actions in terms similar to those of the most radical popular-class insurgents gave credibility to the view that *Cuba Libre* really would break with the economic system and social norms of the Spanish colonial past. Thus, mutuality of action despite differences of interpretation characterized the Revolution's armed movement as much as it did the PRC-led civilian wing. That PRC leaders and conservative white officers tolerated and even endorsed guerrilla strategies despite their naturally ambiguous ideological implications is not difficult to explain. Judging from the financial reports of the PRC during the first two years of the war, the Revolution could not have survived without the collection of planter tribute. Together with similar "taxes" levied on mining companies, the amounts collected in Cuba and funneled to the PRC totaled nearly half a million dollars.[47]

However, Máximo Gómez, as supreme commander of the Liberating Army, and Antonio Maceo, as second-in-command, understood the purpose of such tactics to extend beyond that of merely financing the war. For them, the strategy was in keeping with the promises Gómez and Martí had made in the Manifesto of Montecristi, the Revolution's formal declaration of objectives and principles, before launching the war. As a form of taxing the rich to benefit the poor, revolutionary revenues generated at the front foreshadowed a redistributive role for the state. Under a republic, or so the manifesto had pledged, soldiers of the Liberating Army would be compensated with land and resources.[48] Thus, revolutionary taxation served to instruct planters and rebel soldiers alike on how differently society would be structured after independence. To officers like Gómez, the money collected in tribute meant nothing if the social character of the Revolution was weakened or its goal of demolishing the foundations of colonial society was compromised in the process.[49]

Thus, Gómez cheered on the tactics of Antonio Maceo, whose successful invasion of western Cuba he attributed to Maceo's adamant refusals to accept any bribes from elites, a group he cast as "the powerful ones, partial to the [Spanish] tyrant." In response to such offers, Maceo had ordered his troops to burn every property in sight, "destroying and purifying the origins of such greed." These origins were historical and deeply rooted in the class-color distinctions that had served as the colonial elites' primary rationale for justifiying the exploitation and marginalization to which they subjected black and lower-class Cubans for generations. "Everything is collapsing, and the little that is left standing, Spain herself has determined to destroy. All the better," concluded Gómez.[50] For his part, Maceo declared himself little interested in entering into any compromise for any reason with either colonial aristocrats or the United States.[51] If the United States was genuinely concerned with ending the war for Cuba's sake, he challenged, then let her make possible the shipment of enough arms and munitions to equip the Cuban rebels properly.[52] Otherwise, his terse words imply, no wing of the Revolution should trust the U.S. government or actively court U.S. interests.

Through the lens of imperialist nationalism, Tomás Estrada Palma, together with the first president of the Republic-in-Arms during the 1895 war, Salvador Cisneros Betancourt, were naturally limited in their enthusiasm for methods of war premised on the destruction of private property. Although they appreciated Gómez's respect for and inclusion of civilian leaders like themselves in his plans, they also recognized that neither attitude implied greater flexibility regarding guerrilla strategies.[53] Estrada Palma differed more sharply from Cisneros Betancourt in his interpretation of the degree to which the tax-and-raid approach to financing and spreading the Revolution should be controlled and how it should be understood by those whose interests were attacked. To this end, he frequently met and responded to the concerns of American investors, even writing letters to the Government-in-Arms on behalf of specific investors to request guarantees for the protection of their properties and their right to make improvements on them. He did this in part because he hoped to make investors sympathetic to Cuban independence in order to take advantage of their influence in Washington. But he also did this because he wanted them to feel comfortable with the idea of continuing their investments in a Cuban republic.[54] In a letter to one investor explaining the need for such measures, Estrada Palma rationalized them as less barbaric and more humane to the noncombatant population than the traditional military methods of blockading a town or fortifying its central plaza, normally the local seat of colonial government. Further, he described the future free Cuba as "the home of Cubans and Spaniards, who, as members of the same family, will live in peace and harmony, as members of the same nation. . . . We desire that, once the war ends, those dignified Spaniards should continue living in Cuba, because they, as a [social] element of hard work and order, should serve . . . to give impetus [and] the right direction to the young Republic."[55] At one point in the summer of 1896, Estrada Palma proposed having all payments of taxes go directly to the PRC through the planters' accountants already in New York, a move he felt might inspire more confidence than having planters deal with rebels in the field. He also proposed organizing a planters' association to defend their interests and make the tax collection more efficient.[56]

These activities and proposals, inspired by the tenets of imperialist nationalism, infuriated more radical, revolutionary nationalist members of the Cuban military. Understandably, combatants felt their efforts to destabilize plantation society and punish colonial elites for their tacit support of Spain were being undermined by the very people the Revolution had charged with defending their actions abroad. In September 1896, Gómez responded to Estrada Palma's proposals in no uncertain terms. If a military stalemate had begun to emerge between rebels and royalists, he claimed, it was the fault of PRC leaders in New York, not that of the military. Émigrés' willingness to negotiate with agents of the planting elite abroad and restrict the strategic targets of the Liberating Army had taken away the rebels' greatest weapon—fear. For this reason, Gómez rejected a PRC proposal that would further allow planters to harvest sugar in exchange for money donations by saying,

> In Cuba, it is not possible for anyone to work. Work is a crime against the revolution. Not understanding this from the beginning is the reason that we have seen extended the hours of our triumph. . . . They ought to pay and pay heavily [*pagar gordo*], only and for nothing more, than that we should respect their properties, and to him who does not pay, well he is already lost [to the cause] and he has no reason to make any rational claim, let alone a just one. What is his should be destroyed.[57]

In short, the military leadership turned the PRC leadership's proposals for regulating tax collections down on all counts.[58]

Undoubtedly, Estrada Palma often adopted an accommodating position with officers like Gómez, even recognizing in different moments the positive message of strength that the Revolution sent the world in levying taxes on Cuba's elite. Yet, he was also not afraid to go through extraofficial channels in order to implement the PRC's own plan for ending the war and ensuring a secure beginning for the imperialist nationalist "nation." When dealing with those he assumed to be in agreement, Estrada Palma tended to let down his guard. For example, he instructed "Mario" (a conspirator in the Havana underground) not to ship any dynamite or other explosives sent by émigré clubs in Key West to revolutionaries in the field. Because many of these Florida-based clubs boasted a largely working-class membership with deeply rooted ties to the labor movement, PRC leaders distrusted their objectives and generally dismissed their socially democratic vision for the Revolution as misguided or even dangerous.[59] Ostensibly operating under the same set of assumptions, Mario proceeded to contact Rosario Sigarroa, a principal organizer of arms shipments in Tampa and directed her to turn down the offer of dynamite, originally made by José Dolores Poyo. Though hardly a social radical, Poyo had been a former reader in tobacco factories and a close associate of Martí's in the struggle to bring Florida's émigré tobacco workers to the cause of independence. Apparently, for Mario, the association was enough to make Poyo's intentions suspect. Thus, Mario explained, "in this way, our efforts here will be made easier and our people will not grow accustomed to anarchist methods [in preparation] for the day that we will be alone."[60]

But try as they might, Estrada Palma and the rest of the Revolution's leaders—military and civilian—would not be able to turn back the clock.[61] In fact, by the second year of the war, Estrada Palma and his cohort were convinced that the war had reached an unbridgeable stalemate. As a solution, the PRC began plotting ways outside of military victory to end the war and still gain independence from Spain. It is not clear whether the military leadership at any level (including Máximo Gómez) was ever informed of these plans. However, Estrada Palma and the PRC acted with the full knowledge and consent of civilian leaders like President Cisneros Betancourt of the Government-in-Arms on the island every step of the way.

Beginning in the spring of 1897, PRC leaders concocted various covert schemes meant to win U.S. and/or Spanish recognition of Cuban independence. That May, acting in his role as plenipotentiary delegate of the Revolution, Estrada Palma, vice delegate Joaquín Castillo, José Zayas, and Benjamín Guerra signed a contract on behalf of the PRC and the republic with John R. Dos Passos, a man described in Estrada Palma's official report to the Government-in-Arms as a "rich lawyer from New York." In exchange for the sum of one million dollars in bonds of the Cuban republic, Dos Passos was given six months to orchestrate "the recognition of the Cubans as an independent nation by the United States or Spain" and to arrange with Spain and the Cuban republic "the evacuation of the Island of Cuba by the Spanish forces."[62] However, Dos Passos was apparently able to secure only a private meeting between Estrada Palma and President McKinley's brother.[63] Impatient and increasingly restless, Estrada Palma was already negotiating another deal by June 1897, this time with a syndicate of Wall Street brokers led by Samuel L. Janney. According to the original terms of the contract and amortization scheme signed by both parties on 1 October 1897, the Republic of Cuba agreed to pay Janney and his cronies the sum of $150 million dollars in 4 percent gold bonds of the Republic of Cuba (payment to begin 1 January and end in 1953). In return, Janney would convince the Spanish Crown within three months from the date of the contract to sell the island of Cuba to the Cuban revolutionaries.[64] The money was to be guaranteed by custom receipts under trust to the U.S. Department of the Treasury. U.S. treasury officials were to serve as independent inspectors, ensuring payment and preventing internal graft—a former mainstay of the Spanish colonial government.[65] Although Estrada Palma admitted that the Janney group had not let him in on their precise plans, he assumed that they planned to woo Spain by offering a sale price for the island of $100 million, while keeping $50 million as a commission for themselves.[66]

In his report to the Government-in-Arms, Estrada Palma explained his reasons for seeking out such alternatives. Chief among these, he declared, was his contention that Spain could never defeat the Cubans through force of arms. However, he also doubted the Cubans could defeat the Spanish quickly enough to save the material foundations of production that a new nation would need to grow. In addition, he admitted to having repeatedly failed to obtain U.S. governmental support for an indemnification plan with Spain in exchange for absolute independence.[67] Citing reduced sugar production (the PRC's largest revenue base), declining voluntary contributions, and what he predicted as the eventual demoralization of the Liberating Army, Estrada Palma envisaged no other option but to halt the bloodshed and the "final destruction of the territorial wealth of the island."[68] Following the contradictory logic of imperialist nationalism, Estrada Palma added that relying on U.S. inspection of the Cuban customs house "does not infringe in the most minor way on the sovereignty of the Republic of Cuba, but rather shall serve [. . . to establish] on the basis of our [independent] Republic, morality in that department, which so much depends on the honor of its employees."[69] Sadly, Estrada Palma vested greater faith in those who rejected the tenet of absolute Cuban sovereignty than in the honor of compatriots who were willing to give their lives for it. Because the Government-in-Arms ultimately approved his actions, one can only assume that there were many powerful members who agreed with him.

Such officials—émigré and otherwise—rejected the socially revolutionary principles that informed the nationalism of many rebel officers, popular-class soldiers, and their working-class émigré counterparts in the United States. In so doing, these representatives of Cuban independence facilitated Cuba's development as a neocolony long before the U.S. military ever intervened.

Amazingly, in the early republic, many of the same civilian leaders would claim that other Cubans' efforts to subvert neocolonialism through armed movements or social protest not only undermined, but in fact betrayed the very "nation" for which the Revolution had been fought. Of course, most of them made such a claim because during the 1895 war, they had occupied the highest posts in the PRC and unflinchingly believed their own propaganda: as the supreme representatives of the Revolution abroad, their ideal of "nation" was the highest and dominant ideal. History soon showed that they were gravely mistaken.

As émigrés who had long lived in the United States, PRC leaders constantly sought to gain the attention of U.S. citizens and the validation of the U.S. government for the revolutionary cause of Cuban independence. Through their dealings in Washington and on Wall Street, they understood that for elite Americans, even Cubans like themselves had to prove their worth as cultural and racial equals. Not only did they internalize these beliefs, they transformed them and incorporated them into their own set of assumptions regarding the social and cultural inferiority of Cuba's popular classes. Far distant from the fields of battle where traditional lines of authority and superiority frequently blurred, New York's émigré leaders ignored any signs of emerging discontent among other émigré communities and attempted to thwart the role of military leaders as secondary to their own. At the same time, PRC leaders convinced themselves that gaining U.S. support for their imperialist nationalist "nation" was both supremely necessary *and* the first step toward convincing their own comrades-in-arms of its credibility. Indeed, after 1898, it would be U.S. support for imperialist nationalists like Tomás Estrada Palma that effectively allowed the PRC to marginalize the proponents of revolutionary nationalism from the centers of power, both in Washington and Havana. Ironically, many of their allies in the process were not revolutionaries at all, but imperialist nationalists of a completely different strain: that is, former proponents of continued colonial rule by Spain—those decried as enemies of Cuba during the war.

Nevertheless, in the end, the imperialist nationalists of early-twentieth-century Cuba underestimated the implications that forging a relationship of intimacy with the United States would have for the stability of the Republic of Cuba. More importantly, they also underestimated the power of future revolutionary nationalists and the commitment of their popular-class counterparts to subvert that stability. By marginalizing, ignoring, and undermining the views of their compatriots, PRC leaders opened the door to decades of internal social and political turmoil as generation after generation of Cubans would struggle to see fulfilled alternative, participatory, and socially democratic visions of the nation for which more radical revolutionaries had fought during the 1895 war. In seeking to contain the social and economic objectives of popular-class émigrés and their insurgent counterparts on the island, PRC leaders had relied on external, extraterritorial means to assert their authority and right to determine the nature of the "nation." In doing so, they embodied and consciously espoused a contradictory partnership between U.S. imperialism and a uniquely immigrant vision of Cuban nationalism which survives to this day.

Given the acumen of historical hindsight, it is easy to conclude that émigré leaders' perception of the Cuban cause and their own identity as revolutionaries conflicted with those of the Revolution's armed forces from the start. As we have seen, leaders of the PRC strove to conceive bonds of intimacy with both the citizens and government of the United States even as PRC policies and philosophies increasingly resulted in the social fragmentation and ideological disunification of its émigré and military constituents. What had once been the PRC's original mission—namely, consolidating fragile social pacts and political compromises among émigrés themselves—was consistently relegated to the bottom of the organization's priorities. Despite the coexistence of more radical Cuban nationalisms at home and among émigrés abroad during the war, the PRC concerned itself with promoting its own nationalist ends to the detriment of all others. Its leaders exemplified a vision of "nation" that reflected their own socially conservative values and economically liberal ambitions. As the principle representatives of the Revolution abroad, the imperialist nationalists who shaped PRC activities during the war could not see beyond their own gilded dreams of building a modern civilization in Cuba under U.S. tutelage. By cutting short a military process whose culmination might have rendered an alternative, more radical "nation" as the foundation for the Cuban republic, the U.S. military intervention of 1898 ensured that PRC leaders would not have to see beyond these dreams and encouraged them to believe that in building their vision for the nation-state in Cuba, they would count on official U.S. support.

And yet, the story of Cubans' contradictory identities and conflicted nations does not end in the late 1890s. Nor does it end with the politically violent, socially turbulent years of the republic. What makes our understanding of "imperialist nationalism" during this early period especially relevant is its contemporary analogue among Cuban-American communities today. Certainly Cuban exiles and organizations in the United States are quite diverse, representing at least as many different ideological perspectives as they did a hundred years ago. Yet, undeniably, historical circumstances, partisan political conveniences, and the polarization of debate over forty years of diplomatic isolation have conspired to render the far-right as dominant a force among exiles in the United States as *fidelistas* have traditionally been in Cuba. As a result, not only do alternative interpretations of U.S. policies remain marginalized, but even alternative personal memories of the current revolution and the reasons why people left become obscured or actively silenced. Certainly, the history of Cuba's post-1959 revolutionary state and the disaffection of millions of its citizens (many of them products of the

1959 Revolution itself) can only make us question the Cuban state's commitment to the ideals of social democracy, political freedom, and economic autonomy on which it was founded. But the history of Cuba's earlier, first revolution for national liberation yields important lessons for how today's exiles may affect change and even shape the course of Cuba in this post–Cold War age.

Today's imperialist nationalists of Florida and New York represent a notion of Cuban identity and a vision for the "nation" they wish to see in Cuba that is even more internally conflicted than those visions championed by émigré leaders in the past. Not only are there more exiles than ever before, but the majority of them are naturalized U.S. citizens who have spent more years here than even the most socially conservative leaders of the PRC. No longer must these Cuban exiles lobby the U.S. Congress from without; they have their own exile representatives within. Still, amazingly, a great many exiles—including exile politicians—see their espousal of U.S. imperialist policies toward Cuba as more "nationalist" than many of their historical counterparts ever did. Fueled by the fires of anger and the conscious knowledge that for most Cubans on the island, Cuban exiles who have lived for decades in the United States are no longer "Cuban," the volatility and unpredictability of the "old guard" leaders of the exile community cannot be underestimated. Yet in their refusal fully to entrust the future of Cuba to the younger generation of island Cubans born after the 1959 Revolution, Castro's aging "vanguard" commits a similar mistake—that of marginalizing alternative, creative, and potentially more democratic visions of "nation" for the sake of imposing its own. Clear and open discussions of Cuba's historical legacies should be encouraged on the island and among Cuban communities in the United States since such discussions may provide a brake on the propensity of history to repeat itself—with even more disastrous consequences for all involved.

NOTES

The author wishes to thank Marial Iglesias, Francisco Scarano, Leo Garofalo, and Joseph Hall for their comments on earlier versions of this essay.

1. J. M. Aguirre to Juan Gualberto Gómez, 25 May 1895, in Archivo Nacional de Cuba [hereafter, ANC], Fondo Adquisiciones, Caja 9, Signatura 207, 1–2.

2. For the most part, historians have considered the political dimensions of the émigré experience, especially in discussing the PRC. At the same time, while key historical analysts such as Louis A. Pérez, Jr. recognize ideological differences between émigré leaders and the military, it has generally been accepted that the PRC possessed only a loosely knit sense of its cause, characterized as either annexationist or proprotectorate and not in any way "nationalist." Ramón de Armas may have originated this view in arguing that the vagueness of the PRC proved to be the Revolution's Achilles' heel. See Ramón de Armas, *La Revolución pospuesta: Contenido y alcance de la revolución martiana por la independencia* (Havana: Ediciones Políti-

cas, 1975); Louis A. Pérez, Jr., *Cuba under the Platt Amendment, 1902–1934* (Pittsburgh: University of Pittsburgh Press, 1986), 23–27; and Pérez, *Cuba between Empires, 1878–1902* (Pittsburgh: University of Pittsburgh Press, 1983), 90–99.

3. See Gerald Poyo's otherwise excellent study of émigré politics and the popular nationalist vision of nation espoused by Florida's cigar workers in *"With All, and for the Good of All": The Emergence of Popular Nationalism in the Cuban Communities of the United States, 1848–1898* (Durham, N.C.: Duke University Press, 1989), esp. 57–61.

4. Champions of this view include Jorge Ibarra in *Cuba: 1898–1921, partidos políticos y clases sociales* (Havana: Editorial de Ciencias Sociales, 1992), 224–29; and Lionel Soto in *La Revolución del 33*, 3 vols. (Havana: Editorial Pueblo y Educación, 1985), 1: 47. For an alternative view, see Lillian Guerra, chapters 4–6 of "Crucibles of Liberation in Cuba: José Martí, Nationalisms, and the Search for Social Unity," Ph.D. diss., University of Wisconsin-Madison, 2000.

5. See Emilia Viotti da Costa, *The Brazilian Empire: Myths and Histories* (Chicago: University of Chicago, 1985), xix–xxi, 5–8, 53–60, 69–75; Charles Berquist, *Coffee and Conflict in Colombia, 1886–1910* (Durham, N.C.: Duke University Press, 1978), 8–12; Ralph Lee Woodward, Jr., "Changes in the Nineteenth-Century Guatemalan State and Its Indian Policies," and Carol A. Smith, "Origins of the National Question in Guatemala: A Hypothesis," in *Guatemalan Indians and the State: 1540–1988*, ed. Carol A. Smith with Marilyn M. Moors (Austin: University of Texas Press, 1990), 59–61, 83–90.

6. See Enrique Trujillo, *Apuntes históricos: propaganda y movimientos revolucionarios cubanos en los Estados Unidos desde enero de 1880 hasta febrero de 1895* (New York: Tip. de "El Porvenir," 1896).

7. Poyo, "*With All, and for the Good of All*," 114–18.

8. Rafael Serra, "Filantropía," *La Doctrina de Martí*, New York, 2 September 1896.

9. Rafael Serra, "Con Nuestros Héroes Reales," *La Doctrina de Martí*, New York, 30 March 1897.

10. See Serra's letters to Estrada Palma, 19 January 1902, 13 February 1902, 20 March 1902, and 26 July 1902, in ANC, Fondo Personal de Tomás Estrada Palma, cataloguing still in process.

11. See Eduardo Yero to Domingo Figuerola Caneda, 22 January 1897, in ANC, Fondo Academia de la Historia de Cuba, Caja 168, Signatura 468. This document came to my attention through the generosity of Marial Iglesias. Yero's article in *La Doctrina de Martí*, titled "Vientos de Fronda," appeared in the 15 January 1897 edition of Rafael Serra's paper.

12. Prominent figures in the émigré community seem to have made a habit of putting aside personal differences for the benefit of "unity" in the cause. Two examples that come to mind are that of Martí and Collazo and of Eduardo Yero and Manuel Sanguily in the summer of 1897. Apparently, Yero and Sanguily attacked each other personally at a mass meeting of Cubans in Hardmann Hall that June. Through personal representatives, the two agreed to put their differences aside and contrived a means for tolerating the other's presence at public functions in a legal document signed 9 July 1897. See ANC, Fondo Academia de la Historia, Caja 61, Signatura 66.

13. Hector de Saavedra to Domingo Figuerola Caneda, 9 February 1897, in ANC,

Fondo Academia de la Historia, Caja 167, Signatura 457. From New York, de Saavedra had been trying unsuccessfully for months to convince Estrada Palma that he should use PRC funds to subsidize Figuerola Caneda's émigré newspaper in Paris, *La República Cubana*, an effort to which de Saavedra makes disdainful reference in the same letter. See also de Saavedra to Figuerola Caneda, 20 October 1896, in ibid. According to Yero, de Saavedra was also pressing Estrada Palma for a job as the PRC's vice secretary, a desire that also went unfulfilled. See Yero to Figuerola Caneda, 22 January 1897, cited above.

14. Philip Foner points out that neither New York's nor Massachusetts's congressmen ever voted in favor of Cuban belligerency or independence in the first two years of the war until direct U.S. military intervention became a possibility. Curiously, however, while Foner emphasizes the importance of PRC activities in influencing public opinion and political action in the same work, he ignores the important irony that it was precisely this area of the country in which the PRC exercised its greatest resources. See Foner, *The Spanish-Cuban-American War and the Birth of American Imperialism*, 2 vols. (New York: Monthly Review Press, 1972), 1: 189–90; for a discussion of the role of U.S. public opinion, see esp. 168–70.

15. See Eligio Carbonell to Gonzalo de Quesada, Tampa, Fla., 1 March 1896 and de Quesada to Carbonell, Washington, D.C., 6 March 1896, in *La Revolución del 95 según la correspondencia de la delegación cubana en Nueva York* 3: 238–40.

16. Ibid., 119–20.

17. George Auxier, "Propaganda Activities of the Cuban *Junta* in Precipitating the Spanish-American War," in *Hispanic American Historical Review* 19, no. 3 (August 1939), 294.

18. See Pierra's self-written notes for the publication of a future (but unpublished?) autobiography in Fidel Pierra to Domingo Figuerola Caneda, 3 October 1898, in ANC, Fondo Academia de Historia, Caja 166, Signatura 444. The author gratefully acknowledges the intellectual generosity of Marial Iglesias in bringing this document to my attention.

19. See Tom Chaffin, *Fatal Glory: Narciso López and the First Clandestine U.S. War against Cuba* (Charlottesville: University Press of Virginia, 1996).

20. Fidel Pierra to Tomás Estrada Palma, 25 November 1895, in León Primelles, ed., *La Revolución del 95*, 5 vols. (Havana: Editorial Habanera, 1932), 2: 258–64.

21. See George Reno, "Operating an 'Underground' Route to Cuba," *Cosmopolitan Magazine* 27 (August 1899): 429–432.

22. The Pact of Zanjón, which officially ended the war in 1878, testifies to the extent of these divisions: although the Revolution had taken the abolition of slavery and independence as its goals, white military leaders chose to accept Spain's offer of peace and a general amnesty rather than continue fighting. Unwilling to sanction the double betrayal that the pact represented—of literally enslaved Cubans and of a figuratively enslaved Cuba, Antonio Maceo rejected the treaty and launched a short-lived and poorly funded continuation of the war, known as the Guerra Chiquita. See Ada Ferrer, *Insurgent Cuba: Race, Nation, and Revolution, 1868–1898* (Chapel Hill: University of North Carolina Press, 1999), esp. 15–89.

23. See Ada Ferrer, "The Silence of Patriots: Race and Nationalism in Martí's Cuba," in *José Martí's "Our America": From National to Hemispheric Cultural Studies*, ed. Jeffrey Belnap and Raúl Fernández (Durham, N.C.: Duke University Press, 1998), 228–249.

24. See Guerra, "Crucibles of Liberation," introduction.

25. Hon. Claude Matthews, "The Cuban Patriots' Cause Is Just, the Right Shall Prevail, and in God's Own Time Cuba Shall Be Free" (Philadelphia: Charles F. Simmons, 1895). The pamphlet includes a copy of the petition as well as a reprinting of the transcript of the rally's speeches titled "Matthews on Cuba's Freedom. The Yoke of Spanish Tyranny and Misrule Should Be Lifted. Godspeed Their Holy Ambition," from *The Philadelphia Times*, 22 November 1895.

26. Fidel Pierra and J. A. Gutiérrez to Tomás Estrada Palma, 22 December 1895, in Primelles, *La Revolución del 95*, 2: 339.

27. Both of these works were published separately and as one edition, *Free Cuba: Her Oppression, Struggle for Liberty, History, and Present Condition with the Causes and Justification of the Present War for Independence*, ed. Dr. John Guiteras [a.k.a. Juan Guiteras] (New York: Publishers' Union, 1897).

28. See "Letter of Hon. T. Estrada Palma to Hon. Richard Olney, Secretary of State," 7 December 1895, in *Report of the Committee on Foreign Relations, United States Senate, Relative to Affairs in Cuba, April 13, 1898*, Senate Document No. 885, 55th Congress, 2d sess. (Washington: Government Printing Office, 1898), esp. 10–13.

29. Horatio S. Rubens, *Liberty: The Story of Cuba* (New York: Brewer, Warren & Putnam, 1932), 107–8. Although Rubens disliked de Quesada's more irreverent style, he did acknowledge the positive contributions he made to the cause. See Ruben's description in ibid., 108.

30. "Speech delivered by Mr. Fidel G. Pierra at Washington, D.C. on October 31, 1895," p. 1; see also "Speech delivered by Mr. Fidel G. Pierra, at Chickering Hall, New York, on the night of October 10th, 1895" in pamphlets of the Cutter Collection, Memorial Library, University of Wisconsin-Madison.

31. See the photostatic reproduction of the fair's flyer in Auxier, "Propaganda Activities," 295. Original in the Hoes Papers, Manuscript Collection, United States Library of Congress.

32. Fidel Pierra to Tomás Estrada Palma, 26 June 1896, in Primelles, *La Revolución del 95*, 4: 435–36.

33. Tomás Estrada Palma to Dr. Juan Guiteras, 21 October 1895, in ibid., 2: 75.

34. Fernando Figueredo to Tomás Estrada Palma, 28 April 1896, in ibid., 4: 30–31.

35. "Reglamento Interior del Club Discípulas de Martí" in ANC, Fondo Donativos y Remisiones, Caja 295, Expediente 4.

36. Adelina Sánchez, Presidenta and María Rodríguez Delgado, Secretaria to Rosario Sigarroa, 19 March 1897, in ANC, Fondo Donativos y Remisiones, Caja 308, Expediente 53.

37. See, for example, the 15 September 1897 edition of *Cuba y América* for news about the functions and a photograph of the club Discípulas de Martí, 1: 12.

38. Carmen Mantilla to Francisco Gómez y Toro, Central Valley, 20 April 1895, in ANC, Fondo Máximo Gómez, Legajo 39, Expediente 4858, fols. 5–6. For evidence of Mantilla's relationship with Martí, see José Miguel Oviedo, *La niña de New York: Una revisión de la vida erótica de José Martí* (Mexico, D. F.: Fondo de Cultura Económica, 1989). For the best overview of women's participation in the war and émigré network, see K. Lynn Stoner, *From the House to the Streets: The Cuban*

Woman's Movement for Legal Reform, 1898–1940 (Durham, N.C.: Duke University Press, 1991), esp. 18–33.

39. Adelante [pseudonym of Joaquín Fortún, a rebel spy in Havana] to Tomás Estrada Palma, 8 October 1895, in *La Revolución del 95*, 2: 221–22.

40. Franc R. E. Woodward, *With Maceo in Cuba: Adventures of a Minnesota Boy* (Minneapolis, Minn.: The Scarlett Printing Company, 1896), 14–15.

41. José Dolores Poyo to Tomás Estrada Palma, 1 April 1896, in Primelles, *La Revolución del 95*, 4: 78.

42. Ch. [abbreviation of Francisco Chenard, a revolutionary spy in Havana] to Tomás Estrada Palma, 24 October 1895, ibid., 2: 226.

43. Fidel Pierra to Joaquín del Castillo, 5 March 1896 in *ibid.*, 3: 236–37; and Pierra to Figuerola Caneda, 3 October 1898, in ANC, Fondo Academia de la Historia de Cuba, Caja 166, Signatura 444.

44. Few planters wholeheartedly supported the patriot cause. Only one planter in particular, Marta Abreu, was exceptional in this regard. See Tomás Estrada Palma to Miguel Betancourt, 26 September 1896, in Primelles, *La Revolución del 95*, 5: 368–71. By contrast, planter Emilio Terry, owner of the world's most valuable sugar mill and subsequently touted as a patriot of Abreu's calibre, only grudgingly paid off the PRC while maintaining a squadron of Spanish soldiers [known then as *guerrilleros*] on his plantation. Personal communication with Marial Iglesias, August 1998.

45. Máximo Gómez to Tomás Estrada Palma, Camagüey, 28 August 1895, in Primelles, *La Revolución del 95*, 1: 69.

46. See Ferrer, *Insurgent Cuba*, 141–69.

47. See Primelles, *La Revolución del 95*, 2: 6–10; 3: 5–8; 4: 5–9; 5: 6–9.

48. See José Martí, "Manifesto de Montecristi," in his *Obras completas*, 27 vols., 2nd ed. (1975; reprint, Havana: Editorial de Ciencias Sociales, 1992), 4: 93–103.

49. Máximo Gómez to Tomás Estrada Palma, 11 August 1896, in Primelles, *La Revolución del 95*, 5: 47–48.

50. Máximo Gómez to Tomás Estrada Palma, 29 April 1896, in ibid., 55–56.

51. Antonio Maceo to Tomás Estrada Palma, 21 November 1895, in ibid., 2: 314–15.

52. Antonio Maceo to Tomás Estrada Palma, 14 April 1896, in ibid., 4: 62–63.

53. Salvador Cisneros Betancourt to Tomás Estrada Palma, 22 August 1895, in ibid., 1: 57–58.

54. Tomás Estrada Palma to Secretario de Relaciones Exteriores de Cuba, 11 November 1897, in ANC, Fondo Gobierno de la Revolución de 1895, Caja 44, Signatura 6332.

55. Tomás Estrada Palma to T. E. Culmel[l], 7 December 1895, in Primelles, *La Revolución del 95*, 2: 288–89.

56. Informe General al Gobierno de la República de Tomás Estrada Palma, 30 May 1896, and Tomás Estrada Palma to Máximo Gómez, 29 July 1896, in ibid., 2: 14–25; 37–39.

57. Máximo Gómez to Tomás Estrada Palma, 26 September 1896, in ibid., 5: 267.

58. For Gómez's response to Estrada Palma's proposals for PRC regulation of tax collections, see his letter of 26 September 1896, in ibid., 5: 267.

59. The same attitudes extended toward black émigrés in New York, once closely associated with the PRC during Martí's tenure at its helm. For a discussion of racial

attitudes and émigré workers' dissent, see Guerra, "Crucibles of Liberation in Cuba," esp. chapter 2.

60. "Mario" to Rosario Sigarroa, 8 March 1898, in ANC, Fondo Donativos y Remisiones, Caja 308, Signatura 46.

61. To Salvador Cisneros Betancourt, whom he often addressed by his former title of nobility as the Marquis de Santa Lucía, Estrada Palma honestly revealed the ambivalence he felt toward the promise of social change that the Revolution held out to the bulk of its fighters and more precisely, to the means by which it should be achieved. See Tomás Estrada Palma to Salvador Cisneros Betancourt, 22 July 1896, in Primelles, *La Revolución del 95*, 5: 33.

62. "Memorandum of Agreement made this Eleventh Day of May 1897, between Tomas Estrada Palma, Delegate Plenipotentiary of the Republic of Cuba of the first part and John R. Dos Passos, of the City of New York, of the second part," in ANC, Fondo Gobierno de la Revolución de 1895, Caja 44, Signatura 6306, p. 1. The document is a handwritten transcription of the original contract in English.

63. Tomás Estrada Palma, "Informe de la Delegación de la República de Cuba al Gobierno," 15 October 1897, p. 9. Dos Passos was also given the option of purchasing bonds of the Cuban Republic worth five million dollars upon an advance of five hundred thousand dollars. According to this report, Dos Passos was unable to gather more than one hundred thousand dollars, despite the fact that he had been in London (supposedly lobbying English investors) since September. See idem, "Informe," 9–10; and ibid., 2.

64. "Agreement made this fifth day of August, A.D. 1897, between Señor Don Tomás Estrada Palma, Minister Plenipotentiary and Delegate of the Government of the Republic of Cuba, acting for and on behalf of the said Republic, but subject to the approval of the Constitutional Assembly of said Republic to convene in the month of September 1897, party of the first part, Samuel M. Janney, banker of 6 Wall Street in the City of New York," in ANC, Fondo Gobierno de la Revolución de 1895, Caja 44, Signatura 6329, p. 1. Note that Estrada Palma was so anxious to preserve Cuba's propertied wealth that he wrote to Janney as early as June 1897: "It must be understood that my Government will not be willing to pay such a sum after the time limited, as every day that passes increases the ruin of the island & lessens the value of Spain's sovereignty." See "Copia redactada por J. Zayas de la nota de Tomás Estrada Palma to Samuel L. Janney Esq.," 5 June 1897, in ANC, Fondo Gobierno de la Revolución, Caja 44, Signatura 6329, pp. 1–2.

65. Ibid., 5–6.

66. Estrada Palma, "Informe," 12.

67. Ibid., 4–5.

68. Ibid., 11.

69. Ibid., 13.

4

Imaging a Nation: U.S. Political Cartoons and the War of 1898

Virginia M. Bouvier

Events surrounding the War of 1898 spawned a treasure chest of audiovisual images that has remained virtually unopened by historians. These images include satirical drawings, sheet music, postcards, photographs, posters, and especially thousands of cartoons, some of which will be examined in this chapter. As cultural forms, political cartoons reflect and contribute to the formation of imperial attitudes. They illuminate the myths, references, and experiences upon which U.S. national identity was constructed in the wake of the War of 1898 and reveal a legacy of images that provide the foundation for current U.S. attitudes toward Latin America.

Beyond their aesthetic value, political cartoons can help illuminate a wide range of historiographic issues by providing evidence of variations in regional interpretations of an event, challenging previous periodization schemes, and illustrating continuities and changes in historical representations. They can also provide data that might not be obtained from more traditional, scholarly sources. Thomas Milton Kemnitz writes that cartoons "can provide insights into the popular attitudes that underlay public opinion, insights that may be more difficult to glean from written material or from other evidence of behavior."[1] In his classic study on political cartoons about Latin America, John J. Johnson notes that cartoons "provide invaluable clues to the mood and mores and underlying attitudes of the society that produced and accepted them."[2] Sudden shifts in imagery provide clues about changes in popular attitudes, and the suppression or absence of certain images or themes likewise alert us to cultural blind spots or to the deliberate exclusion of groups or perspectives.[3]

An analysis of cartoons likewise provides students of the press with clues as to the import and timing of certain issues in the public consciousness and can serve as a reminder of the dangers inherent in applying general labels such as "pro-interventionist," "jingo," or "anti-interventionist" to an individual newspaper or group of papers. Images of any era offer a wealth of opportunities for insights into concepts of national identity, particularly when relationships between nations are shifting.

Work conditions and technology, as well as editorial policies, affected the output of cartoons in the 1890s. In their study of American political cartoons during the nineteenth century, Allan Nevins and Frank Weitenkampf divide the production of political cartoons into four somewhat vaguely defined periods.[4] At the beginning of the nineteenth century, the few political cartoons produced were restricted to expensive woodcuts and copper engravings and were generally issued as separate publications. By the 1830s, commercial lithography made the production of cartoons more cost effective, but cartoons of that period were still cluttered with public figures and dense text in balloons, making for difficult reading. By the last third of the century, weekly publications such as *Harper's Weekly, Vanity Fair, Frank Leslie's Weekly, Puck, Judge*, and *Life*, provided the primary venue for talented political cartoonists such as Thomas Nast, William Newman, Matt Morgan, Joseph Keppler, Bernhard Gillam, and William H. Walker.

Beginning in 1884, however, the *New York World* set the standard for newspapers by introducing political cartoons as a regular feature.[5] In the wake of the circulation wars spawned by Joseph Pulitzer and William Randolph Hearst, virtually every major daily newspaper soon added political cartoons to their menu of attractions. By the late 1890s, newspapers supplanted the weeklies, which were unable to keep pace with the daily commentary that newspapers could offer on issues of the day. As a result, many cartoonists left the weeklies to join the newspaper ranks. Well-known cartoonists for the dailies included John T. McCutcheon, R. C. Bowman, Clifford K. Berryman, Fred Morgan, Frederick B. Opper, Charles G. Bush, Homer Davenport, Charles R. Macauley, and Charles Nelan.[6]

As full-time professionals at the dailies, cartoonists were expected to produce social commentary with great rapidity. Charles Nelan, cartoonist for the *New York Herald* in 1898, noted that a cartoonist was "often called on to make a cartoon in two or three hours and sometimes in less time."[7] Such time constraints meant that an individual artist had little time to consider the subtleties of argumentation and was often forced to adopt simpler drafting techniques. These sketches, perhaps even more succinctly than the freestanding lithographs of the earlier period, were able to capture mood swings related to unfolding events of the day. However, a direct relationship usually existed between the positions advocated in the individual cartoons and the editorial policy of the publication. As W. A. Coupe observed, "Few editors can afford to lose favour or circulation in the interests of a cartoonist's freedom of expression."[8] In his brief introduction to a volume of his printed cartoons on the war with Spain, Nelan noted diplomatically, "If we do anything towards moulding [*sic*] public opinion, do not blame us entirely, but remember the editor, whose name does not appear on the cartoon."[9]

Through symbols, metaphors, analogies, distortion, and prosopopoeia, political cartoons convey information and a point of view quickly and tend to appeal to emotions rather than reason, making no attempt to be objective. Their power often resides in the strength of their editorial position. Political cartoons differ from editorials or news stories in that they depend on the reduction of issues to simple lines and allegorical representations. They create, reinforce, and mirror an attitudinal subtext which, whether in an imperial or a revolutionary context, may contribute to mythic understandings of past events as well as expectations for the future. Furthermore, political cartoons can help explain how the causes of war were understood and explained on a popular level. Content analysis of cartoons reveals the complexity of the press, the evolution of public opinion over time, and the collective fears and concerns of large sectors of society. A monitoring of the frequency and nature of issue-specific cartoons assists in measuring how, when, and if public attitudes changed over time, as well as the intensity of public sentiment over immediate issues.

Leaving aside a judgment as to the actual impact of the press in general and political cartoons in particular, what can political cartoons reveal about the mood of the United States and U.S. attitudes toward Spain and Cuba during the pivotal year of 1898? In that year, public debate about intervention overseas centered around a number of key events: the 9 February publication in the *New York Journal* of derogatory remarks about U.S. President William McKinley made by Spanish minister Enrique Dupuy de Lôme; the mysterious explosion of the U.S.S. *Maine* in Havana harbor; the congressional appropriation of fifty million dollars in defense spending to be used at the president's discretion; Senator Redfield Proctor's report to the Senate on his fact-finding mission to Cuba; the president's war message to Congress on 11 April, calling for armed intervention in Cuba; the congressional decision to go to war; the subsequent battles; the resolution of the conflict; and revelations about U.S. government corruption during the war effort. Related to these themes were cartoons whose images spoke to questions of U.S. economic policies and military preparedness, the changing identity of the United States as it emerged as a global power, and the role of the yellow press in the policy debates about the war. The cartoons documented evolving representations of Spain, and, when depicted at all, images of the inhabitants of the territories that would come under U.S. control in the course of the year, namely Cuba, the Philippines, Puerto Rico, Guam, and Hawaii.

Historians have devoted considerable attention to debates about the role of the press in the War of 1898 and its relationship to public opinion and the U.S. decision to go to war.[10] Many have focused on the relationship between the rise of "yellow journalism" and interventionist tendencies in the population at large.[11] The importance of cartoons as one element of the press is suggested by the origins of the term "yellow journals." The epithet was derived from a comic-strip character known as the Yellow Kid, so-called because his smock sported a splash of bright yellow ink, an innovation made possible because of inexpensive new press technology.[12] Created by illustrator Richard F. Outcault for Pulitzer's paper, the Yellow Kid soon became a feature of *The World* when Hearst hired the illustrator away from his competitor. Both papers then ran the cartoon strip, and "yellow journalism" soon became a generic term used to describe any of the numerous major dailies throughout the United States that shared the Pulitzer-Hearst sensational style of journalism.[13]

The *New York Herald*, under the leadership of James Gordon Bennett, a Scottish immigrant born in 1795, had pioneered the journalistic techniques of sensationalism and popular appeal, which would be cultivated to an extreme by Pulitzer when he took over the *New York World* in 1893 and by Hearst when he assumed ownership of the *New York Journal* in 1895. Since its founding in 1835, the *New York Herald* had become the foremost U.S. daily by the mid–nineteenth century.[14] The *New York Herald* of the 1890s, now under the editorship of James Gordon Bennett, Jr., prided itself on providing even-handed, authoritative news, and disdained the shrieking headlines and sensational exploits of its newly arrived competitors.[15] On the eve of the Cuban uprising in 1895, the *New York Herald* boasted in its daily tally that, at 217,600 copies, its circulation was greater than that of any daily in the United States.[16] And throughout 1898, at a time when the population of Manhattan was close to two million inhabitants,[17] the *New York Herald* boasted a circulation of over 500,000 people. Readership levels hovered at 503,200 throughout the first eleven months of 1898, and by 31 December registered a high water mark of 511,900 subscriptions.[18] The war was apparently good for the newspaper business.

The *New York Herald*, the "favorite newspaper of the wealthy," was not aligned with any party and was considered to be "incorruptible and independent of political or other influence."[19] Newspapers throughout the country reprinted its war dispatches. The editor, himself a former third lieutenant of the union navy, considered himself to be a watchdog of U.S. foreign policy. "My foreign policy," Bennett once noted, "is simply this: If a nation is friendly to America, I wish the *Herald* to be friendly to that nation, but if a nation shows an unfriendly policy, I wish the *Herald* to adopt an unfriendly tone. This may not be patriotism, but it is the course I wish the *Herald* to follow."[20] Given that Bennett resided in Paris, where he oversaw production of a European edition of the *Herald*, the *New York Herald* also had an international flavor absent from most U.S. dailies of the time.

The *New York Herald* was replete with illustrations of the war, including sketches of maps, warships, cavalry, local scenes, military officials, and soldiers in action. For the most part, the cartoons did not appear in an "editorial" section per se. In 1898 the *New York Herald* generally ranged from twelve to twenty pages of text on weekdays, with Sunday papers running some four times longer. The first two pages were dedicated to densely set material lacking in illustrations or bold headlines. The front page of the paper included death notices, marriage announcements, religious notices, lost and found items, rewards, personals, and advertisements by local merchants. The second page included listings of real estate and housing, as well as advertisements from resorts, hotels, and restaurants. In general, cartoons and illustrations adorned the following pages, which contained news and features of local, state, national, and international import. Topics relating to crimes (particularly sensational court cases), scandals, corruption, blackmail, bankruptcies, lawsuits, thefts, and larceny were common on these inner pages. The standard format included on page eight information about the newspaper, editors, circulation, and weather, as well as unsigned editorials. The remaining pages included more sketches and illustrations, occasional letters to the editor, reprints from other newspapers, sports, extensive shipping news, society pages, legal notices, several pages dedicated to financial and commercial notices and opportunities, and additional advertisements.

Charles Nelan was the artist responsible for most of the political cartoons on the war that ran in the *New York Herald*.[21] Nelan was born in Ohio and studied at the National Academy of Design in New York.[22] He worked as a cartoonist for the *Cleveland Press* and the Scripps-McRae league of Western newspapers for ten years before joining the permanent staff of the *New York Herald* in 1898; he served as an illustrator and cartoonist there until 1901.[23]

Images about what would become known as the War of 1898 began appearing in the U.S. press subsequent to the *Grito de Baire*, the call by Cuban rebel leaders on 24 February 1895 that launched Cuba's second war for independence from Spain. Since early 1895, news items and political cartoons denouncing Spanish misdeeds and atrocities in suppressing Cuba's second war for independence were, according to historian Joseph Smith, "virtually a permanent fixture on the front pages of the American popular press."[24] Yet the portrayal of the war and its protagonists was far from uniform and varied over time and by publication.

The *New York Herald* has been described by historians alternatively as no less jingoistic than the Pulitzer-Hearst dailies and as opposed to U.S. intervention in the Cuban-Spanish conflict.[25] Understanding the nature, rationale, and evolution of the *New York Herald*'s editorial position on the war and its protagonists as viewed in Nelan's cartoons may help to explain this apparent contradiction. A study of Nelan's cartoons reveals an editorial policy that called for reasoned restraint prior to the outbreak of war, based initially on fears of potential military defeat, the economic consequences of war, and concerns over European reactions to U.S. intervention. As the war

Figure 4.1
"If I Have Another War, I'll Be Broke," *New York Herald*, 14 December 1897.

proceeded and the United States gained stature, the cartoons (penned under heightened war censorship) were mostly supportive of the war. Following the initiation of peace talks in late July 1898, however, Nelan's cartoons raised serious questions about the expansion of the war to Asia.[26] In the aftermath of the war, the *New York Herald* spearheaded efforts to expose U.S. military incompetence in Cuba, as well as administration attempts to conceal Secretary of War Russell A. Alger's mismanagement of the war effort.[27]

In late 1897 and early 1898, Nelan's cartoons raised two key concerns, namely that war would threaten U.S. economic prosperity and that the United States was not prepared militarily to engage Spain. In a 14 December 1897 cartoon, the artist showed Uncle Sam turning in distress from a huge box labeled "U.S. Treasury," to ponder the Spanish war cloud looming on the horizon (see Figure 4.1).[28] In one hand, Uncle Sam holds up a pension list showing $141 million due, a reference to the Dependent Pension Bill passed under the Harrison administration, which guaranteed dependent veterans of the Civil War a pension of at least six dollars a month.[29] In the other, Uncle Sam holds the handle of a small, tattered, closed-up umbrella. The editorial posture of the cartoon underscores the financial commitments required by war and, on a more subtle level, the lack of U.S. military preparedness. Symbolically, the umbrella's inadequacy to protect its owner from a transpiring or impending storm was a leitmotif that cartoonists of the time employed to symbolize both U.S. and Spanish naval deficiencies.[30]

Nelan's lack of confidence in the status of U.S. military readiness for a war with Spain was underscored in his cartoon "It Looks Bad for the Gunner."[31] A U.S. Marine wearing a patched life preserver stands on the deck of a ship under attack by a warship; he holds a rifle labeled "the U.S. Navy." Nelan's cartoon echoed the theme of a series of *New York Herald* articles written by naval experts that week that stressed the "utter unpreparedness" of the United States for war, given the inferiority of its medium-caliber guns, the lack of dry docks and submerged torpedo tubes on its ships, and other deficiencies in ammunition and equipment.[32]

In another Nelan cartoon in early 1898, Uncle Sam, shopkeeper par excellence, examines the U.S. ledger for 1897 (see Figure 4.2).[33] The record shows no sign of indebtedness; rather it portrays a healthy economy and an optimistic outlook for the future. Uncle Sam's annual statement notes abundant crops, restored confidence, a rise in national wealth and population, peaceful foreign relations, and general improvement in business. In sum, it shows that prospects for the coming year are "excellent." In this cartoon, war is conspicuously absent, and peace is seen as part of an overall package for economic stability. Behind Uncle Sam, his hat and a closed umbrella await a rainy day. Here Uncle Sam is portrayed as a businessman, ever calculating the costs and benefits of his actions and looking to the future.

While on the one hand, Nelan expressed an editorial preference for steering clear of war with Spain, he also demonstrated confidence in the future expansion overseas of U.S. foreign trade. In his cartoon "Wake Up!" Nelan depicted New York as a merchant marine asleep on a dock in severe disrepair, as ships steamed past from Havre, Antwerp, Liverpool, and Hamburg on their way to New Orleans, San Francisco, Baltimore, and Boston (see Figure 4.3).[34] In the cartoon, a horrified Statue of Liberty has dropped the arm holding up her torch, and she leans forward with her other hand cupped to her mouth to sound the alarm to the fair city to wake up. This cartoon responded explicitly to a Chamber of Commerce report that showed that in 1897 foreign commerce at New York's port had declined by $3,153,044 whereas it had increased at all other U.S. ports by $135,994,713. Nelan's cartoon was a wake-up call to New Yorkers to take advantage of commercial opportunities overseas, which were passing them by.

At the close of the nineteenth century, commercial expansion was considered the future of America's manifest destiny. The desire for greater foreign

Figure 4.2
"Good!" *New York Herald*, 3 January 1898.

trade had escalated during the last decade of the nineteenth century, fostered by the closing of the Western frontier, the depression following the panic of 1893, and the subsequent economic expansion occasioned by technological advances in industry and agriculture. A surplus of U.S. manufactures and cheaply made American goods increasingly required U.S. control of and access to foreign markets.[35]

Closely linked to the expansion of foreign markets was the ability to protect them. The navy was the lynchpin of this strategy. In a seminal article published in 1890, influential naval strategist Alfred Mahan warned that as the welfare of the United States became increasingly linked to the world outside its own borders, greater naval preparedness was imperative.[36]

The issue of military preparedness would become more pressing following the explosion on 15 February 1898 of the U.S. battleship *Maine* in the Havana harbor, which killed 266 U.S. Marines. Louis A. Pérez, Jr. has argued convincingly that privileging the *Maine* incident as a causal factor of

Figure 4.3
"Wake Up!" *New York Herald*, 13 January 1898.

the war is misleading.[37] Pérez has noted the contradiction in the historiographic literature between historians who believe that the sinking of the *Maine* prompted an immediate and sudden shift of popular attitudes in favor of U.S. intervention in Cuba in February 1898 and those who link the shift in U.S. attitudes to the 28 March release of the findings by the U.S. Naval Court of Inquiry implicating Spain in the explosion. An analysis of the *New York Herald* supports a third alternative suggested by Pérez, namely, that on a popular level, a retroactive mythification of the *Maine* incident occurred once the war officially began. Such a mythification effectively absolved U.S. policymakers of the belligerent policies they enacted to acquire new territories in the Far East and the Caribbean.

In the days immediately following the sinking of the *Maine*, Nelan steered clear of images that might have provoked a battle cry or fueled war fever. In his cartoon "The Nation's Grief," Nelan paid tribute to the victims of the *Maine*.[38] He showed an image of a U.S. Marine lying in an open casket, as Uncle Sam turns away in sorrow, hat off and eyes downcast. The floor is covered with wreaths of flowers from numerous states, suggesting the national dimension of the tragedy. The cartoon is a poignant but hardly provocative image, somber in tone. In the following weeks, Nelan called explicitly for his readers to renounce immediate vengeance. In his cartoon of 19 February, Uncle Sam is seen writing a note, "Suspend Judgement Until the Investigation Is Finished!" The doorknob is draped in a large black mourning bow, a symbolic but conspicuously nonincendiary reminder of the *Maine* victims.[39] Behind Uncle Sam sits a dove with the additional counsel "Let us have peace." The caption "Good Advice" further reinforces the editorial call for prudence.

In the wake of the *Maine* explosion (and in honor of George Washington's birthday), the cartoonist invoked the ghost of George Washington to support a variety of sometimes-contradictory positions. In one Nelan cartoon, Washington stands draped in the American flag, eyes closed in prayer-like dignity, with his hat off, quietly mourning the loss of the *Maine*, which sinks before his eyes. The caption of the cartoon, "Observe good faith and justice toward all nations, cultivate peace and harmony with all," is a quotation taken from Washington's Farewell Address.[40] In a Nelan cartoon the following day, however, the founding father chastises Thomas B. Reed, the passionately antiwar Speaker of the House, noting, "Timely disbursements to prepare for danger—frequently prevent much greater disbursements to repel it."[41] Nelan here seemed to advocate the opposite of the previous day's editorial position, as he satirizes Reed's efforts to stave off militarization and labeled them as "anti-national."

For the next two weeks, Nelan exhibited a decidedly restrained attitude toward going to war with Spain. In "Keep Your Head Cool," free-floating hands reach out toward Uncle Sam's head with a Fan of Judgment; other anonymous hands hold pincers with a huge block of ice, labeled "common sense," which melts as it rests on the back of Uncle Sam's head (see Figure 4.4).[42] Within sight, but studiously avoided by Sam's eyes, buzz several yellow jackets, which symbolize the "yellow press." On their long stingers, these bees carry newspapers whose headlines call for war.

The *New York Herald* cartoons suggest that the decision to go to war rested squarely in the hands of the policymakers in the U.S. Congress and the president and that their decision was at no point inevitable. Far from inflaming interventionist sentiment, in the period prior to the war, the *New York Herald* encouraged restraint following both the explosion of the U.S.S. *Maine* and the release of the U.S. naval inquiry report about the causes of the explosion. Such temperance stemmed not from anti-imperialist ideologies, but from misgivings about the economic costs of war and the state of U.S. military readiness, as well as fears anticipating European opposition to such military intervention.

In the immediate aftermath of the *Maine* explosion, other periodicals ran

Figure 4.4
"Keep Your Head Cool," *New York Herald*, 24 February 1898.

cartoons that depicted a variety of editorial positions. The cartoons of the *Chicago Tribune* are peopled with the forgotten, impatient, translucent ghosts of the *Maine* victims, who demand immediate retribution. In one cartoon, Uncle Sam sits cross-legged in a chair at the shore's edge, whittling a piece of wood. He remains coolly oblivious to a diaphanous U.S. Marine, who has emerged dripping wet from the water dragging a U.S. flag labeled "The *Maine*" on the ground. The Marine reaches out to Uncle Sam for assistance. At Uncle Sam's side, an eagle hangs his head in apparent shame.[43] The caption "Are we so soon forgotten?" is meant to shame the reader into action. On the other hand, cartoons that appeared in papers such as the *Washington Post* and the *Philadelphia Inquirer* shared the *New York Herald*'s view to withhold judgment on the affair until more information was available.[44]

During this time, the editorials of the *New York Herald* continued to note that the United States was not prepared militarily to engage in war.[45] As the U.S. military and their allies in Congress struggled to secure additional military resources in preparation for war, Nelan supported such disbursements but warned that giving the military too much power could threaten the democratic process at home. In the five weeks between the explosion of the *Maine* and the release of the naval court findings, Nelan depicted a Congress trying desperately to hold firm before demands for increased military expenditures.[46] In "Appropriations for Everything But National Defense," a raging Marine has seized the gavel and overturned the chair of the Speaker of the House.[47] With a black mourning band on his arm (a reference to the *Maine*), the usurper of congressional power thrusts out a basket "for National defence" above piles of relatively frivolous congressional appropriations for sundries, including Goose Creek and Huckleberry Swamp. An editorial earlier that week had pointedly criticized Congress's reluctance to appropriate sufficient funds for defense while "enormous sums" were "wasted on the so-called improvement of obscure harbors and useless creeks."[48] The reference to Huckleberry Swamp appears to have been connected to local news regarding corruption scandals.[49]

When the U.S. Congress unanimously approved fifty million dollars in discretionary funds for national defense and the president signed the bill into law on 9 March 1898, Nelan's cartoons called for the reader to reflect on the purpose of the money. In "He Wouldn't Be Happy Till He Got It," Nelan depicted a U.S. Marine with an overflowing basket of coins labeled "50 million for national defence."[50] The Marine grins from ear to ear, revealing a few blackened teeth. He has a crazed look in his eyes and wears bell-bottomed pants that are too short and expose frivolous looking star-spangled socks. The man spills the coins from the basket, leaving a trail behind him as he waddles off. The image hardly suggests the responsible use of funds to prepare for war or to compel Spain to negotiate for peace. Subsequent cartoons documented the effort to prepare a military defense in the event of war.[51]

Until mid-March, there was still some question as to both U.S. military preparedness and Spanish ability to muster European support in the event of a war with the United States. In his 12 March cartoon, Uncle Sam and a personified Spain appear to be equal in size and strength as they engage in a fistfight, literally and figuratively, over the Western Hemisphere.[52] On the other side of the globe, the Old World powers fight amongst themselves—Germany battles it out with Japan, England with Russia, and France cheers England on. On the surface, this cartoon appears to be simply a condemnation of wars. The accompanying text supports this reading. Looking on from outer space, Jupiter comments to Mars, "Gracious! They are a bad lot on the Earth; they are all fighting at once." In addition, however, the cartoon suggests that if the United States were to go to war, the Old World powers might be too absorbed in their own struggles to intervene on the side of Spain.[53]

According to the cartoons in the *New York Herald*, even with the 28

March 1898 release of the naval court findings on the causes of the explosion of the *Maine*, war was still not a foregone conclusion. In the following two weeks, Nelan portrayed in a variety of ways the choices that stood before the president and the nation. In Nelan's "Peace or War?" Uncle Sam looks over McKinley's shoulder as the latter prepares to unlock a treasure chest identified as the Board of Inquiry report.[54] In "Columbia's Easter Bonnet, Which Shall It Be?" Miss Columbia, the female symbol for the United States, has just taken off the bonnet of peace and is viewing herself in the mirror to see how the bonnet of war fits.[55] In another cartoon, the dove of peace asks, "Must I get out?" as a scrub brush held by an anonymous hand in a star-spangled sleeve drips suds and water on her nest inside the barrel of a cannon.[56] Other cartoons emphasize the leadership demonstrated by the president's steadfast resistance to the war cries of the jingoist press.[57]

After McKinley's war message on 11 April, the responsibility for deciding the fate of the country shifted from the president to the Congress.[58] Nelan made few references to other prominent actors, such as the business sectors or the press.[59] Other segments of American society were even more conspicuously absent. Democracy, in the view of the cartoonist, was primarily a game of patience—waiting for the naval report, waiting for the president to make a decision, waiting for Congress to act on McKinley's war message.

By the second week of April, Nelan confirmed that Europe was likely to maintain neutrality in the event of war with Spain. In "She Has Troubles of Her Own," a desperate man representing Spain comes running inside a house to solicit help from a huge washerwoman identified as Europe. The latter is wearing a warrior's helmet, and her temples drip with sweat. With shirtsleeves rolled up, she struggles to get her laundry, labeled "China," clean. Other dirty laundry, labeled "Africa" and "India," wait their turn.[60] The panicking Spain gestures toward Uncle Sam, who waits outside the door, but the laundress ignores Spain's pleas and continues scrubbing away on her washboard.

With the official declarations of war in the third week of April, the policymakers (and the press) disappear from the cartoons, and the *Maine* is converted into the sole cause of war. In his 22 April cartoon "Rally Round the Flag," Nelan draws on powerful imagery from the patriotic storehouse. Holding on firmly to a large American flag, which bears the words "Remember the *Maine*," Uncle Sam fires the cannon of war against an invisible enemy (see Figure 4.5).[61] This cartoon is noteworthy for its reliance on the trilogy of Uncle Sam, the American flag, and the *Maine*; its self-absorption; and the absence of other referents, such as Cuba or Spain.

Once war was declared, the cartoons ceased to support a noninterventionist stance and relied on a range of patriotic images, especially that of the *Maine*, to promote the war. The U.S.S. *Maine* became the symbol that could best represent the war for the public. References to and images of the sunken battleship continued to be prominent in Nelan's cartoons as the

Figure 4.5
"Rally Round the Flag," *New York Herald*, 22 April 1898.

United States defeated Spain in subsequent battles.[62] Likewise, Nelan occasionally reminded the public that there was a cost to the war, as manifested by new war taxes placed on goods including wine, flour, sugar, tea, tobacco, and petroleum.[63] When peace was finally attained, the *Maine* again figured into the cartoonist's iconography.[64]

The cartoons do not support the historiographic interpretation that U.S. intervention stemmed primarily from humanitarian or altruistic motives.[65] In fact, images that might support that interpretation are conspicuously absent from the repertoire of *New York Herald* cartoons that appeared in 1898.

Analysis of the cartoons published from April until July must be considered in light of the wartime restrictions under which the press was operating. In the first months of the war, Nelan's cartoons lack a critical edge, attributable in part to wartime censorship practices. Following the initiation of peace talks in Washington, D.C., on 26 July and subsequent modifications in the censorship laws, however, a more critical stance in Nelan's cartoons is evident.[66] In late July, the *Herald* cartoons begin to raise pointed questions about the direction of U.S. foreign policies, and in the aftermath of the war, the *Herald* became a fierce critic of U.S. wartime policies, corruption, and mismanagement.

Throughout 1898, images and symbols mirrored popular attitudes about the United States and its changing relationships with the rest of the world. In virtually all of the Nelan cartoons, Uncle Sam is the main actor, and he relates to others according to his evolving national identity. While these images generally dictated that the United States deserved to rule, in the period before and following the war, the cartoonist steps back and questions the new U.S. role.

During the war, Nelan's cartoons stressed primarily the positive aspects of the war in promoting national unity. The War of 1898 had contributed to national reconciliation by bringing together the North and South in common cause. In "If the War Brings Nothing Else, We Are Thankful," the North and South are personified as two figures who join right hands as they hold the hands of Uncle Sam's British counterpart, John Bull, who stands behind the flag of England.[67] The war also boosted U.S. prestige and its sense of self-importance, and Nelan's images show Uncle Sam's newfound acceptance in Europe, particularly with England. In "Cousins," a tall and assured Uncle Sam leans down from his towering height to light his cigar from the pipe of John Bull. The diminished European nations huddle nearby in apparent concern over Sam's readmission to the family fold.[68] In "Concert of Europe," Uncle Sam is shown as an equal to his European counterparts.[69] He performs with and becomes a member of the European orchestra of nations. In another cartoon, he seeks and secures greater economic integration with Europe.[70] In defeating the Spanish in Manila, Philippines, on 1 May, and at Santiago, Cuba, on 3 July, he establishes his military prowess and perceives himself to be held in greater esteem by France, Germany, England, Russia, Austria, and Italy.[71] As in "The Birth of a Marine Giant," however, Nelan's cartoons continue to suggest a certain fear on the part of the European nations over the new, growing, and seemingly uncontrollable role of the United States in the world (see Figure 4.6).

Immediately following the relaxation of press censorship on 29 July, the cartoons in the *New York Herald* became increasingly critical. The very next day, in Nelan's 30 July 1898 cartoon, "My Goodness, How He Is Mutilating That Beautiful Map!" Europe, who is personified as a chambermaid with a dusting broom, looks on in horror as Uncle Sam cuts from a world map swatches that represent the regions the United States hopes to acquire in the peace negotiations.[72] The following day, "A New War Map of the United States," a small cartoon signed by Huntington, appeared in the lower right-hand corner of the *Herald* (see Figure 4.7). In Huntington's illustration, Uncle Sam is represented as a map of North America—his nose

Figure 4.6
"The Birth of a Marine Giant," *New York Herald*, 8 July 1898.

is Florida; his beard is Texas; Mexico is his shirtsleeve; and his hand, which is Central America, reaches out to grab the island of Cuba.[73] The caption calls into question the direction of U.S. foreign policies as it asks, "Would George Washington Turn in His Grave If He Could See This?" Significantly, the cartoon was peripheral to a feature article about Grant Squires, the New York war censor, whom the *Herald* called the "Frankenstein of the Press." The cartoon underscores an editorial position which, by reference to George Washington, challenges the ultimate "Americanness" of U.S. intervention in Cuba. Its placement next to an article that describes the censorship regulations just lifted seems intended to alert the readers to the nature of the *Herald*'s "new," stronger editorial position.

The transformation of U.S. national identity wrought by the war can be seen in the shifting representation of Uncle Sam throughout the year. While in the first quarter of 1898 Nelan's Uncle Sam was a tall, slender, healthy

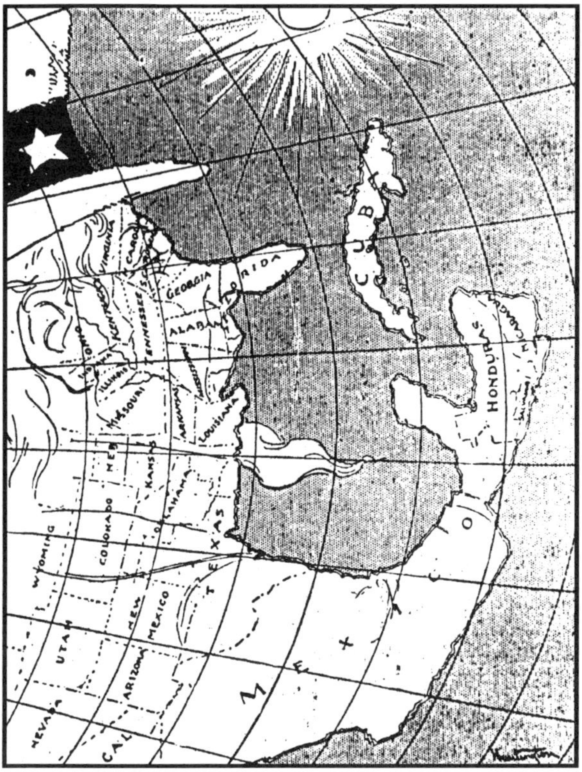

Figure 4.7
"A New War Map of the United States,"
New York Herald, 31 July 1898.

character who embodied entrepreneurial wisdom and responsibility, by August he had grown quite rotund, reflecting his expanding world power. In "Before and After Taking," a full-page, color spread which ran on the cover of one of the sections of the Sunday paper, Nelan expresses a certain discomfort with the new U.S. role as an imperial power (see Figure 4.8).[74] The artist provides before-and-after pictures of Uncle Sam. Before the war Uncle Sam is gaunt, emaciated, and sickly. After four months, however, his waistline has expanded to include Santiago, Puerto Rico, Hawaii, the Ladrones,[75] and the Philippines. Uncle Sam, who has literally consumed the globe, seems to be quite content with his new shape, but his size appears to interfere with his ability to see or move, and the diminutive Europeans appear to be concerned over the changes they have observed. The cartoonist notes in an ironic subtitle "Uncle Sam Proudly Informs His Physician That the Treatment Has Been a Success." Such metaphors about eating and physical growth provide the cartoonist with an opportunity to critique the shifting national identity and are used elsewhere with the same intent.[76]

Figure 4.8
"Before and After Taking," *New York Herald*, 7 August 1898. Original caption also reads,"Uncle Sam Proudly Informs His Physician That the Treatment Has Been a Success."

Likewise, Nelan's cartoons occasionally criticized the nation's new role in cartoons about the U.S. congressional debates over what to do with the new imperial territories. One such cartoon raises questions about whether the

Figure 4.9
"Troubles Which May Follow an Imperial Policy," *New York Herald*, 3 July 1898.

United States could exert its hegemony over the Philippines without compromising its own democratic principles. Following U.S. Admiral George Dewey's victory in Manila, Filipino revolutionary Emilio Aguinaldo declared the Philippines to be an independent republic on 12 June 1898. In Nelan's cartoon of 3 July 1898, "Troubles Which May Follow an Imperial Policy," House Speaker Thomas Reed sits at the head of the Congress before a dark-skinned figure with Negroid features who sports a sash over his naked torso indicating that he is a Representative from the Philippines. The Filipino carries a spear and shield and wears a skirt and earrings in his nose and ears. Six interconnected primitive spears cage in the Speaker, who has just been coerced into passing an appropriation for the ninety-ninth Philippine district (see Figure 4.9). The Congress is up in arms and congressmen are fleeing in the background. The humor in the cartoon is precisely in the reversal of the accepted roles for the United States, as ruler, and the Philippines as subject. The cartoon suggests a conflict between the political systems of the Americans who governed through a Congress, and the Filipinos, who apparently ruled by brute force.[77] The image of the Filipino (which appeared

Figure 4.10
"A Good Motto," *New York Herald*, 19 January 1898.

only rarely in the cartoons) suggests that the Filipino character is incompatible with that of the United States. The cartoonist fans the fears of racial difference to drive home a basically anti-imperialist position.

Images of the various nations involved in the war demonstrate that an iconographic battle was being fought in the cartoons of the war. These images reflected the ebbs and flows of wartime activity. In the course of 1898, Uncle Sam photographs, bottles, threatens, fights with, and triumphs over Spain. From the beginning of 1898, Nelan portrayed the United States as being in command and culturally superior to Spain. In "A Good Motto," the artist availed himself of prosopopoeia to personify Spain as a man in a fancy jacket, striped sash around his waist, knickers, white stockings, slippers, and a large hat with the word "Spain" written across it. To the left, "Spain" stands on tiptoe on a ladder as he assists Uncle Sam in putting up a plaque that reads "Let us have peace"[78] (see Figure 4.10). The symbols of intellectual rationality—an inkwell, paper, and a quill pen labeled "mightier than the sword"—are graphically associated with the United States. These objects sit on a star-spangled tablecloth located on the right-hand, U.S.-

dominated side of the picture. Spatially and symbolically, this cartoon shows the United States clearly in charge of the prospects for peace in the era prior to the outbreak of war. Uncle Sam and his symbols dominate the drawing: the quotation on the plaque is attributed to the U.S. Civil War hero General Ulysses S. Grant (again a subtle reference to the potential unity which the United States could achieve in its position toward Spain); Uncle Sam is twice as large as the diminutive Spaniard; and Uncle Sam holds the plaque securely in both hands as "Spain" plays a supportive, but not essential, role in holding up the sign.

By mid-April, images in the *New York Herald* began to show Spain in a less auspicious light. The first cartoon to appear in the *New York Herald* following the declaration of war, "Now Will You Fight?" portrayed Spain as reluctant to go to war.[79] Even in the throes of battle, Nelan's cartoons never presented Spain as a real threat to the United States. Nor, with one possible exception, did Nelan demonize the so-called enemy.[80] Rather, the *New York Herald* cartoons avoided attacking Spanish policies in Cuba and personified Spain as a white male, often Premier Práxedes Mateo Sagasta, for whom Nelan displayed considerable sympathy. As riots besieged Spain during the first week of May and Admiral Dewey proclaimed victory at the Battle of Manila Bay, Nelan portrayed Sagasta caught in an untenable position between revolution at home and U.S. opposition overseas.[81] In "She's Tumbling!" Sagasta struggles desperately in the throes of war to prop up the collapsing brick wall of Spanish government.[82] In another cartoon, Nelan depicted Spain as a hungry Spanish peasant coerced into fighting.[83] Other cartoons published in the *New York Herald* repeatedly personified Spain as the mangled victim of U.S. force.[84] Often, the cartoons prematurely anticipated Spain's demise.[85]

In his cartoons, Nelan mocked Spain's cultural icons and suggested that a culture built on dreams and antiquated notions of honor was futile and had left Spain incapable of governing its colonies. In "Our Modern Don Quixote," Don Quixote, representing Spain, is seated on a mule and charges at a windmill, whose blades represent the Cuban rebellion, the *Maine* disaster, the Philippines Island Uprising, Puerto Rico, and the United States.[86] Nelan consistently portrayed the concept of Spanish honor, a fundamental tenet of Spanish cultural imagery, in a derisive manner that equated Spain's military defeats with satisfying Spanish honor.[87] In "The Spanish Ignis Fatuus," a proud Spaniard with clenched fists holds his head high and, blinded by the rays of "Spanish honor," walks off a cliff toward destruction.[88] In "Your Only Salvation," Premier Sagasta staggers toward the medicine bottle of peace, and a miniature, doll-like figure of Spain hangs on the wall with the note "Spanish Honor is Satisfied."[89] The subtext about honor here suggests that it provided, at least for Spain, a false premise for going to war. Ironically, the U.S. Congress justified its own bellicose actions with a rhe-

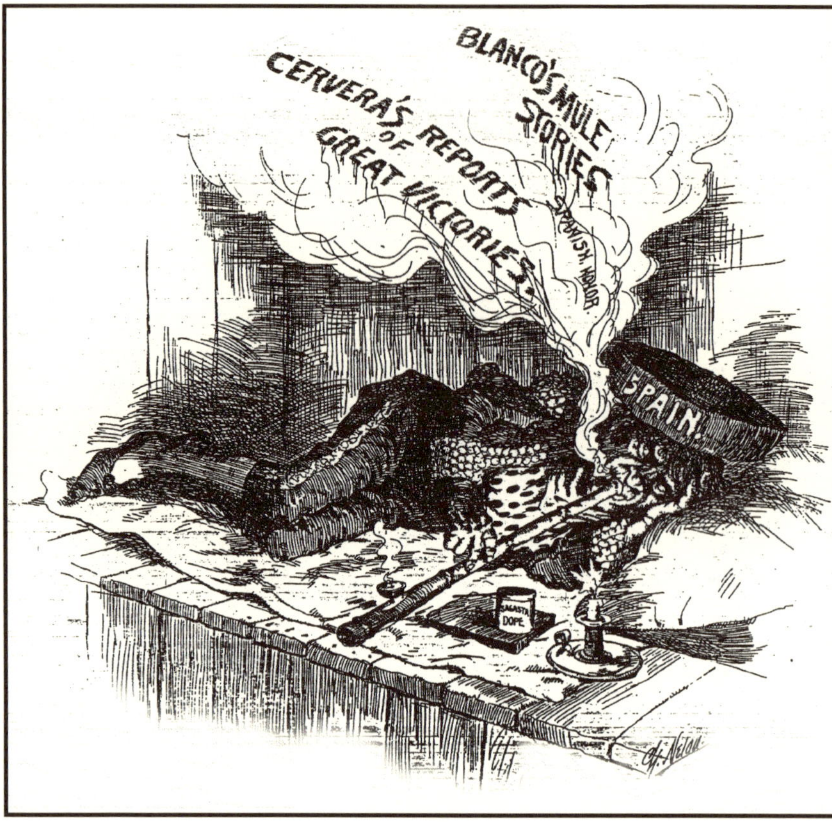

Figure 4.11
"How Will He Feel When the Pipe Gives Out?" *New York Herald*, 7 June 1898.

torical discourse which underscored the concept of honor as a reflection of American manhood (see Hoganson chapter, this volume).

Nelan, like other cartoonists of the time, repeatedly drew on the Spanish Golden Age concept that "Life is a dream" to suggest that Spain was living in a fantasy world.[90] In "The King's Jester," King Alfonso III, the twelve-year-old heir to the Spanish throne, sporting an oversized crown, is seated on Prime Minister Sagasta's knee. He laughs as Sagasta, decked out in a jester's cap, reads him cables from Spanish Admiral Pascual Cervera y Topete and General Ramón Blanco about the recurring but nonexistent defeats they have dealt to the Americans. In case the reader misses the point, *Sagasta's Joke Book* leans against the bench where the Spanish authorities are seated.[91] In the cartoon "How Will He Feel When the Pipe Gives Out?" the artist depicts Spain, personified as Sagasta, smoking a dope pipe and dreaming of honor and victory (see Figure 4.11).[92] The implication of course is that the

Spanish authorities are choosing to ignore their own inevitable defeat and dishonor.

Cuba was conspicuously absent from most of the *New York Herald* cartoons and was referred to or represented in only about 10 percent of the approximately 140 war cartoons Nelan produced in 1898. The marginalization of Cuban history and culture in the cartoons served as a metaphor for both the transformation of the war from Cuba's war for independence into the Spanish-American War and the isolation of Cuba from military and political events once the United States intervened.[93] In both cases, the axis of power passed directly from Europe to the United States without regard for Cuba.[94]

In the Nelan cartoons where Cuba was represented at all, it was as a name on a map being clipped and reconstructed by Uncle Sam, as an appendage of Uncle Sam's attire, or as an appetizer item on Uncle Sam's menu.[95] When Cuba was personified, it was usually as a boy or man-child, or, in one case, as a group of terrified men fleeing in panic from Uncle Sam.[96] Only in the cartoon "May All Our Hopes for '98 Be Realized!" (not penned by Nelan) was Cuba represented as a black man. The illustrator of that cartoon, published on 2 January, shows Father Time amidst a collage of pictures representing aspirations for the New Year. One reads "Cuba at Peace" and shows a black worker harvesting sugar from the fields.[97] In no case did Nelan personify Cuba as anything other than a white male, despite the dominance of blacks and mulattos in the Cuban population, particularly among the insurgents.[98] Nor did Nelan rely on female figures to represent Cuba, a practice commonly used by other cartoonists to create sympathy for the Cuban rebels or to encourage U.S. intervention on behalf of the damsel in distress, the suffering women and children, or Lady Liberty.[99]

Just before McKinley's war message to Congress, the *New York Herald* ran a cartoon that anticipated future tensions over Cuban sovereignty. In "He Seems To Be Looking For Trouble," Uncle Sam glares disapprovingly at a mustached man-child half his size who carries a knife and a *Cuba Libre* (Free Cuba) flag with a banner proclaiming "We accept nothing but independence."[100] This cartoon reinforced headlines from the previous day that indicated that the Cuban insurgents had rejected U.S. and Spanish efforts to negotiate an armistice and eventually establish Cuban autonomy under the Spanish flag.[101] At a time when U.S. diplomats were pushing for Cuban autonomy, Nelan portrayed independence as an immature position worthy of U.S. censure. In a 22 May cartoon "Before and After Intervention," Nelan further discredited the insurgents, not only for their intransigence but also for their cowardice and duplicity.[102] The left half of Nelan's drawing is labeled "The Cuban Revolutionist as Described by the Junta" and portrays a tall, swarthy soldier with a hefty sword, intimidating a Spaniard whom he holds hostage in the branches of a tree. On the right side, entitled "The

Figure 4.12
"All Sizes and Good Fits for All the Family," *New York Herald*, 13 May 1898.

Cuban Revolutionist as Discovered by the United States Army," the roles are reversed, and it is the Spaniard who waves a triumphant sword at an insurgent clinging to the tree in terror. In effect, the cartoon discredits the Cuban revolutionaries and invalidates the Cuban role in securing independence from Spain. Such images paved the way for four years of U.S. military occupation after the war, followed by continued U.S. dominance guaranteed by the Platt Amendment of 1902.

Once the war was in full swing, cartoons helped to establish a myth of benevolence by underscoring the generosity of Uncle Sam toward his new acquisitions. In Nelan's 13 May cartoon "All Sizes and Good Fits for All the Family," Uncle Sam assists a tall, smiling, bare-footed, dark-skinned youth identified as the Philippines in putting on a long, star-studded coat, striped trousers, and suspenders (see Figure 4.12).[103] The male personifications of Cuba, Puerto Rico, and Hawaii patiently sit on a bench and await their turns. A sign on the wall reads "Leave your orders and avoid the rush."

Figure 4.13
"Wanted—A Good Licking," *New York Herald*, 17 September 1898.

Behind the benevolent Uncle Sam is a row of star-spangled jackets. A bureau to his side is filled with clothes, a reference to the abundance of U.S. products available to Spain's former colonies.

The distribution of clothing and food to a welcoming population was a leitmotif employed by cartoonists during the war.[104] This theme both reflected and reinforced assumptions about the beneficence of U.S. purpose and expectations of gratitude and appreciation on the part of the recipients. Only rarely and inadvertently did Nelan provide a glimpse of the gap between these images and reality. That such expectations were not always fulfilled is illustrated in "Wanted—A Good Licking," the only cartoon published in 1898 in which Nelan caricatured a known Cuban personality[105] (see Figure 4.13). In that cartoon of 17 September 1898, penned a few weeks after the Spanish and U.S. governments signed a peace protocol and shortly before the Paris peace conference from which Cuban and Philippine independence leaders would be excluded, Nelan depicts Cuban insurgent General Máximo Gómez and Philippine independence leader Emilio Aguinaldo as naughty boys (although Gómez, sporting a beard, is a sort of manchild) engaged in throwing rocks at the American flag. Uncle Sam, puffing on a corncob pipe, angrily gets out of his chair and heads for a barbed-wire switch. By virtue of their depiction as children, the insurgents are thus denied stature. Their opposition to the flag, the symbol of American empire, is shown to be improper, disrespectful, and deserving of punishment. In the context of supposed U.S. beneficence, the colonial subjects appear to be ungrateful as well.

In all of Nelan's cartoons, the United States defined, dictated, and enforced the parameters of "acceptable" behavior. Nelan portrayed Uncle Sam as the omniscient, omnipotent, benevolent, paternal figure who knew best the needs of the childlike colonies. While these images reinforced notions that citizens of Cuba (and Hawaii, Puerto Rico, the Philippines, and Guam) lacked the maturity and knowledge required for self-government, they also called on readers to evaluate the evolving relationship of the United States with these "other" entities.

The representation of other Latin American nations varied little over the course of the year.[106] Latin American countries were often portrayed interchangeably as unreasonable, childish, and culturally inferior to the United States (particularly in their politics) and as ungrateful for U.S. guidance and assistance. Such images have persisted in the national imagery and provided the foundation for later images of Latin America.[107]

This chapter on cartoon images published in one newspaper, the *New York Herald*, has been limited to a single, albeit critical year, 1898. These cartoons confirm the importance of the War of 1898 in documenting the emergence of the United States as a global power and the transformation of concepts of national identity which that new role implied. The cartoons discussed and reproduced here show how certain representations and themes (particularly of the *Maine*, the United States, Spain, and Cuba) changed in accordance with the shifting contours of the international landscape, the trajectory of the war, and the imposition or removal of press restrictions. Comparative studies are needed to determine to what extent the *New York Herald* represented a unique case. Studies of cartoons from Latin America, Canada, Asia, and Europe would provide fascinating counterpoints against which to measure the U.S. perceptions of itself and others found in Nelan's cartoons.[108]

NOTES

1. Thomas Milton Kemnitz, "The Cartoon as a Historical Source," *Journal of Interdisciplinary History* 4, no. 1 (1973): 90, 93.

2. John J. Johnson, *Latin America in Caricature* (Austin: University of Texas Press, 1980), 26.

3. Lawrence H. Streicher, "On a Theory of Political Caricature," *Comparative Studies in Society and History* 9, no. 4 (1967) 427–45.

4. Allan Nevins and Frank Weitenkampf, *A Century of Political Cartoons: Caricature in the United States from 1800 to 1900* (New York: Charles Scribner's Sons, 1944), 11–16.

5. James Melvin Lee, *History of American Journalism* (New York: Houghton Mifflin Company, 1923), 362.

6. Nevins and Weitenkampf, *A Century of Political Cartoons*, 15.

7. Charles Nelan, *Cartoons of Our War with Spain* (New York: Frederick A. Stokes Company, 1898), n.p.

8. W. A. Coupe, "Observations on a Theory of Political Caricature," *Comparative Studies in Society and History* 11, no. 1 (1969): 82.

9. Nelan, *Cartoons of Our War with Spain.*

10. For a review of the Cuban historiography, see Duvon C. Corbitt, "Cuban Revisionist Interpretations of Cuba's Struggle for Independence," *Hispanic American Historical Review* 43, no. 3 (1963): 395–404; and Louis A. Pérez, Jr., *Essays on Cuban History: Historiography and Research* (Miami: University Press of Florida, 1995), 3–25. For a review of the Spanish literature, see Sylvia L. Hilton, "Democracy Goes Imperial: Spanish Views of American Policy in 1898," in *Reflections on American Exceptionalism*, ed. David K. Adams and Cornelius A. van Minnen (Staffordshire: Keele University Press, 1994), 97–128; and Sylvia L. Hilton, "The Spanish-American War of 1898: Queries into the Relationship between the Press, Public Opinion and Politics," *Revista Española de Estudios Norteamericanos* 7 (1994): 71–87.

11. Carmen González López-Briones, "The Indiana Press and the Coming of the Spanish-American War, 1895–1898," *Atlantis* (*Revista Española de los Estudios Angloamericanos*) 12, no. 1 (1990): 165–76; Joyce Milton, *The Yellow Kids: Foreign Correspondents in the Heyday of Yellow Journalism* (New York: Harper and Row, 1989); Charles H. Brown, *The Correspondents' War: Journalists in the Spanish-American War* (New York: Charles Scribner's Sons, 1967); George W. Auxier, "Middle Western Newspapers and the Spanish-American War, 1895–1898," *Mississippi Valley Historical Review* 26, no. 1 (1939–40): 523–34; George W. Auxier, "The Propaganda Activities of the Cuban *Junta* in Precipitating the Spanish-American War, 1895–1898," *Hispanic American Historical Review* 19, no. 3 (1939): 286–305; Joseph E. Wisan, *The Cuban Crisis as Reflected in the New York Press, 1895–1898* (New York: Columbia University Press, 1934); and Marcus M. Wilkerson, *Public Opinion and the Spanish-American War: A Study in War Propaganda* (Baton Rouge: Louisiana State University Press, 1932).

12. Marion Tuttle Marzolf, *Civilizing Voices: American Press Criticism, 1880–1950* (New York: Longman, 1991), 23; and David Traxel, *1898: The Birth of the American Century* (New York: Alfred A. Knopf, 1998), 82.

13. Traxel, *1898*, 82.

14. James L. Crouthamel, *Bennett's New York Herald and the Rise of the Popular Press* (Syracuse, N.Y.: Syracuse University Press, 1989), ix.

15. Richard O'Connor, *The Scandalous Mr. Bennett* (Garden City, N.Y.: Doubleday and Co., 1962), 229.

16. *New York Herald*, 23 February 1895.

17. John D. Stevens, *Sensationalism and the New York Press* (New York: Columbia University Press, 1991), 57.

18. *New York Herald*, 1 January 1898; *New York Herald*, 1 December 1898; and *New York Herald*, 31 December 1898.

19. Wisan, *The Cuban Crisis*, 33.

20. O'Connor, *The Scandalous Mr. Bennett*, 185.

21. *New York Herald* cartoons directly related to the war in 1898 totaled more than 150. Some fifteen of these were by artists other than Nelan. Not included in this count are the multitude of other images and sketches related to the war. The period of greatest saturation was from April (nineteen cartoons), May (twenty-four cartoons), and June (eighteen cartoons).

22. *Who Was Who in America*, a component volume of *Who's Who in American History*, 5 vols. [Volume 1, 1897–1942] (Chicago: A. N. Marquis Co., 1943), gives Nelan's birthdate as 1859. Peter Hastings Falk, ed., *Who Was Who in American Art: Compiled from the Original Thirty-Four Volumes of American Art Annual—Who's Who in Art, Biographies of American Artists Active from 1898–1947* (Madison, Conn.: Sound View Press, 1985), 445, says Nelan was born in 1854.

23. Falk, *Who Was Who*, 445.

24. Joseph Smith, "The American Image of the Cuban Insurgents in 1898," *Zeitschrift feur Anglistik und Amerikanistik* 40, no. 4 (1992): 319.

25. Wisan, *The Cuban Crisis*, 38; and O'Connor, *The Scandalous Mr. Bennett*, 230.

26. See the cartoons, "What Will He Do with It?" *New York Herald*, 3 June 1898; and "My Goodness, How He Is Mutilating That Beautiful Map!" *New York Herald*, 30 June 1898. Unless otherwise noted, all *New York Herald* cartoons cited are the work of Charles Nelan.

27. "Let Us Look Into This Matter," *New York Herald*, 27 August 1898; "I Am Pleased With the Situation," *New York Herald*, 28 August 1898; "And The Fall Elections Are Coming On!" *New York Herald*, 2 September 1898; "The President Has Ordered Mr. Alger to Investigate Himself," *New York Herald*, 8 September 1898; "Are There Not Some Things Worse Than the Bad Dollar?" *New York Herald*, 10 September 1898; "The Present 'Organization' of the Army," *New York Herald*, 13 September 1898; "Better Hurry That Job, Alger," *New York Herald*, 15 September 1898; "Their Busy Season," *New York Herald*, 16 September 1898; "Alger: Say, Haven't I Been a Good War Secretary?" *New York Herald*, 22 September 1898; "Appointed For the War," *New York Herald*, 23 September 1898; "A Game of Blind-man's Buff [*sic*]," *New York Herald*, 13 October 1898; "Is There Anything in These Halloween Souvenirs?" *New York Herald*, 1 November 1898; and "Say, Alger, That Date Means a Great Deal to Us," *New York Herald*, 5 November 1898.

28. "If I Have Another War, I'll Be Broke," *New York Herald*, 14 December 1897.

29. Nevins and Weitenkampf, *A Century of Political Cartoons*, 172.

30. See [Berryman], "It's Hard to Carry Eggs in a Paper Bag During a Cyclone," *Washington Post*, 11 May 1898; and "Perhaps It Ain't Going to Rain Much, Anyhow," in Manuel Méndez Saavedra, *1898: la guerra hispanoamericana en caricaturas/The Spanish American War in Cartoons* (Puerto Rico: Comisión Puertorriqueña para la Celebración del Quinto Centenario del Descubrimiento de América y Puerto Rico, 1992), 52.

31. "It Looks Bad for the Gunner," *New York Herald*, 20 January 1898.

32. The articles were cited in *Herald* (Paris, European edition), 21 January 1898. See also Herald Bureau, "Navy Too Weak to Go to War; Experts Point Out Deficiencies Which Would Put the United States at the Mercy of Foreign Enemies," *New York Herald*, 21 January 1898; and Herald Bureau, "Navy Needs Guns and More Men," *New York Herald*, 22 January 1898.

33. "Good!" *New York Herald*, 3 January 1898.

34. "Wake Up!" *New York Herald*, 13 January 1898.

35. Walter LaFeber, *The New Empire: An Interpretation of American Expansion, 1860–1898* (Ithaca: Cornell University Press, 1963), 370–79.

36. Alfred Mahan, "The United States Looking Outward," *The Atlantic Monthly* 66 (1890): 816.

37. Louis A. Pérez, Jr., "Meaning of the *Maine*," *Pacific Historical Review* 58, no. 3 (1989): 293–322.

38. "The Nation's Grief," *New York Herald*, 18 February 1898.

39. "Good Advice," *New York Herald*, 19 February 1898.

40. "Observe Good Faith and Justice Toward All Nations, Cultivate Peace and Harmony with All," *New York Herald*, 22 February 1898.

41. "Our Great Objector," *New York Herald*, 23 February 1898.

42. "Keep Your Head Cool," *New York Herald*, 24 February 1898.

43. *Cartoons of the War of 1898 with Spain from Leading Foreign and American Papers* (Chicago: Belford, Middlebrook and Co., 1898).

44. R. Swayze, "Keep Cool—We've Had Enough Explosions!" *Philadelphia Inquirer*, 20 February 1898; R. Swayze, "Waiting for the Facts," *Philadelphia Inquirer*, 18 February 1898; and Clifford K. Berryman, "Waiting for the Facts," *Washington Post*, 25 February 1898.

45. Herald Bureau, "More Men Needed to Man the Guns," *New York Herald*, 21 February 1898.

46. "No Appropriation Can Get Past Us," *New York Herald*, 4 March 1898; and "Shut Out By 'Maine' Strength," *New York Herald*, 7 March 1898.

47. "Appropriations for Everything But National Defence," *New York Herald*, 21 February 1898.

48. "Everything for Dingley 'Protection,' Nothing for National Protection," unsigned editorial, *New York Herald*, 19 February 1898.

49. A "Huckleberry" railroad franchise had been granted in 1893 under provisions similar to those which were being applied to favor the Citizens' Water Supply Company. See "Big Profits in a Water Contract," *New York Herald*, 17 February 1898.

50. "He Wouldn't Be Happy Till He Got It," *New York Herald*, 8 March 1898.

51. "A Cash Customer with Money to Burn," *New York Herald*, 10 March 1898; "A Hard Race Against Time," *New York Herald*, 17 March 1898; and "As Spain Views the Approaching Conflict," *New York Herald*, 3 April 1898.

52. "Gracious! They are a Bad Lot on the Earth; They are All Fighting at Once," *New York Herald*, 12 March 1898.

53. See also, "It Begins to Look As If These Gentlemen Agreed With Me," *New York Herald*, 22 March 1898.

54. "Peace or War?" *New York Herald*, 28 March 1898. See also "Which Shall It Be?" *New York Herald*, 5 April 1898.

55. "Columbia's Easter Bonnet, Which Shall it be?" *New York Herald*, 9 April 1898.

56. "Must I Get Out?" *New York Herald*, 4 April 1898.

57. "Peace Hath Her Victories No Less Renowned Than War," *New York Herald*, 26 February 1898; and "Don't Bother the Pilot," *New York Herald*, 28 February 1898.

58. See Nelan's cartoons, "Before and After Taking Responsibility," *New York Herald*, 12 April 1898; and "Well, I'm Waiting Now," *New York Herald*, 13 April 1898.

59. "Which Shall It Be?" *New York Herald*, 17 January 1898; "Danger of Asphyxiation," *New York Herald*, 31 January 1898; "Keep Your Head Cool," *New York Herald*, 24 February 1898; [artist unknown], "What Is Behind the War Scare," *New York Herald*, 27 February 1898; and [Company (?)], "Eager to Get War Bonds," *New York Herald*, 15 June 1898. Interestingly, Nelan rarely personified businessmen in his cartoons except to poke fun at the trusts. See "Don't You Put That On Me!" *New York Herald*, 10 June 1898.

60. "She Has Troubles of Her Own," *New York Herald*, 16 April 1898.

61. "Rally Round the Flag," *New York Herald*, 22 April 1898.

62. "Remember the Maine," *New York Herald*, 3 May 1898; "Will I Ever Forget It?" *New York Herald*, 7 May 1898; "Well, Who'll be Next?" *New York Herald*, 11 May 1898; and "Their First Decoration Day—Keep Their Graves Green," *New York Herald*, 30 May 1898.

63. "He Isn't Handsome, But He Comes High," *New York Herald*, 12 June 1898; and "This Isn't Too Much for a Good Thing," published in Nelan, *Cartoons of Our War with Spain*.

64. "The Bitter End," *New York Herald*, 14 August 1898; and "Victor—and Victim," *New York Herald*, 30 August 1898.

65. Ruhl Bartlett, *Policy and Power: Two Centuries of American Foreign Relations* (New York: Hill and Wang, 1963), 126–27; Albert Frederick Pollard, *Factors in American History* (New York: Macmillan Company, 1925); Robert Endicott Osgood, *Ideals and Self-Interest in America's Foreign Relations: The Great Transformation of the Twentieth Century* (Chicago: University of Chicago Press, 1953); and H. Wayne Morgan, *America's Road to Empire: The War with Spain and Overseas Expansion* (New York: Wiley, 1965), 8–9, 61, 113.

66. See "Sketch of General A. W. Greely, head of the Censor's Department," *New York Herald*, 14 June 1898; "New York's Boss, The War Censor," *New York Herald*, 31 July 1898; and "A Boss? Well, I Should Say We Had. He is New York's War Censor," *New York Herald*, 31 July 1898.

67. "If the War Brings Nothing Else, We Are Thankful," in Nelan, *Cartoons of Our War with Spain*.

68. "Cousins," *New York Herald*, 23 May 1898.

69. "The Concert of Europe," *New York Herald*, 2 June 1898.

70. "The Tide Is Coming Our Way Now," *New York Herald*, 31 May 1898.

71. "The Birth of a Marine Giant," *New York Herald*, 8 July 1898.

72. "My Goodness, How He Is Mutilating That Beautiful Map!" *New York Herald*, 30 July 1898.

73. "A New War Map of the United States," *New York Herald*, 31 July 1898.

74. "Before and After Taking," *New York Herald*, 7 August 1898.

75. The Ladrones, literally "thieves," was the name for the Mariana Islands, an archipelago of fourteen volcanic islands to the east of the Philippines. These included Guam, one of the islands ceded to the United States following the war.

76. For other examples, see "Uncle Sam's Thanksgiving Dinner," *New York Herald*, 25 November 1898; "I Won't Skate on Your Pond," *New York Herald*, 26

November 1898; and "Goodbye, Mr. Monroe," *New York Herald*, 27 November 1898.

77. "Troubles Which May Follow an Imperial Policy," *New York Herald*, 3 July 1898.

78. "A Good Motto," *New York Herald*, 19 January 1898.

79. "Now Will You Fight?" *New York Herald*, 26 April 1898.

80. See Nelan, *Cartoons of Our War with Spain*. Interestingly, this cartoon appears never to have been published in the *New York Herald*.

81. "Will This Be the Bitter End?" *New York Herald*, 5 May 1898; "Between Two Fires," *New York Herald*, 6 May 1898; and "Spain's Dilemma," *New York Herald*, 12 May 1898.

82. "She's Tumbling!" *New York Herald*, 17 May 1898.

83. "It's Bread, Not War, He Wants," *New York Herald*, 14 May 1898.

84. Leon Barritt, "Will I Ever Forget It?" *New York Herald*, 7 May 1898; "I Wonder If He Wants Some More?" *New York Herald*, 7 May 1898; and "Don't Smile—Til You Hear From Sampson," *New York Herald*, 10 May 1898.

85. See "Only a Question of Time," *New York Herald*, 27 May 1898; "Is This the 'Bitter End'?" *New York Herald*, 6 July 1898; "The Boy Stood on the Burning Deck," *New York Herald*, 9 July 1898; "Your Only Salvation," *New York Herald*, 12 July 1898; and "Nero Fiddled While Rome Burned," *New York Herald*, 22 July 1898.

86. "Our Modern Don Quixote," *New York Herald*, 10 April 1898.

87. "Satisfying Spanish Honor," *New York Herald*, 15 May 1898; and "A Comparison," *New York Herald*, 25 June 1898.

88. "The Spanish Ignis Fatuus," *New York Herald*, 25 June 1898.

89. "Your Only Salvation," *New York Herald*, 12 July 1898.

90. See "A Rude Awakening in Store," *Detroit News*, n.d.; "Entertaining a Delusion," *Syracuse Herald*, n.d.; and "About to Burst," *Chicago Journal*, n.d.; all in Méndez Saavedra, *1898: la guerra hispanoamericana*, 44, 46, 54.

91. "The King's Jester," *New York Herald*, 5 June 1898.

92. "How Will He Feel When the Pipe Gives Out?" *New York Herald*, 7 June 1898.

93. For an insightful analysis of this theme, see Pérez, *War of 1898*.

94. This shift was represented in numerous cartoons throughout the country and was referred to allegorically in a cartoon by R. C. Bowman, "Don't Forget What You Are Fighting For, Uncle." In the cartoon, a white man-child in rags (representing Cuba) holds out his hand to Uncle Sam, who is busy beating up an already defeated Spain. In the caption, Cuba says to Uncle Sam, "Excuse me for interrupting you, but can't you find time to give me a bite to eat?" See "Don't Forget What You Are Fighting For, Uncle," *Minneapolis Tribune*, n.d., in Méndez Saavedra, *1898: la guerra hispanoamericana*, 77.

95. "A New War Map of the United States," *New York Herald*, 31 July 1898; "My Goodness, How He Is Mutilating That Beautiful Map!" *New York Herald*, 30 July 1898; "Uncle Sam Revising the International Atlas," *New York Herald*, 23 October 1898; "Before and After Taking," *New York Herald*, 7 August 1898; and "Uncle Sam's Thanksgiving Dinner," *New York Herald*, 25 November 1898.

96. "Yankee Doodle in Cuba," in *New York Herald*, 26 June 1898.

97. H. C., "May All Our Hopes for '98 Be Realized," *New York Herald*, 2 January 1898.

98. For a discussion of the changing U.S. notions of Cuban ethnicity, see Smith, "The American Image," 319–29.

99. See "Easter Greetings to the Pearl of the Antilles," *Chicago Tribune*, n.d., and untitled, *St. Louis Globe-Democrat*, n.d., in Méndez Saavedra, *1898: la guerra hispanoamericana*, 101, 129. See also "Behold! I Stand at the Door and Knock!" *Chicago Tribune*, n.d., in Nelan, *Cartoons of the War of 1898 with Spain.*

100. "He Seems To Be Looking For Trouble," *New York Herald*, 8 April 1898.

101. "Cuban Defiance Angers Congress; H. S. Rubens, Junta's Counsel, Stirs Hornet's Nest By Declaring that Intervention Before Recognition Would Turn Insurgent Guns on Us," *New York Herald*, 7 April 1898.

102. "Before and After Intervention," *New York Herald*, 22 May 1898.

103. "All Sizes and Good Fits for All the Family," *New York Herald*, 13 May 1898.

104. See "Will Wear the Stars and Stripes," *Minneapolis Journal*, n.d., in Méndez Saavedra, *1898: la guerra hispanoamericana*, 114.

105. "Wanted—A Good Licking," *New York Herald*, 17 September 1898.

106. See "It Begins to Look As If These Gentlemen Agreed With Me," *New York Herald*, 22 March 1898.

107. See Martha L. Cottam, *Images and Intervention: U.S. Policies in Latin America* (Pittsburgh: University of Pittsburgh Press, 1994); and Lars Schoultz, *Beneath the United States: A History of U.S. Policy toward Latin America* (Cambridge: Harvard University Press, 1998).

108. Some work has been done on the Spanish cartoons of the war. See Aurora G. Morcillo, "Satire, Journalism, and Madrid's *Gedeon*: National Images and National Characters in the Spanish-American War of 1898," *Colonial Latin American Historical Review* 8, no. 1 (1999): 43–78. For a study of political cartoons in *La campana de gracia*, *El motín*, and *Blanco y negro*, see Antonio Elorza, "Con la marcha de Cádiz (imágenes españolas de la guerra de independencia cubana, 1895–1898)," *Estudios de historia social* [Spain] 1–4 (1988): 327–86.

5

"Honor Comes First": The Imperatives of Manhood in the Congressional Debate over War

Kristin L. Hoganson

Among the panoply of explanations offered by historians for the U.S. entry into the Spanish-Cuban War is that partisan considerations made jingoist stances seem politically astute. According to this line of thought, in the wake of the *Maine* disaster Democrats and Republicans alike thought that clamoring for war would help their parties win future elections. Added to this ambition was the hope that war would unite the country after the divisive presidential election of 1896. This political explanation has withstood the test of time well. Members of Congress undoubtedly did formulate policy with an eye on the voting public and their own future political prospects. Furthermore, as their frequent calls for greater fraternity suggest, national unity was a topic of some concern. It seems highly plausible that jingoistic political leaders had hopes of rallying the nation behind a common cause.[1]

Yet questions remain about the political explanation. Why did leaders from both major parties (and Populist leaders as well) view war as an opportunity for partisan gain and national unity? Given that eighteen years later Woodrow Wilson won reelection with the platform "He kept us out of war," why was there not a political premium on avoiding war in the spring of 1898? To understand the political appeal of jingoism, we need to look at the issue from the perspective of contemporaries. How did they conceptualize the war issue? Foremost among the concepts invoked by congressmen in the post-*Maine* debate over war was *honor*. It is this word and the meanings attached to it that can help us unravel the mystery of politically motivated militancy. Tracing the use and significance of the chivalric term can illuminate how cultural assumptions—and more specifically, assumptions about the imperatives of manhood—had the power to shape decisions of peace and war.

Although militant jingoes had called for U.S. intervention virtually from the start of the Cuban war for independence from Spain initiated with the *Grito de Baire* in February 1895, the issue had little political weight until the U.S. battleship *Maine* exploded and sank in Havana harbor on the night of 15 February 1898. In response, President William McKinley appointed a court of naval inquiry and urged Americans to suspend judgment until the investigators had filed their findings. The court's report, submitted on 25 March, attributed the explosion to an external source. Although the commission admitted that it could not determine who was responsible, suspicion came to rest on the Spaniards. Not only did Spain have a reputation for perfidy, but also, to many Americans, it appeared that only the Spanish government had the technological capabilities to commit such an act. Members of Congress, no less than other Americans, were outraged at the thought of Spanish villains striking in the dark without giving the sleeping crew a chance to fight. "Splendid sport, indeed! How chivalric!" exclaimed one senator, whose biting sarcasm punctuated his view of the incident as a manifestation of Spanish treachery.[2]

Those who blamed the disaster on Spain regarded it as a challenge to American men, particularly because Spain refused to apologize or offer reparations and instead suggested that the men of the *Maine* were at fault. Senator Richard R. Kenney (D, Del.) captured the leading sentiment of the day in his response to what was perceived as a Spanish insult: "American manhood and American chivalry give back the answer that innocent blood shall be avenged, starvation and crime shall cease, Cuba shall be free. For such reasons, for such causes, America can and will fight. For such causes and for such reasons we should have war."[3]

The reference to American manhood and chivalry was by no means unusual in the halls of Congress. As it waited for the investigators' report on the cause of the incident, Congress passed a $50 million defense appropriation to move the U.S. military to a wartime footing. Congressmen were eager to show their support for the measure. The Senate did not debate the issue at all, passing the $50 million bill without discussion or an opposing vote. The House also passed the bill unanimously. On the Democratic side, Representative John F. Fitzgerald (D, Mass.) announced he would vote for the appropriation "to defend the honor and maintain the dignity of this Republic. [Great applause.]" From across the aisle, Representative Stephen A. Northway (R, Ohio) proclaimed that, if necessary, "we will vote to spend not only this appropriation, but millions more in defense of our country and our country's honor. [Applause.]" As these statements suggest, the word *honor* surfaced repeatedly in the discussions over the appropriation.[4]

After the *Maine* report had been submitted, congressmen continued to invoke honor in debates over the appropriate response to the presumed attack. "I am one who believes in peace with honor, and I say now and again there can be no peace with honor until Cuba is free and the crime of the *Maine* is atoned," said Representative William Sulzer (D, N.Y.). "I have been and am for peace," said Representative David B. Henderson (R, Iowa), but not, he insisted, at the expense of his country's honor. Senator George Turner (Pop., Wash.) joined in the clamor by calling for a "declaration of war, pure and simple" because "every dictate of national honor" demanded it.[5]

Many of the congressmen who cited honor exhibited an unfettered enthusiasm for war, but even those who professed to want peace often admitted that war would be preferable to dishonor. Representative James A. Norton (D, Ohio) said that although he deplored "the infinite woe of war, yet better far that this war should come, though at the cost of untold treasure, of countless wealth, and human life, than the degradation of our country's honor." In a similar vein, Representative Mahlon Pitney (R, N.J.) said he hoped that there would be no conflict. "We desire peace with honor," he said, "but we lay a solemn emphasis upon the word honor. Honor comes first. It is most important; it is the end ever to be held in view. [Applause.]"[6]

Republicans, Democrats, and Populists alike used the chivalric standard of honor to explain their support for a militant response to the supposed Spanish insult. According to jingoist congressmen, a slight of honor as great as the *Maine* incident must be avenged. This claim was more than a rhetorical flourish—jingoes regarded honor as a legitimate and persuasive rationale for war. To understand how their commitment to honor and their manipulation of the standard affected the war debate, it is first necessary to look at what the term meant to the congressmen who used it.

Although *honor* had a feminine component—in 1895 the *Century Dictionary* defined it as "loyalty and high courage in men and chastity in women, as virtues of the highest consideration"—in the context of the debate over war in 1898, *honor* implied male courage rather than female virtue. It referred to a male code of behavior; being honorable meant being manly. Congressmen showed that they connected the chivalrous standard of honor with ideals of manliness by declaring that the opposites of honor were effeminacy and childishness. As Representative John J. Lentz (D, Ohio) questioned, would the nation defend its honor or "remain impotent"? Earlier Lentz had associated dishonor with immaturity: "We have not yet awakened to a realization of what 'national honor' means when we can go waddling and wabbling along, day in and day out, refusing to hear the cry of the people—'Remember the *Maine*!' "[7]

That congressmen connected manliness and honor is also shown by their tendency to use the word *honor* alongside words that evoked manly qualities, such as *bravery*, *liberty*, *glory*, and *manhood* itself. Senator George F. Hoar (R, Mass.) implied that honor was related to manhood when he expressed fears that "manhood and courage and honor will follow athletics to Yale" if Harvard men did not repudiate Charles Eliot Norton, a professor who discouraged Harvard students from enlisting. At times, congressmen substituted the word *manhood* for *honor* with no perceptible change in meaning, as in a speech by Representative James R. Mann (R, Ill.): "We do not fight for a fancied slight; we do not fight for a commercial wrong; we do not fight for an increase of territory; we do not fight because our commercial spirit has been outraged; we do not fight because our land has been invaded; we fight because it has become necessary to fight if we would uphold our manhood."[8] In sum, as used in Congress in 1898, *honor* referred to a male code of valorous and self-respecting behavior. Honor was an attribute of a potent, mature, and chivalrous man, a man who wielded power, who was poised to fight.

The militant understanding of honor that guided the war debate reflected the new standards of passionate manhood that were in the ascendance in the late nineteenth century. As E. Anthony Rotundo and other men's historians have noted, at the end of the century, older standards of self-controlled manhood were giving way to ideals that exalted aggression, toughness, and physical prowess. Late-nineteenth-century standards of manhood valued combativeness; new words like *sissy, pussyfoot*, and *stuffed shirt* expressed the rising disfavor with self-restraint. According to the prevalent standards, it was not so much his specific objectives that signaled a man's character but his willingness to fight for his beliefs. An advertisement published in the *Boston Journal* at the time of the war debate conveyed this point. The pitch for Dr. Pierce's patent medicine (which promised to cure white-livered men) ran as follows: "A woman judges a man from appearances. If he is energetic and forcible she doesn't always stop to reason why. She . . . applauds the man who fights bravely. He may win, he may lose; but he must never flag; he must fight."[9]

The idea that bellicosity was, in itself, a mark of manliness also surfaced in late-nineteenth-century political reporting. A glowing profile of Representative Charles H. Grosvenor (R, Ohio) published by the *Washington Post* in late February 1898 illuminates the enthusiasm shown for militant qualities in political leaders. The article, tellingly titled "A Manly Fighter is He," said that Grosvenor "delights in crossing blades with those worthy of his steel. . . . He prefers the battle-ax to the broadsword; yet he can use the rapier with exquisite skill. . . . He's ever rambling in the arena of discussion, looking for a fight, and he usually gets it." The valorization of militant qualities in men benefited jingoes after the *Maine* disaster, as an appreciative editorial from the *Rochester Democrat and Chronicle* attests: "We may call these war orators, 'hot-heads,' but what would a nation be without hot-heads? . . . Impatience that needs restraint is better than sluggishness that requires prodding."[10] The late-nineteenth-century propensity to prefer hotheads to sluggards gave rise to and legitimated jingoes' martial understanding of honor.

The congressmen who cited honor as a rationale for war were highly vested in the term because it represented their self-worth and identity as men. They used the concept of honor to connect deeply held individual ideals to public policies. What made this tactic effective was the widespread conviction that the standards that guided individual men should be the standards that guided nations. This certainty led jingoist congressmen to draw on a men-and-nations analogy to argue for war. The analogy was often only implicit in jingoes' pro-war arguments, but at times they stated it straightforwardly. As Representative Lorenzo Danford (R, Ohio) maintained, "No man ever went to the assistance of a weak and defenseless fellow-being who was being tortured by a brutal master and did not feel that he had done a good act, and did not receive the encouragement and plaudits of manly men; and so, no nation that goes to the relief of an oppressed people but will grow in the respect of other nations, and what is better than all, in the self-respect of its own people."[11] In his men-and-nations analogy, Danford suggested that intervention would reflect positively on both American men and their nation, for the virtues admired in one were the virtues admired in the other.

Taking the men-and-nations analogy to heart, jingoist congressmen applied their personal standards of behavior to international affairs. One congressman who concluded that violence was the only appropriate response to the *Maine* incident was Representative Sulzer. "I am no jingo crying for war for the sake of war," he said, "but there are things more horrible than war. I would rather be dead upon the battlefield than live under the white flag of national disgrace, national cowardice, national decay, and national disintegration." Sulzer invoked the specter of male cowardice and disgrace to convey the magnitude of the nation's cowardice and disgrace should it fail to intervene. He cited his personal convictions to justify war. Assertive personal standards also led a number of Sulzer's fellows to conclude that it was better to be too precipitous than too prudent in a case involving honor. "I have no sympathy with those rash, intemperate spirits who would provoke war simply for the sake of fighting," said Representative Joseph W. Bailey (D, Tex.), "and yet I would rather follow them, and suffer all the miseries and misfortunes their heedlessness would bring than to follow those other contemptible and mercenary creatures who are crying out for 'peace at any price.' [Great Applause.]" Bailey elaborated on this point in a later speech: "If in order for a man to preserve his equanimity and to appear cool he must allow insults to pass unanswered, then I prefer to be classed with those who lose their heads. I would infinitely rather lose my head in resenting an insult than to lose my self-respect by submitting to be insulted."[12] Believing that the nation should live up to his personal code of conduct, Bailey called for war.

The conviction that an affront to honor mandated combat led jingoist congressmen to conclude that submitting the *Maine* and Cuban independence issues to arbitration would be unacceptable. "There can not be and must not be any arbitration," Representative William C. Arnold (R, Penn.) said to loud applause. "Our honor is at stake and our flag insulted. If I insult any gentleman in this house should there be arbitration to decide and inform that gentleman whether or not he has been insulted?" Senator George C. Perkins (R, Calif.) agreed. Although he had voted in favor of an arbitration treaty the previous year, he said he could not countenance arbitration of the *Maine* issue. "There are questions that do not admit of arbitration," he said. "Men do not arbitrate questions of honor. Neither do nations." The problem with arbitration in a case of honor was that it could not address the core of the grievance; the implication was that the aggrieved party could not command respect. Arbitration could lead to conciliation, but it could not reinstate the insulted party before his peers. To the contrary, it would undercut his position by implying that he was unable to settle his own affairs without assistance. War, in contrast, promised to demonstrate that the nation was not devoid of honor. Indeed, according to the jingoist logic, war would foster greater honor among American men. By strengthening their fiber (an assumption fostered by nostalgic accounts of the Civil War that presented combat as a crucible of character), it also would strengthen their political system, for the health of American democracy commonly was seen as resting on the well-being, both physical and moral, of the masses of American men. The belief that war would benefit American men and their nation led jingoes to regard the likelihood of war with enthusiasm. As Representative Norton said, "I welcome war."[13]

Those who welcomed war did so not only because of their desire to redeem American honor vis-à-vis Spain, but also because they believed that American men *needed* a war—that their manly fiber was in doubt. The ascendance of militant ideals of manhood can be seen, in large part, as a response to the troubling suspicion that American manhood was in peril. Men hit hard by the depression of 1893 discovered that their self-respect had suffered along with their ability to provide for their families. As hard times raised doubts about the evolutionary fitness of struggling men, the comforts of the wealthy raised questions about upper-crust men's continued vitality. The growing cohort of middle-class men who held soft, white-collar jobs in what was an increasingly industrialized, urbanized, and bureaucratized society found that declining occupational independence was not the only thing that distinguished them from their fathers' generation. They started to worry about "overcivilization," by which they meant emasculating luxury, ease, and overrefinement. Added to these anxieties were concerns about the moral grounding of middle-class and wealthy men, whose Gilded Age obsession with moneymaking seemed to come at the cost of civic virtue and whose self-seeking materialism boded ill for the future of fraternalism.[14]

If white, middle-class men were beset by uncertainty about their ability to compete against, much less forge a common cause with, hardened working-class men, they worried equally that seemingly degenerate lower-class men would reduce the virility of the national "stock." Mired in the pervasive racism of the time, a number of white people feared that, in the absence of the allegedly civilizing influence of slavery, black men were regressing toward their "natural" bestial state, turning into savage rapists.[15] In addition, many native-born Americans regarded the influx of immigrants as fraught with peril for American manhood, for they interpreted immigrant men's social customs, labor protests, and support for machine bosses as signs of unmanly character.[16] Reports of homosexual acts, impotence, mental deterioration, and a loss of vital energy suggested that the social changes of the 1890s were causing degeneracy in middle-class as well as lower-class men, an alarming thought in a world assumed to be governed by Darwinian laws.[17] Since the well-being of the nation commonly was seen as resting on the character of its citizens (and particularly on the character of the men who could vote and hold office), the fate of the nation seemed to hang in the balance.

What made these apparent changes exceptionally worrisome for the northern middle- and upper-class men who fretted most about American manhood was the lack of a remedy. Casting about for solutions, they concluded that old methods of inculcating manhood were becoming increasingly obsolete or inefficacious. The aging pool of Civil War veterans meant that there were fewer robust heroes to serve as models for younger men, and the apparent closing of the frontier meant that young men had to search for new tests to replace the challenges of the Wild West. Perhaps most significantly, assertive New Women, highly visible on their bicycles and in their forthright business attire, seemed determined to elide gender differences, thereby making it more difficult for men to define themselves relative to women. To those late-nineteenth-century Americans who worried about the character of American men, it appeared that modern times demanded new ways of inculcating manhood. The appeal of war lay as much in its character-building potential as in its usefulness for attaining policy objectives.[18] Disregarding the death and debility sure to result from a war, jingoes instead imagined combat as a means to build a powerful manhood.

Besides promising to toughen American men physically, war promised to foster greater moral character. Jingoist congressmen believed war would expose the hollowness of the mercenary values so prominent in the Gilded Age. Representative James Hamilton Lewis (D, Wash.) avouched that war would show "that the wealth of our nation's Treasury is not in the gold of her chests, but in the glorious patriotism of her noble sons." Senator Hernando de Soto Money (D, Miss.) agreed. He averred that "any sort of a war is better than a rotting peace that eats out the core and heart of the manhood of this country. [Applause in the galleries.]" He continued:

War brings out not the commercial trait, not the business instinct, not the training faculties, not the skill to corner articles of general consumption at the cost of the consumer, not short cuts to wealth, but war brings out all the best traits of character.

It teaches us devotion, self-abnegation, courage. It teaches us to offer upon the altar of our country everything dear to us—sons and brothers and fathers and all that goes to make life happy and holy. It teaches us to rise above the petty, the unworthy, the selfish. It broadens our nature, and in my opinion a wholesome war, like one for human liberty and human life, will have its purgatorial effect upon this nation and we will come out of it, like the Phoenix from its ashes, renewed and with glory.[19]

As this panegyric to war suggests, Money regarded war as a means to replace ascendant commercial values with honor, to the mutual benefit of American men and their nation.

What made a militant defense of honor particularly appealing to jingoes was their assuredness that such a noble undertaking would foster a greater sense of brotherhood in American men. Representative Mason S. Peters (Pop., Kans.) conveyed this idea in his statement that war would bring men from different parties together "as one man in defense of our country's honor." Other congressmen predicted that war would lead wealthy men to enlist alongside poor men and northern men to serve alongside southerners. The remarks of Representative Reese C. De Graffenreid (D, Tex.) illustrate the conviction that war was an unparalleled opportunity to foster brotherhood: "The boys who wore the blue and the boys who wore the gray, reconciled and reunited in the great and grand bonds of true brotherhood and love, side by side, heart in heart, and hand in hand, will go marching on with the one purpose, the one intention, and one exclamation, that is, woe, irretrievable woe, shall betide that country, that nation, and that people against whom a brother American's blood shall cry to us from the ground."[20] Congressmen like Peters and Graffenreid welcomed the prospect of a war waged in the name of brotherhood because they thought it would engrave the value of fraternalism on American men's hearts.

Along with reminding American men of their common citizenship, war promised to draw attention to the differences between men and women stipulated by the chivalric paradigm. Representative Joseph Wheeler (D, Ala.) declared that war would enable American men to recapture a bygone era, an era in which mothers "taught their sons that the highest possible honor and greatest possible privilege was to fight for [their] country, its safety, and its honor . . . that an ounce of glory earned in battle was worth more than a million pounds of gold."[21] Wheeler assumed that war would restore an imagined past in which women dedicated themselves to their families and men won political authority on the battlefield, a past in which women respected men because of their fighting capacities and male honor reigned supreme in public life. According to jingoes, war would keep American politics virile.

The final reason jingoist congressmen welcomed war was that they thought it would increase their standing in the eyes of the watching world. For Senator William E. Mason (R, Ill.), one of the most steadfast jingoes in Congress, this matter was of great personal interest: a Spanish nobleman had challenged him to a duel over his assertions about Spanish atrocities in Cuba. Rather than fight this individual challenger, Mason urged the nation to take on the entire Spanish army. Mason's jingoist colleagues, too, were eager to stand up to Spain because they believed that Spain had issued a collective challenge to all American men. Newspaper reports that Spanish men taunted American men as cowards and blustering braggarts, as men of commerce "wholly unacquainted with the martial spirit," buttressed this conviction. Congressmen who were convinced that Spain had impugned the honor of American men thought war was necessary to demonstrate both their own and their constituents' honor. The desire to win respect for American men can be seen in Representative Lentz's proclamation, in support of an appropriation to ready the nation for war, that he wanted to "lift our American manhood high upon that appropriation as upon a pedestal, there to unfurl our flag."[22] Lentz regarded the prospect of war with enthusiasm because he expected that the watching world would see that American men did not value money more than manhood, that they had not lost their sense of fraternal obligation, and that they were not degenerate or effeminate. By conveying these points, war would secure American men a preeminent place in the hierarchy of nations. By proving their honorable character, it would prevent future insults.

Claiming a desire to defend and strengthen the honor of American men, jingoist congressmen rejected further deliberation. As Representative Levin I. Handy (D, Del.) exclaimed in the middle of a pension discussion, "I am restraining and holding back the thoughts that swell in my breast lest I might inquire whether the honor of the Government of the United States has been upheld and is likely to be upheld in that matter [the sinking of the *Maine*]. I trust the gentleman will not appeal to my patriotism. I am wild when I get on that subject. I am not safe in a body like this." Representative Ferdinand Brucker (D, Mich.) also voiced a strong preference for action. "This is no time for discussion," he impatiently said in reference to the Cuban issue. "That time has passed. This is the time for action, and 'vigorous action,' too, at that." The belief that men must aggressively defend their honor filled some jingoes with an almost overwhelming sense of frustration with the slow pace of congressional proceedings. Convinced that the manly response to an insult such as the *Maine* was, as Senator Lee Mantle (Silver R, Mont.) put it, "open, aggressive, decisive action," jingoes clamored for war.[23]

The overwhelming desire to act made it impossible for some congressmen to continue sitting at their desks, legislating, in the middle of such a crisis. Motivated by their commitment to martial ideals, several congressmen offered their services to the military. At the start of the war, Representatives Sulzer and Lewis accepted positions as colonels. Lewis was such a firebreather on the war issue that a fellow congressman, Henry U. Johnson (R, Ind.), jested that the best solution to the crisis was to "harness up the gentleman from Washington [Lewis] and turn him loose upon Spain." Johnson then went on to note a possible objection to his proposal: "We are a Christian nation. We should not engage in a war of absolute extermination."[24] Another leading jingo, Joseph Wheeler, a former Confederate general, took command of a cavalry division in Cuba during the war. This surprised no one, for the general-turned-congressman, craving a fight, had offered his services to the military in earlier diplomatic crises, even stating a willingness to serve as a private if that would secure him a position.[25]

Although the congressmen who entered the military demonstrated an unusual commitment to action, they were not alone in their desire to fight. One senator who confessed a strong temptation to volunteer was Henry Cabot Lodge (R, Mass.). "It is most splendid and most uplifting the way our boys are going in everywhere, and it makes one love the country better than ever," he wrote to his friend Henry Lee Higginson. "I want to go, but I should be a fool, I suppose, and only fill a place some younger man could fill better, while here I can be of use."[26] The strange proceedings in the Capitol lobby on the night of 18 April also illustrate the general desire to jump into the fray. Knowing that war was imminent, a large group of congressmen gathered to sing "Hang General Weyler to a Sour Apple Tree as We Go Marching On," a modified version of a rousing Civil War song.[27] These legislators saw the war issue less as a matter to be soberly decided after lengthy deliberation than as an opportunity to rally with their fellows, to imagine themselves marching among the ranks in defense of the nation's honor. Their undisguised enthusiasm for war indicates that their insistence on action was not just a rhetorical ploy but also a reflection of their personal codes of behavior. After weeks of deliberating the *Maine* issue, these congressmen could restrain themselves no longer.

The most vivid demonstration of the belief that action was the manly response to a slight of honor was the hullabaloo in the House on 13 April. On that day, according to the *New York Times*, the House was in a state of "frenzied excitement" as it considered the prospect of war. Representative Henderson "made an impassioned appeal to the men of the American Congress to act like men. This remark was met with a storm of hisses." Democrats and Republicans accused each other of playing for political advantage. In the discussion, Representative Charles N. Brumm (R, Penn.) called Representative Charles L. Bartlett (D, Ga.) a liar. "Instantly," ran the description in the *New York Times*, "Mr. Bartlett reached for a large bound copy of the *Congressional Record* in the desk before him, and, raising it aloft, hurled it at his adversary. It fell short and then the two antagonists rushed for each other."[28]

The House was immediately in an uproar. Some of the ladies in the galleries screamed. Congressmen crowded into the aisles, "clinching, tugging, hauling at each other like madmen. It was like free fight in the street." Congressmen Bartlett and Brumm tried to "get at each other over the benches, but they were borne back by friends." In the end, the Speaker commanded the sergeant at arms to restore order. Armed with the great silver mace, he "repeatedly charged the thick mass of struggling members, but was as often swept aside." Another House employee was "felled by a blow on the jaw." Finally, a dozen "muscular members" of the House separated the belligerents and a semblance of order was restored. As the House again considered the resolutions before it, Representative Henderson said the Republicans were "overwhelmingly in favor of action, not talk." His Republican colleagues applauded his pronouncement.[29] The brawl in the House suggests that congressmen's aggressive personal standards of honor helped make fighting seem a legitimate, if not a desirable, option for the nation. Congressmen who saw violence as an appropriate response to personal insults viewed war with Spain as an appropriate way to resolve international disputes.

Not surprisingly, those who opposed U.S. intervention in the Spanish-Cuban War responded to the outbreak in Congress with horror. After the incident, the Boston reformer Henry B. Blackwell questioned, "How can we expect a Congress which in a grave national emergency resorts to blows and personal violence, to exercise national self-restraint and intelligent adaptation of means to ends?" Blackwell interpreted the nation's path toward war as the result of misguided standards of male behavior. An ardent women's suffrage supporter, he thought the war debate demonstrated the need to enfranchise women. That, he opined, would shift the tone of political debate from aggressive posturing to intelligent reflection. As the language of honor drowned out other ways of viewing the war issue, thus leading the nation into war, his daughter, Alice Stone Blackwell, the editor of the prosuffrage *Woman's Journal*, cited the war debate to prove suffragists' point that Congress did not represent American women. "Congress is composed exclusively of men," wrote the younger Blackwell, "the chosen representatives of all the men of the nation. Assuming for the sake of argument that this war is . . . utterly inexcusable . . . it is a Congress of men that has declared it. We must all admit that there is much division of opinion among the women of our acquaintance, while Congress is practically unanimous for war."[30]

Alice Blackwell's assertion that the jingoist Congress did not represent U.S. women appears well-founded, at least for middle-class women, for they were more visible on the anti-interventionist side of the debate than the jingoist side. This is not to say that U.S. women were unsympathetic to the Cuban cause. For the past few years, women belonging to groups such as the Woman's Christian Temperance Union had protested Spanish soldiers' mistreatment of Cuban women. Seeing women's honor as a central issue in the conflict, they expressed sympathy for the beleaguered Cubans and called for U.S. aid. But they stopped short of demanding war.[31] As Judith Papachristou has argued in a study of American women and turn-of-the-century foreign policy, activist women generally viewed the prospect of a war between the United States and Spain as a reflection of male values.[32] The lack of modern polling data for this period makes it difficult to gauge the sentiments of women (and of men, for that matter) who did not take public stances on the issue, but it does seem likely that women were less enthusiastic about war than men because women experienced the dictates of honor differently. If a women-and-nations analogy had guided political debate, war would have seemed absurd, for chivalric traditions did not teach women to respond to insults with violence. To the contrary, one mark of a true woman was that she did not engage in fisticuffs. Furthermore, as the protected class in the chivalric paradigm, women had little reason to think that the *Maine* issue had bearing on their self-worth and identity as women. Unlike men, U.S. women were under little pressure to assume a bellicose stance.

In contrast to women, men faced considerable pressure to assume a bellicose stance on the *Maine* issue because of the standard of honor. Jingoes regarded honor not only as a guide for their own behavior, but also as a potent political tool. They realized that honor signified the manly character so necessary for wielding political authority and thus invoked the term to push their associates toward war. Reversing the men-and-nations analogy, they proclaimed that an honorable man should act according to the standards of his nation. When, in patent disregard for anti-interventionist men, jingoes contended that the nation stood "as one man" for war, they implied that any man who failed to join with his bellicose peers was no longer part of the men-and-nations analogy. He would lose his political status and suffer a kind of social death. If the nation as a whole determined that its honor had been affronted, then every man in the nation had an obligation to rally behind the flag. Failure to do so would betray a lack of manly character.[33]

Jingoes' efforts to present war as the manly course of action can be seen in Representative David A. De Armond's (D, Mo.) claim that warlike sentiments represented "an assertion of American manhood by American representatives." It also can be seen in pleas exhorting men to act like men by supporting war. Representative Sulzer conflated fighting with manly character in his appeal: "Let us be men. Let us do our duty. Let us be true to the people and to our constituents." Representative Samuel B. Cooper (D, Tex.) suggested that fighting was as necessary to men's honor as marriage was to women's in his assertion that men from his state would "rush to the nation's defense as swiftly and as cheerfully as ever maiden rushed to the marriage altar." Political cartoons that depicted effeminate or puny men trying to stop the nation (depicted by a tall, resolute Uncle Sam) from going to war buttressed the contentions that war was the manly course of action. By portraying themselves as honorable men and their opponents as "nervous old ladies," jingoes inside and outside of Congress equated martial policies with manly character.[34] They left no place in this dichotomy for men to oppose war or, for that matter, for women to support it.

Jingoes' conflation of military intervention with manly character can help explain why women were not very visible on their side of the war debate. Although few prominent women clamored for war in the aftermath of the *Maine* disaster, thousands of women later mobilized to aid the war effort. The discrepancy between women's eventual support of the war effort and their earlier reluctance to join the jingoes can be explained by their ability to manipulate honor in political debate. Prior to the *Maine* disaster, women cited the honor of Cuban women to plead for intervention, but when attention shifted to avenging the dead men of the *Maine*, Cuban women's status became a secondary concern. In effect, the disaster reframed the Cuban issue in the United States so as to push women further to the margins. As jingoes proclaimed that the main issue in the war debate was manly honor, they implied that vengeance was a matter best left to men. At times they explicitly stated that war was a matter that men alone should decide. This can be seen in calls for the approval of "good men" and in claims that a failure to act would reveal American men to be "lost to all sense of brotherhood."[35] Representative Harry Skinner's (Pop., N.C.) remark that those who would resolve the war issue were "standing on an isthmus connecting the dead and unborn—the fathers of liberty who have gone before us and the sons that are to come after us," reflected the jingoist view that deciding whether or not to declare war was a choice that only men could make.[36]

Jingoes' efforts to associate intervention with militant standards of honor made interventionist women reluctant to call for war. Such hesitancy can be seen in the women assembled for a Daughters of the American Revolution convention a week after the *Maine* incident. Some of the delegates urged their organization to protest the "outrage" and advocate war, but the assembled women decided that it was not women's place to call for vengeance. Rather than passing a prowar resolution, they discussed how to render "womanly assistance" in the event of war.[37] By setting up the war issue as a matter of male honor, male jingoes inhibited like-minded women. In turn, women's inclination to express militant views privately or not at all helped jingoes argue that militancy was the manly approach to take toward Spain.

Building on their argument that true men advocated war, congressional jingoes urged their less bellicose colleagues to show their manhood. It was time for "the doubting, the hesitating, the opposing to go to the rear," announced Senator Joseph B. Foraker (R, Ohio), "while the virile, strong-minded, patriotic, liberty-loving masses" should rally around the military. Embedded in Foraker's exhortation was an implicit threat—a man who did not rally around the military would no longer seem virile. The threat was not always so veiled. Senator William V. Allen (Pop., Neb.) said that men who failed to heed the nation's honor would prove themselves unfit to continue the nation's political traditions. Deserting Cuba, he said, would be "base cowardice"—a cowardice that "the men of other generations would not palliate or excuse." In addition to proving themselves cowards, those who contemplated arbitration supposedly would reveal a mercenary streak at odds with manly honor. "No man who loves the flag of his country, no man who loves its honor, believes that the outrage can be wiped out by the payment of money," said Senator William B. Bate (D, Tenn.). "It is the trembling coward, the sordid huckster, who teaches such doctrine."[38] In the hands of jingoes, honor served a coercive function, for the claims that men who shirked war would appear to lack honor implied they would face a grim political future.

Lest the links between honor and political authority be overlooked, jingoes reminded their colleagues that the masses of American men demanded militant honor in their leaders. Representative Lentz conveyed this point when he said, "Our American manhood—the youth of this country—will not rest until that matter [the *Maine*] has been adjusted to their satisfaction, and to the honor of this country." Lentz implied that if Congress failed to declare war, then restless American men would seek new leaders. Constituent letters underscored Lentz's point that voters demanded leaders who would uphold the nation's honor. As one Ohio man wrote his senator, "Nine-tenths, yes 99% of the voters of this country want done what you have been driving at—the upholding of American honor and manhood through thick and thin."[39]

Lentz's jingoist associates also drew attention to the links between honor and political viability by saying that the men they represented were committed to defending the nation's honor. Representative James T. McCleary (R, Minn.) pledged immigrant men's support for honor: "Every man beneath the flag, whether native born or naturalized, will, with genuine pleasure, contribute of his substance and his strength that the honor of the nation may be vindicated." In response to stories that Catholics would not support their government in a war against Catholic Spain, Representative Fitzgerald testified on their behalf: "If war does come, no more valiant, brave and heroic defenders of the national honor . . . will be found than the members of the Catholic church." Congressmen also hastened to show that no state or region was deficient in honor. Said Representative Albert S. Berry (D, Ky.), "We who were defeated in the late unpleasantness will be glad as citizens of a common country to touch elbows with the men of Massachusetts and see who can go farthest for the honor of our country." Representative Samuel S. Barney (R, Wis.) expressed similar sentiments when he said that the "sons of the old Badger State will do their full measure in maintaining our national honor," and Representative James G. Maguire

D, Calif.) spoke for the far West when he said that the men of California would not tolerate a "dishonorable peace."[40]

Assertions that men from various walks of life valued honor as a standard for individual and national behavior made it clear that a man who denied that honor was at stake or who hesitated to defend it would no longer represent American men. Such assertions made it seem politically imperative to join the jingoes in their defense of honor. Their manipulation of honor had partisan implications—clearly, if one party seemed to disregard honor, it would lose the respect of American men—but jingoes also manipulated honor to sway individual men, irrespective of party. Recognizing that the Republican, Democratic, and Populist parties all had jingoist members, jingoes maintained that honor outweighed partisanship. Honor, they held, should transcend ideological differences and unite all the men in Congress. Representative George E. Foss (R, Ill.) revealed this conviction when he said, "To-day, when the honor of our country is at stake, we know no party." Representative Alexander M. Dockery (D, Mo.) agreed: "Divided we may be, among ourselves, upon questions of domestic policy; as to our relations toward other nations we present an unbroken front. [Applause.] Party lines fade away, and we are ready on this side of the Chamber to join the other side in support of all proper measures to protect the country and to uphold the national dignity and the national honor. [Applause.]"[41]

According to the jingoist line of argument, the fact that honor was at stake made war politically imperative not only for individual men and their parties, but also for the nation. All men, they implied, had a shared interest in preserving the nation's honor, for honor underlay their common status as men and as Americans. The belief that honor and the manhood it signified were more fundamental than partisanship can be seen in Representative Thomas C. McRae's (D, Ark.) appeal: "In this hour of threatened and impending war, every man who claims to be an American, and who would desire to exalt American manhood, should bury his partisanship and . . . say that the honor of this Government and the liberty and rights of our citizens everywhere shall be protected by it without regard to cost. [Loud applause.]"[42]

When jingoes spoke of exalting American manhood, one of the referents they had in mind was American women. Thinking that the war issue had bearing on men's privileged political position relative to women, jingoes warranted that women would lose their respect for American men if they failed to act. Senator Mason reckoned that a failure to fight would cause American men to be disgraced in the eyes of the wives and mothers rendered bereft by the *Maine* disaster. Representative Samuel J. Barrows (R, Mass.) went a step further and claimed that *all* American women were "weeping in sympathy with the mothers and sisters of 266 unavenged American citizens." He thus implied that no women would excuse inaction. The suspicion that American women expected action underlay Senator Lodge's assertion that Congress could not "anymore negotiate about it [the *Maine*] than a man can negotiate about an insult to his mother."[43] Such a man would be scorned by all women because of his patent inability or unwillingness to uphold his end of the chivalric bargain: protection in exchange for power. To prevent women from publicly denouncing American men and taking the matter into their own hands, American men had to act.

Just as jingoes argued that American men were obligated to fight lest they lose standing relative to women, they argued that they must fight to avoid dishonoring American men in the eyes of the watching world. Senator Foraker spelled out the implications of failing to respond to such an insult. It would lead the United States to be "written down before all the nations of the earth as pusillanimous—as wanting in pluck and courage." Representative Sulzer echoed these thoughts: "We must fight now for the independence of Cuba and our national honor, or we must retire in disgrace. We must bring about the freedom of Cuba and wipe out the stain Spain has put on our flag, or we must forever hereafter hold our heads in humiliation and shame before the civilized powers of the world." He continued, "Unless something is speedily done to vindicate American honor and the glory of our flag, unless something is speedily done for the freedom of Cuba, unless something is speedily done to demonstrate that we are a brave people and a great people, conscious of our rights and willing to maintain them, the world will charge us with cowardice. We are no cravens, no cowards. Let us prove it now. [Applause.]"[44] Sulzer presented the vindication of American honor as a collective responsibility, one that implicated all American men.

Jingoist congressmen took the threat of international disgrace as seriously as they took the threat of disgrace in women's eyes. They regarded it as nothing less than a danger to national integrity, for they were convinced that just as a dishonored man would suffer a kind of social death, a dishonored nation would cease to exist. As Senator Edward O. Wolcott (R, Colo.) said, "This national honor which we evoke is intangible. . . . The existence of it makes nations survive and fit to live. The loss of it, or the trading upon it, or the abandonment of it, makes nations fit to die and perish from the face of the earth." Senator Turner employed equally florid prose to contend that without honor the nation would die. "There is a crucifixion of the soul when honor dies," he said, "there is a death of a nation 'when the jingle of the guinea heals the hurt that honor feels'; there is an existence, when patriotic pride is dead, 'that doth murder sleep' and life becomes a horrid nightmare, and men shun their fellows, and the laugh of little children becomes a taunt and a mockery. True, there have been men who could exist and thrive and fatten without national honor or pride or patriotism, like worms in a muck heap, but that nation has been the scorned of all time and has quickly died."[45] In making these claims, Wolcott and Turner were in keeping with the Darwinian theorists who warned that nations that lost the "instinct of pugnacity" would soon perish.[46] Jingoes drew on the idea of honor as a bedrock of male and national character to cast the debate over war as nothing less than a debate over the viability of American men and their nation.

The certitude that honor was at stake made it politically foolish to argue that a naval accident of uncertain provenance was insufficient grounds for war because honor framed the issue as essential to the preservation of American manhood and the American political system. Jingoes believed that if the issue were understood as a choice between war and dishonor, American men would conclude, as Representative Lewis did, "there is no choice left us."[47] According to Lewis, war was not a choice but an obligation. American men had a responsibility to uphold their manhood because of its larger political implications.

Admonitions to follow the honorable course of action resonated among congressmen because honor was too important a component of male identity and political authority to take lightly. Congressmen hastened to prove that their honor was sound by citing their commitment to the principle. The desire to appear manly by associating themselves with honor helps explain why Representative Pitney asserted that "honor comes first" and Representative Norton avowed that war was preferable to dishonor. Such invocations of honor displayed congressmen's respect for the standard. Congressmen also were quick to assert that their political parties were committed to honor. Speaking for the Democrats, Representative Leonidas F. Livingston (D, Ga.) said that every member of the party would rise to "defend the flag and the honor of this country." On behalf of the Republicans, Senator Hoar emphasized that he and his associates would follow their fellow Republican, President William McKinley, "an honorable American patriot," as he acted to resolve the issue in a way "creditable and honorable to American manhood."[48]

Jingoes' concerted effort to paint the *Maine* issue as a choice between fighting and dishonor proved so persuasive that few congressmen expressed strong opposition to war in congressional debate. Because congressmen faced so much political pressure to support war, much of the argument against it was developed not on the floors of Congress but in the press and among the wider public. When it came time to vote on a declaration of war, both houses of Congress voted unanimously in favor of it—the Senate in a closed executive session, the House in a resounding chorus of ayes that sparked a round of applause and some cheers from the floor and the galleries.[49] The congressmen who had reservations put them aside lest they or their nation appear less than completely committed to honor.

Anti-interventionists' tendency to agree that honor mattered strengthened the standard. But although anti-interventionists accepted the importance of honor and its relevance to international affairs, they differed over what the standard implied. In the debate over war, anti-interventionists tried to promote a more restrained definition of honor. As Representative Albert J. Hopkins (R, Ill.) contended, "Moderation and firmness . . . will accomplish quite as much as bustle and bravado." Senator Orville H. Platt (R, Conn.) also presented self-control as a higher virtue than passion. "Hot talk," he said, "should give way to calm judgment and dispassionate utterances."[50] Anti-interventionists argued that honorable nations, like honorable men, should exercise self-control and avoid using force if other means were available to settle disputes. An editorial in the *Boston Journal* made the point as follows: "An honorable nation, like a manly man, fights only when forced to fight." Only robbers, tyrants, and pugilists, it declared, fight for the sake of fighting. Writing in *Harper's Weekly*, the Republican senior statesman Carl Schurz maintained that honor did not require the nation to "swagger about among the nations of the world with a chip on its shoulder, shaking its fist under everybody's nose, and telling the world on every possible occasion that we can 'whip' any power that might choose to resent this, that we would be rather glad of an opportunity for doing so." Arguing that "a private individual taking such an attitude would certainly not be called a gentleman . . . [but] a vulgar bully," Schurz went on to say that the same would be true for the nation. Drawing on the men-and-nations analogy, anti-interventionists reasoned that because men no longer subscribed to a dueling mentality, neither should nations. "Why should not the policy usually adopted by the sensible men in their private affairs also govern in public controversies?" questioned an article in the *New York Times*, which maintained that war over a point of honor was akin to murder.[51]

Because anti-interventionists criticized bellicose standards of honor, women did not feel as excluded from their side of the war debate as from the jingoist side. Like anti-interventionist men, women who opposed intervention tried to promote a more restrained definition of honor. May Wright Sewall, a women's club movement leader and suffragist, sent a letter to President McKinley arguing that just as the defense of honor among men no longer justified killing, neither should honor justify war. Similarly, the author Elizabeth Stuart Phelps Ward wrote to President McKinley, " 'Honor' can no longer mean killing and being killed. . . . the honor of a nation must hereafter be rated by its success in the exertion of the peace-compelling power."[52] Unlike interventionist women, anti-interventionist women did not view their position on the war issue as unladylike; rather, they deemed it an expression of feminine values.

Anti-interventionists buttressed their argument that war was not the honorable course of action by describing Spain as a weak and unworthy foe. They argued that just as an honorable man would not fight an inferior opponent, neither should a nation, for no honor was to be gained from such a conflict. "What will we gain by war?" questioned Senator George L. Wellington (R, Md.). "Glory? Nay; there can be no glory in defeating a nation than whom we are stronger as 5 to 1." Indeed, it would dishonor the nation to demand satisfaction from such an unworthy adversary. "Saying that our honor in the bellicose sense requires us to fight Spain is absurd," ran an article in the *Nation*. "It is like saying that a brawny pugilist's 'honor' requires him to meet a slight and consumptive youth in the 'twelve-foot ring.' " According to anti-interventionists, instead of demonstrating the nation's honor, war would reveal the nation to be a dishonorable bully.[53]

The anti-interventionists who said that fighting a weak opponent was dishonorable and hence unmanly may have disagreed with the jingoes' argument that American honor demanded war to avenge the *Maine*, but they sometimes conceded the underlying point that a truly honorable war would prove manly character. As a letter in the *New York Times* said, "It is much better to maintain a dignified peace than to rush into a conflict with an arrogant and emasculated race, a race entirely unworthy [of] a great Nation's hostile anger. If the country must have war—and, unless all signs fail, it will come sooner or later—let it be a contest with a power equal to our own, and one which it will be an honor to meet in respectable combat, rather than with an effervescent and quixotic race, whom it would be no credit to ourselves to thrash."[54] The letter disapprovingly hinted that honor, rather than a specific policy objective, was driving the nation into war. Even as it denounced the possibility of a war with Spain, however, it suggested that once the nation found a worthy opponent, it should not shirk battle, for a good fight would redound to the nation's credit.

As this letter indicates, although both interventionists and anti-interventionists cited honor in the debate over war, jingoist congressmen benefited from the assumption that honor must not be impinged, for implicit in the term was a willingness to fight. Because bellicose standards of manhood were in the ascendance in the late nineteenth century, congressmen who appeared cowardly ran a greater risk of losing political authority than congressmen who seemed too aggressive. More congressmen spoke in favor of bellicose manhood than against it because the political system equated a fighting spirit with leadership. Try as anti-interventionists might to redefine the term, most Americans thought that "honor" implied the inability to let pass an affront as grave as the sinking of the *Maine*. The belief that "men do not negotiate questions of honor" enabled jingoist congressmen to manipulate the standard of honor to limit dissent and present war as a desirable option. Anti-interventionist congressmen realized that they had to support war or be stigmatized as dishonorable. They feared that a failure to fight would undercut their own standing, that of their parties, and, indeed, their entire political system. The coercive use of gender ideals in political debate made war seem imperative to the reluctant congressmen who joined their jingoist fellows in voting unanimously for war.

NOTES

I have incurred many debts while working on this project but particularly wish to thank Nancy F. Cott, Gail Bederman, Peter Filene, Akira Iriye, Ernest May, Kathleen

Dalton, and Warren Center colloquia participants for their comments and advice. I also would like to thank Yale University Press for giving me permission to draw from my book, *Fighting for American Manhood: How Gender Politics Provoked the Spanish-American and Philippine-American Wars* (1998).

1. On partisan motivations, see Ernest R. May, *Imperial Democracy: The Emergence of America as a Great Power* (New York: Harcourt, Brace, and World, 1961), 147; H. Wayne Morgan, *America's Road to Empire: The War with Spain and Overseas Expansion* (New York: John Wiley and Sons, 1965), 55; John L. Offner, *An Unwanted War: The Diplomacy of the United States and Spain over Cuba, 1895–1898* (Chapel Hill: University of North Carolina Press, 1992), 180–81, 193; and Walter Karp, *The Politics of War: The Story of Two Wars Which Altered Forever the Political Life of the American Republic (1890–1920)* (New York: Harper and Row, 1979), 74. Harold U. Faulkner argues that Americans regarded war as an opportunity to end partisan strife and unite the country. See his *Politics, Reform, and Expansion, 1890–1910* (New York: Harper, 1959), 228.

2. Sen. Charles W. Fairbanks, *Congressional Record* [hereafter *CR*] 31, pt. 4, 14 April 1898, p. 3845.

3. On Spain's refusal to apologize, see Henry Cabot Lodge, *The War with Spain* (New York: Harper, 1899), 30. Sen. Richard R. Kenney, *CR* 31, pt. 4, 5 April 1898, p. 3547.

4. Rep. John F. Fitzgerald, *CR* 31, pt. 3, 8 March 1898, p. 2606; Rep. Stephen A. Northway, *CR* 31, pt. 3, 8 March 1898, p. 2604.

5. Rep. William Sulzer, *CR* 31, pt. 4, 7 April 1898, p. 3673; Rep. David B. Henderson, *CR* 31, pt. 4, 13 April 1898, p. 3813; Sen. George Turner, *CR* 31, pt. 4, 14 April 1898, p. 3829.

6. Rep. James A. Norton, *CR* 31, pt. 5, 28 April 1898, p. 4370; Rep. Mahlon Pitney, *CR* 31, pt. 3, 8 March 1898, p. 2605.

7. William Dwight Whitney, ed., *The Century Dictionary*, 10 vols. (New York: Century, 1895), 4:2874; Rep. John J. Lentz, *CR* 31, pt. 5, 27 April 1898, p. 4331; Rep. John J. Lentz, *CR* 31, pt. 4, 31 March 1898, p. 3444.

8. George F. Hoar, pamphlet, "Quality of our Honor," 189, Pamphlet box 49, George F. Hoar Papers, Massachusetts Historical Society; Rep. James R. Mann, *CR* 31, pt. 5, 28 April 1898, p. 4362.

9. On late-nineteenth-century manhood, see E. Anthony Rotundo, *American Manhood: Transformations in Masculinity from the Revolution to the Modern Era* (New York: Basic Books, 1993), 5–6; E. Anthony Rotundo, "Body and Soul: Changing Ideals of American Middle-Class Manhood, 1770–1920," *Journal of Social History* 16 (summer 1983): 23–38; Gerald Franklin Roberts, "The Strenuous Life: The Cult of Manliness in the Era of Theodore Roosevelt" (Ph.D. diss., Michigan State University, 1970), 5, 18–20; Elliott J. Gorn, *The Manly Art: Bare-Knuckle Prize Fighting in America* (Ithaca: Cornell University Press, 1986), 187; Michael Kimmel, *Manhood in America: A Cultural History* (New York: Free Press, 1996), 120; Gail Bederman, *Manliness and Civilization: A Cultural History of Gender and Race in the United States, 1880–1917* (Chicago: University of Chicago Press, 1995), 18; Stephen Kern, *Anatomy and Destiny: A Cultural History of the Human Body* (New York: Bobbs-Merrill, 1975), 103–4. On epithets, see John Higham, "The Reorientation of American Culture in the 1890s," *Writing American History* (Bloo-

mington: Indiana University Press, 1970), 73–102, 79; on cure for white-livered men, see "The Way to Win a Woman," *Boston Journal*, 5 March 1898.

10. Amos J. Cummings, "A Manly Fighter Is He," *Washington Post*, 20 February 1898; "The Value of War Oratory," *Rochester Democrat and Chronicle*, 1 April 1898.

11. Rep. Lorenzo Danford, *CR* 31, pt. 8, 28 April 1898, p. 313. Michael Kammen notes that analogies between individuals and the nation were pervasive in political talk at the turn of the century, *A Season of Youth: The American Revolution and the Historical Imagination* (New York: Alfred A. Knopf, 1978), 196.

12. Rep. William Sulzer, *CR* 31, pt. 4, 7 April 1898, p. 3673; Rep. Joseph W. Bailey, *CR* 31, pt. 3, 8 March 1898, p. 2616; Rep. Joseph W. Bailey, *CR* 31, pt. 4, 15 April 1898, p. 3907.

13. Rep. William C. Arnold, *CR* 31, pt. 4, 24 March 1898, p. 3193; Sen. George C. Perkins, *CR* 31, pt. 4, 4 April 1898, p. 3498; Rep. James A. Norton, *CR* 31, pt. 3, 16 March 1898, p. 2879.

14. On the 1893 depression, see Joe L. Dubbert, *A Man's Place: Masculinity in Transition* (Englewood Cliffs, N.J.: Prentice-Hall, 1979), 101. On white-collar work and "overcivilization," see Roberts, "The Strenuous Life," 98–139; Peter Filene, *Him/Her/Self: Sex Roles in Modern America*, 2nd ed. (Baltimore: Johns Hopkins University Press, 1986), 73; Tom Lutz, *American Nervousness, 1903: An Anecdotal History* (Ithaca: Cornell University Press, 1991), 28; Rotundo, "Body and Soul," 32; Rupert Wilkinson, *American Tough: The Tough-Guy Tradition and American Character* (Westport, Conn.: Greenwood, 1984), 147; Gorn, *The Manly Art*, 187, 192–93; T. J. Jackson Lears, *No Place of Grace: Antimodernism and the Transformation of American Culture, 1880–1920* (New York: Pantheon, 1981), 98–139. On moneymaking, see John P. Mallan, "The Warrior Critique of the Business Civilization," *American Quarterly* 8 (fall 1956): 216–30, 218. On declining numbers of self-employed men, see Michael Kimmel, "The Contemporary 'Crisis' of Masculinity in Historical Perspective," *The Making of Masculinities: The New Men's Studies*, ed. Harry Brod (Boston: Allen and Unwin, 1987), 121–53; David I. Macleod, *Building Character in the American Boy: The Boy Scouts, YMCA, and Their Forerunners, 1870–1920* (Madison: University of Wisconsin Press, 1983), 46.

15. On racist thought about black men, see Joel Williamson, *The Crucible of Race: Black-White Relations in the American South since Emancipation* (New York: Oxford University Press, 1984), 111.

16. On middle-class concerns about working-class men, see Bederman, *Manliness and Civilization*, 14.

17. On social changes and degeneracy, see Bederman, *Manliness and Civilization*, 30, 88; David F. Greenberg, *The Construction of Homosexuality* (Chicago: University of Chicago Press, 1988), 413; George Chauncey, *Gay New York: Gender, Urban Culture, and the Making of the Gay Male World, 1890–1940* (New York: Basic Books, 1994), 39, 44; Kevin J. Mumford, " 'Lost Manhood' Found: Male Sexual Impotence and Victorian Culture in the United States," *American Sexual Politics: Sex, Gender, and Race since the Civil War*, ed. John C. Fout and Maura Shaw Tantillo (Chicago: University of Chicago Press, 1993), 75–99, 75–77; Higham, "The Reorientation of American Culture," 92; Mary W. Blanchard, "The Soldier and the Aesthete: Homosexuality and Popular Culture in Gilded Age America," *Journal of American Studies* 30 (April 1996): 25–46; Daniel Pick, *Faces of Degeneration: A European Disorder, c. 1848–c. 1918* (Cambridge: Cambridge University Press, 1989), 23–24.

18. Richard Slotkin, *Gunfighter Nation: The Myth of the Frontier in Twentieth-Century America* (New York: Atheneum, 1992), 11–12, 61; David M. Wrobel, *The End of American Exceptionalism: Frontier Anxiety from the Old West to the New Deal* (Lawrence: University Press of Kansas, 1993), 3, 36; Filene, *Him/Her/Self*, 93. On war as an opportunity for body-building, see Amy Kaplan, "Romancing the Empire: The Embodiment of American Masculinity in the Popular Historical Novel of the 1890s," *American Literary History* 2 (winter 1990): 659–90.

19. Rep. James H. Lewis, *CR* 31, pt. 3, 8 March 1898, p. 2610; Sen. Hernando de Soto Money, *CR* 31, pt. 4, 28 March 1898, pp. 3280–82.

20. Rep. Mason S. Peters, *CR* 31, pt. 3, 8 March 1898, p. 2613; Rep. Reese C. De Graffenreid, *CR* 31, pt. 3, 7 March 1898, p. 2615. On wealthy and poor men, see Rep. Charles H. Grosvenor, *CR* 31, pt. 5, 28 April 1898, p. 4416.

21. Rep. Joseph Wheeler, *CR* 31, pt. 3, 8 March 1898, p. 2607.

22. "Which War Does Mason Mean?" *Washington Post*, 16 March 1898. On American men as cowards, see "Bluster," *New York Times*, 17 April 1898; on men of commerce, see "If War Should Come," *Atlanta Constitution*, 9 March 1898; and Rep. John J. Lentz, *CR* 31, pt. 3, 8 March 1898, p. 2613.

23. Rep. Levin Handy, *CR* 31, pt. 3, 4 March 1898, p. 2503; Rep. Ferdinand Bruckner, *CR* 31, pt. 3, 8 March 1898, p. 2613; Sen. Lee Mantle, *CR* 31, pt. 4, 4 April 1898, p. 3499.

24. George W. Blake, ed., *Sulzer's Short Speeches* (New York: J. S. Ogilvie, 1912), 18; "James Hamilton Lewis," *National Cyclopaedia of American Biography* (New York: James T. White, 1940), 28:38. Rep. Henry U. Johnson, *CR* 31, pt. 4, 31 March 1898, p. 3434.

25. "Joseph Wheeler," *National Cyclopaedia of American Biography* (New York: James T. White, 1899), 9:19.

26. Henry Cabot Lodge to Henry Lee Higginson, 3 July 1898, in Bliss Perry, *Life and Letters of Henry Lee Higginson* (Boston: Atlantic Monthly, 1921), 427.

27. Everett Walters, *Joseph Benson Foraker: An Uncompromising Republican* (Columbus: Ohio History, 1948), 151.

28. "Blows Averted in the House," *New York Times*, 14 April 1898; on hisses, see clipping, 13 April 1898, Scrapbook of Emily Carow, Theodore Roosevelt Collection, Houghton Library, Harvard University.

29. "Blows Averted in the House," *New York Times*, 14 April 1898; see also "Startling Episode," *Boston Journal*, 14 April 1898.

30. Henry B. Blackwell, "The War with Spain," *Woman's Journal*, 16 April 1898, p. 124; Alice Stone Blackwell, "Mr. Garrison on Women and War," *Woman's Journal*, 30 April 1898, p. 140.

31. Kristin Hoganson, *Fighting for American Manhood: How Gender Politics Provoked the Spanish-American and Philippine-American Wars* (New Haven: Yale University Press, 1998), 46, 56–61. On depicting Cuba as a victimized maiden, see Michael H. Hunt, *Ideology and U.S. Foreign Policy* (New Haven: Yale University Press, 1987), 60–62; and Kaplan, "Romancing the Empire," 666–72.

32. Judith Papachristou, "American Women and Foreign Policy, 1898–1905: Exploring Gender in Diplomatic History," *Diplomatic History* 14 (fall 1990): 493–509, 495, 498, 501.

33. On standing "as one man," see Rep. Romulus Z. Linney, *CR* 31, pt. 3, 7

March 1898, p. 2613. See also Rep. William D. Vincent, *CR* 31, pt. 8, 18 April 1898, p. 304; Rep. George Spalding, *CR* 31, pt. 3, 8 March 1898, p. 2616.

34. Rep. David A. De Armond, *CR* 31, pt. 3, 8 March 1898, p. 2610; Rep. William Sulzer, *CR* 31, pt. 4, 7 April 1898, p. 3669; Rep. Samuel B. Cooper, *CR* 31, pt. 3, 8 March 1898, p. 2606; see cartoons in *Review of Reviews* 17 (May 1898): 548; and *Literary Digest* 16 (12 March 1898): 303; on nervous old ladies, see "The Horrors of War," *Rochester Democrat and Chronicle*, 14 March 1898.

35. On women's support for the war effort, see Hoganson, *Fighting for American Manhood*, 125–26. Among the militant women were the members of a New York City art class who sent President McKinley a telegram saying, "To h— with diplomacy!" cited in John Joseph Leffler, "From the Shadows into the Sun: Americans in the Spanish-American War" (Ph.D. diss., University of Texas at Austin, 1991), 24. On the honor of Cuban women, see "Women and Cuba," *Woman's Journal*, 16 April 1898, p. 124; on good men, see John Coit Spooner to O. A. Ellis, 27 April 1898, Letterbook, 9 April–5 May 1898, box 135, John C. Spooner Papers, Library of Congress; on brotherhood, see Sen. Henry C. Lodge, *CR* 31, pt. 4, 13 April 1898, p. 3784.

36. Rep. Harry Skinner, *CR* 31, pt. 4, 24 March 1898, p. 3211.

37. Gertrude B. Darwin, *Second Report of the National Society of the Daughters of the American Revolution, Oct. 1, 1897–Oct. 11, 1898* (Washington: Government Printing Office, 1900), 45.

38. Sen. Joseph B. Foraker, *CR* 31, pt. 4, 13 April 1898, p. 3781; Sen. William V. Allen, *CR* 31, pt. 4, 31 March 1898, p. 3412; Sen. William B. Bate, *CR* 31, pt. 4, 16 April 1898, p. 3966.

39. Rep. John J. Lentz, *CR* 31, pt. 4, 12 April 1898, p. 3766; John Bergen to Joseph Benson Foraker, 6 April 1898, folder 1, box 13, Joseph Benson Foraker Papers, Cincinnati Historical Society.

40. Rep. James T. McCleary, *CR* 31, pt. 3, 8 March 1898, p. 2614; Rep. John F. Fitzgerald, *CR* 31, pt. 3, 8 March 1898, p. 2606; Rep. Albert S. Berry, *CR* 31, pt. 3, 8 March 1898, p. 2610; Rep. Samuel S. Barney, *CR* 31, pt. 3, 8 March 1898, p. 2612; Rep. James G. Maguire, *CR* 31, pt. 3, 8 March 1898, p. 2619.

41. Rep. George Foss, *CR* 31, pt. 3, 8 March 1898, p. 2614; Rep. Alexander Dockery, *CR* 31, pt. 3, 8 March 1898, p. 2603.

42. Rep. Thomas McRae, *CR* 31, pt. 1, 8 March 1898, p. 2604.

43. Sen. William E. Mason, *CR* 31, pt. 4, 29 March 1898, p. 3295; Rep. Samuel J. Barrows, *CR* 31, pt. 4, 7 April 1898, p. 3688; Sen. Henry C. Lodge, *CR* 31, pt. 4, 13 April 1898, p. 3784.

44. Sen. Joseph B. Foraker, *CR* 31, pt. 4, 13 April 1898, p. 3781; Rep. William Sulzer, *CR* 31, pt. 4, 7 April 1898, pp. 3669, 3672.

45. Sen. Edward O. Wolcott, *CR* 31, pt. 4, 15 April 1898, p. 3892; Sen. George Turner, *CR* 31, pt. 4, 5 April 1898, p. 3547.

46. Henry Childs Merwin, "On Being Civilized Too Much," *Atlantic Monthly* (June 1897): 838–46, 840.

47. Rep. James H. Lewis, *CR* 31, pt. 3, 8 March 1898, p. 2610.

48. Rep. Leonidas F. Livingston, *CR* 31, pt. 3, 8 March 1898, pp. 2603–4; Sen. George F. Hoar, *CR* 31, pt. 4, 14 April 1898, p. 3835.

49. On the House vote, see "Declaration of War," *Boston Transcript*, 25 April 1898; on both votes, see *CR* 31, pt. 5, 25 April 1898, pp. 4244, 4252.

50. Rep. Albert J. Hopkins, *CR* 31, pt. 3, 8 March 1898, p. 2605; Orville Platt to Rev. William B. Carey, 23 March 1898, in Louis A. Coolidge, *An Old-Fashioned Senator: Orville H. Platt* (New York: G. P. Putnam's Sons, 1910), 270.

51. "Not Choice, But the Right," *Boston Journal*, 11 March 1898; Carl Schurz, "National Honor," (1898) in *Speeches, Correspondence, and Political Papers*, 6 vols., ed. Frederic Bancroft (New York: G. P. Putnam's Sons, 1913), 5: 452; J. J. Russell, "Against War with Spain," *New York Times*, 29 March 1898.

52. Sewall cited in David S. Patterson, *Toward a Warless World: The Travail of the American Peace Movement, 1887–1914* (Bloomington: Indiana University Press, 1976), 49; Elizabeth Stuart Phelps Ward to President McKinley, 18 March 1898, Microfilm Series 1, reel 3, William McKinley Papers, Library of Congress.

53. Sen. Stephen M. White, *CR* 31, pt. 4, 16 April 1898, pp. 3960, 3962; Sen. George L. Wellington, *CR* 31, pt. 4, 16 April 1898, p. 3953; "Deliberation," *Nation* 66 (7 April 1898): 258; on revealing the nation as a bully, see Rep. Albert J. Hopkins, *CR* 31, pt. 3, 8 March 1898, p. 2605; and "Trust the President," *Washington Post*, 24 March 1898.

54. Samuel Essmond Shipp, "Spain an Unworthy Foe," *New York Times*, 24 February 1898.

PART III

LEGACIES OF 1898

6

1898 and the Legacies of Intervention: The Case of Cuba

Louis A. Pérez, Jr.

I

This chapter seeks to explore the events culminating in 1898 as context for an understanding of the larger circumstances of the Cuban post-colonial condition. That the U.S. intervention in 1898—what is known in the United States as the Spanish-American War—signified something of an imperial transfer is commonly understood and generally acknowledged.[1] Not as well appreciated, however, is the degree to which 1898 served as a conjuncture of far-reaching consequences, the occasion for a transfer of another kind. These were the circumstances by which foreign normative hierarchies insinuated themselves into the realms of the everyday Cuban familiar as a cultural system, and thereupon proceeded to metabolize into the ordinary and commonplace assumptions by which vast numbers of Cubans arranged their lives and assembled their world and gave meaning to both—the means, too, by which the terms of North American hegemony obtained simultaneously acquiescence and resilience.

II

The war for *Cuba Libre* cost Cubans dearly. Not all suffered equally, of course, but most suffered some, and many suffered much. In all, the separatist project spanned thirty years of intermittent upheavals and periodic uprisings, random depredations alternating with systematic devastation, successive acts of reprisal and revenge, of pillage and plunder, of homes destroyed and lives disrupted. The war for independence (1895–98) was a particularly brutal affair, a war of excesses, disruptive and destructive at every turn. Spaniards were ruthless in their defense of colonial rule; Cubans were relentless in their demand for national sovereignty.[2]

Peace arrived in August 1898, and only then was it possible to comprehend fully the dimensions of the devastation. The war of independence had been total war, a campaign in which fire was adopted as a cost-effective means of engagement and in which the systematic destruction of property became an acceptable if not preferable means of defeating the enemy. Total, too, in that the war had implicated almost everyone in nearly all the one thousand towns and villages of the island, where the distinction between civilians and combatants lost any useful meaning, where neutrality was suspect, and where security was often obtained only behind one or the other battle line, rarely ever outside them, and never between them.

The losses were incalculable. The war was won through much sacrifice and great suffering. Hundreds of thousands of Cubans had perished, and only a fortunate few could comprehend that they had survived a population disaster of frightful proportions. A population of 1.8 million people had declined to less than a million and a half, a net loss of more than 15 percent.[3] Households had been shattered, families scattered. Some went from the countryside to the city to escape the fighting; others went from the city to the countryside to join the fighting. Tens of thousands of families went into exile, in sufficient numbers to assume fully the proportions of a diaspora. Thousands had been sent to prison: on the island, on the peninsula, and to the penal colonies in Africa. The losses were incalculable: the countless numbers of orphans, parents who lost children, children who lost parents, the untold numbers who lost entire families, the maimed, the infirmed, the aged, the homeless, the jobless—all whom could not even remotely begin to imagine how to put their lives together again. "The starving children live on the streets and how it made my heart ache," wrote Mrs. W. A. Candler from Havana in December 1898. "There are thousands left wandering about the streets begging for bread. They are emaciated until their hands as they stretch them out to you [and] look like bird claws and their nakedness is embarrassing. There [are] tiny little ones whose parents are all dead and they are left to fight life's battle alone and unprotected."[4] Many thousands of Cubans emerged from war with no hope; others had little else. Few indeed were the numbers of Cubans who had not suffered in direct and very personal ways.[5]

Cubans had, to be sure, triumphed against Spain, but the cost was enormous. The war had shattered the world as previously known by most Cubans. They returned to ruin, to incalculable material losses and irreplaceable human ones. Many of the things that people had used as reference points in their lives had disappeared or no longer worked; places to which they had been previously anchored by memories no longer existed. Familiar markers had vanished, old boundaries had disappeared.

Cubans had sacrificed personal assets and family fortunes, great and small. Many had abandoned their shops, businesses, and professions; others had interrupted their educations and disrupted their careers to dedicate themselves to *Cuba Libre*. Some of the most prominent military and political leaders of the insurrection had come from families of means, with property and professions, with plans and prospects. After the war they had nothing.

As Cubans surveyed what their victory had wrought them, not a few contemplated a cruel denouement indeed: perhaps they had created a future in which there was no place for them. General Alejandro Rodríguez confided to a friend in 1899:

> You know that abandoning my interests and family, I was among the first to reach for arms and support the revolution. I, who have served my country, for which I have sacrificed everything, cannot even have my family at my side for a lack of means to support it. I cannot embark on any business or reconstruct my farm due to a lack of funds. I see myself perhaps forced to emigrate in search of bread in a strange land.[6]

III

The war had indeed ended in 1898, but not entirely the way Cubans had envisioned the end. Spain had been defeated, to be sure, and at least that part of the Cuban purpose had been achieved. But the U.S. intervention changed everything. The separatist project had been successful on every count except perhaps the one that mattered most: it failed to deliver power to Cubans.

A vast and heterogeneous constituency had organized around *Cuba Libre*, for whom free Cuba had promised advancement, improvement, and betterment: always the possibility of mobility, the creation of a nation in which Cuban interests formed the sacred trust for which the republic was to be created and charged to defend and uphold. They had entered into a covenant, as they had understood the nature of their commitment, a social contract in which they devoted themselves to bringing into being a republic dedicated to the defense of their interests.[7]

It is in this context that the impact and importance of the U.S. intervention assumes larger meanings. A war inaugurated for Cuban independence had resulted instead in a North American intervention. The intervention changed everything. It was meant to. The larger significance of the North American intervention, certainly the enduring consequences of this presence, had less to do with subsequent political relationships than with ensuing social realignments, specifically the ways by which North American normative standards and moral hierarchies worked their way into everyday life, principally in the form of a vast cultural transfer, one that was facilitated by the magnitude of material impoverishment in which Cubans found themselves in 1898. Conditions existing in 1898 severely limited the Cuban capacity to articulate and advance national forms independent of North American structures. That they succeeded in the defense of a separate nation did not mean that they were able to define the terms of nationality. The experience shaped decisively the forms around which they subsequently constituted themselves as a nation and gave form to the dominant categories of national identity.[8]

The North American presence assumed its most visible form in postwar reconstruction, an undertaking that was as sweeping as it was thorough. It was a time of putting lives back together again, of fresh beginnings and new hopes. But this was also reconstruction on North American terms, rearranging Cuban institutions in ways to make room for the North American presence and accommodate North American interests. The project of recovery was appropriated by North Americans, largely on their terms, under their direction, conceived almost wholly within the moral order of the North and into which Cubans were routinely incorporated, unremarkably, as a matter of fact and in the ordinary course of events.[9] Most of all, it implied realigning social relationships and reassembling what commonly served as the means of security in such a manner as to guarantee that success would come easiest to those most conversant with and adept at North American ways.

The scope of reconstruction under North American auspices is perhaps incalculable. New forms were injected directly into Cuban institutional representations, virtually uncontested and unchallenged. What was especially noteworthy about the postwar condition was the North American capacity to mobilize vast resources, made all the more potent in an environment of widespread want and desperate need. The larger significance of these developments was the degree to which North American forms so thoroughly gained ascendancy and in the aggregate served to define a market culture derived from North American sources and from which Cubans obtained models of identity and modes of self-representation.

IV

After 1898 the island filled with North Americans, first as a vast army of occupation, followed by legions of colonists and tourists and almost as many merchants, agents, and an assortment of social types who would loosely qualify as "business people." So large was this presence as to constitute itself fully a market driven by North American necessities and preferences and which simply by virtue of availability could not but have influenced Cuban needs and wants. North American hotels, guesthouses, and boarding houses expanded across the island. Bars and restaurants multiplied. New entertainment forms replaced old Spanish productions. Cabarets, bistros, and theaters contracted vaudeville acts, minstrel shows, and burlesque companies from the United States. Baseball expanded, boxing took hold. Retail shops of all types opened, serving as the conduit by which a seemingly endless supply of consumer goods satiated the Cuban market. New North American clothing lines arrived, principally as inexpensive ready-made women's dresses and men's suits, all represented as "the latest fashion." As early as 1904, the U.S. minister reported: "Articles of American manufacture or production are . . . offered for sale almost everywhere. The demand for American shoes has largely increased. . . . American watches and clocks are frequently seen as are also American soaps, shirts, corsets, hosiery, dry goods in general, typewriters and foodstuffs of every description in which we control the market."[10]

A new market emerged in Cuba, one that replicated demands of the U.S. market and, aided by the Reciprocity Treaty of 1903, one into which North American manufacturers were uniquely qualified to expand. North American products transformed Cuba in very fundamental ways: from simple household appliances to complex industrial technology, from advanced transportation modes and expanded communication systems to the newest conveniences and latest advances, and always with an emphasis on modernity and progress.[11]

The relationship between national forms and market culture was from the outset complex, always in a state of flux, contingent and changing in response to context and circumstances. National sensibilities evolved under specific historical circumstances in which the affirmation of "Cuban" could not but draw upon those forms that were most readily available. The postcolonial condition by definition implied transition and transformation, often as a conscious effort to create distance from the discredited past. Circumstances provided ample occasion to affirm and act out rejection of old ways, through new conventions and conduct, new patterns of association, and new forms of recreation. The lasting impact of the U.S. presence and, indeed, in the end, its very capacity to implicate Cubans in things and ways North American was related to the degree to which new forms themselves provided the moral and material basis upon which daily life in Cuba resumed after the war.

The old colonial elites were among the first incorporated into North American structures. Many managed to escape total ruin by exchanging deeds for stocks and relinquishing positions of ownership of property for places of membership on corporate boards. Many were transformed into resident managers and administrators—employees, in a word—and lived off salaries and commissions. Others found salvation through employment with North American enterprises. An entire generation of entrepreneurs, businessmen, and managers were formed by their association with U.S. corporate interests. They earned a living distributing North American manufactures and managing U.S. franchises. Others made careers of serving North American interests as sales representatives, advisers, agents, and attorneys, as notaries and negotiators, as translators and interpreters.

What was especially striking about the character of the postwar recovery was the degree to which Cubans incorporated North American representations of material progress and moral well-being as the basis upon which to prepare themselves for the future. The process provides suggestive insight into the revival of class structures in postcolonial Cuba. The emerging middle class acquired its definitive characteristics in function of collaborative linkages with North American enterprises, with far-reaching implications. The new middle class was obliged to invent itself with the social material most commonly available. It derived its principal characteristics from North American market forms, which implicated the first generation of the republic in behaviors noteworthy for their emphasis on consumption and display.

V

The expansion of North American market structures presented new consumption options and served to foster new fashions, new habits, and new modalities of self-representation. Some of this was familiar, of course, but what was different after 1898 was the sheer scope of the North American presence, the power of its appeal, the ubiquity of its forms, and the ways it seemed endowed with the capacity to affirm status and security. North American ways resonated modern and offered a means by which to proclaim success and material well-being and in the end became elements routinely appropriated as a means of self-invention seemingly available to all.

The infusion of capital goods, industrial organization, and technology from the United States meant too that the North American presence provided the structural basis around which Cuba reconstituted itself. North American forms insinuated themselves at every turn. They served as the material context in which Cubans arrived at a sense of themselves and suggested the categories from which to contemplate alternatives and possibilities. Cubans could choose only from what was commonly available, from what was at hand and within reach with which to make a place for themselves in their own country. Styles and fashion began to change almost immediately and indeed under the circumstances, it perhaps could not have been otherwise.

Observed Cuban writer Wenceslao Gálvez as early as 1900:

> The youth who previously imitated French Styles and combed and cut their hair with a certain distinction now use suspenders and part their hair in the middle, leaving them with a hairstyle that was always associated with philosophers. The university is full of students with hair cuts *a la americana* and hair styles of the same origins, with a part down the middle and two pigtails on the side. Everyone can comb their

hair as they wish, of course, but the youth of today will soon shape our future, and so it is natural that upon seeing them so fond of *yanquismo* one becomes alarmed.[12]

Much of what was incorporated into national identity after 1898 was assembled from an environment dominated by North American forms. Cubans were surrounded by the artifacts of U.S. market culture and the ethos that gave it social meaning. The power of these forms lay in their capacity to incorporate Cubans into their assumptions, the degree to which they could presume these forms to be universal—and indeed superior—and worthy of emulation and adoption. These were assumptions to which countless numbers subscribed, the propositions around which they pieced their world together again. Values associated with North American market culture gained usage and utility precisely because they served as a means by which to mediate the Cuban encounter with the new order of things, a way to make space inside Cuba. It was only a matter of time before most Cubans ceased to pay any attention at all to the origins of the material structures and normative standards of their everyday lives. Market culture became so well understood, so fully integrated into daily existence, that it assumed the appearance of the ordinary, with which most felt more or less at home because it was, in fact, home.

North American forms expanded into communities across the island, not only as goods and services but also as the moral order that those goods and services implied. They were present in republican architecture, in recreational forms, in new technologies: in short, in almost everything.[13] North American ways were everywhere. Under some circumstances these ways were all-encompassing, a condition that made it all but impossible to contemplate alternatives or, for that matter, to entertain doubts that these ways were anything less than predominant and permanent. They served as the choices from which Cubans routinely selected the means of self-definition and personal advancement. They insinuated themselves into public and private spheres, into households and at workplaces, into the meanings assigned to daily life and the preparations made to meet the future. Much of what passed for everyday and ordinary—what was "Cuban," in a word—was in fact the product of a normative foundation of reality derived in large measure from North American formulations, henceforth inalterably part of the physiognomy of postcolonial Cuba.

VI

The expanding U.S. presence changed profoundly the character of the Cuban economy and the role of Cubans in that economy, no less than Cuban attitudes, social values, and habits. It was a presence to which vast numbers of Cubans were obliged to acquiesce, as a means of security and mobility, in the role of employees, debtors, renters, and customers. These relationships served to place Cubans in a new cultural context and within new ideological structures. The pursuit of security and success necessarily obliged Cubans to adapt to those forms that most promised to provide a measure of well-being for themselves and their children. This relationship served also to influence psychological needs, suggest new economic possibilities, and shape behavior codes, both private and public, individual and collective. Increasingly large sections of the Cuban population were incorporated into U.S. cultural forms. Tens of thousands of Cubans were bilingual and, in varying degrees, bicultural. Consumption patterns and lifestyles, no less than personal definitions of self-fulfillment and public perceptions of success, were derived from North American standards. That Cubans came in such close contact with U.S. society guaranteed that vast numbers of them would think like North Americans, act like North Americans, look like North Americans, and generally derive their cultural, social, and ethical orientations from North American sources. In the end, Cubans would construct many of their expectations and aspirations around these experiences.

All through the early decades of the twentieth century, Cubans and North Americans expanded contacts, and continued to pull each other into the orbit of their respective charms. These were two peoples who seemed to possess the capacity to meet each other's needs well, finding in one another fulfillment of their fantasies, a kind of complementary coexistence in which each had something to offer—something each seemed to lack and could find only in the other. In the minds of many on both sides, the connection seemed to promise completion to both. North American tourists traveled to Cuba to escape an old morality; Cubans traveled to the United States in search of a new morality. Americans found in Cuba relief from work; Cubans traveled north in pursuit of work. Americans arrived in Cuba seeking a tropical adventure, to lose themselves in the primitive and the exotic; the Cubans traveled north to find modernity: for business, for an education, to guarantee themselves a future, to learn English, to master technology, and to learn to compete and prevail in a world—their own world, dominated by North American capitalist structures, and from which they could not escape: not in Cuba, not in the United States.

VII

This must be considered as an enormously complex condition in which to arrive at nationality and national identity. Forms of the North, unchallenged and in some instances unchallengeable, were in the ascendancy through much of the first half of the twentieth century. Cubans in growing numbers acquiesced to the new order to get on with their lives the best way they could. Accommodation and adaptation were entirely practical responses to reality as encountered in its daily forms—ways to take measure of what needed to be done and proceed to make due, always with the expectation that these ways could solve some of the most urgent and immediate needs confronting vast numbers of households. Many found themselves almost daily obliged to negotiate encounters with North American ways, an interplay that over time shaped the way Cubans arrived at definitions of selfhood and nationhood. By assembling much of which was formed and informed by North American normative structures out of the offerings of everyday life in the post-colonial environment, Cubans developed a complex but highly usable means to define nationality.

There was nothing especially dramatic about these adjustments and certainly nothing that was immediately apparent. They were, rather, simply decisions made and actions taken, often in routine ways, to cope and make do, and it is not reasonable to suppose that more than a handful were alive to the larger implications of these transformations. These were a people longing to resume normality and get on with their lives as best as possible. They were mostly ordinary people trying to get by, choosing to adapt and accommodate rather than to change or challenge. They were, in the end, formed by this world, in which they participated daily in unremarkable fashion. They acquiesced to the everyday and commonplace assumptions of the world as they found it, in the conviction that compliance to prevailing norms would deliver the material bounty, the economic security, and personal well-being that were the central promises upon which North American market culture rested.

This was a gradual and complicated process that spanned fully the early decades of the republic. Much of it was made possible by the expanding availability of U.S. manufactured products, consumer commodities, and household merchandise—goods mass-produced and priced within the reach of large numbers of people. The possibility of possessing these goods was perhaps one of the most powerful sources of Cuban productivity and played a central role in developing and defining the Cuban middle class. Ordinary people in large numbers were disposed to work harder and longer, for they saw the prospect for mobility and improving their status and raising their standard of living through hard work. The greater the availability of consumer products, the greater the incentive for emulative consumption. The promise of the North American ethic, to which vast numbers of Cubans increasingly subscribed, was contained in the proposition of the material basis of happiness and the availability of these products through hard work.

VIII

The implications of these developments were far-reaching indeed. From the beginning of the century, the United States had set out purposefully to "Americanize" Cuba, but never considered the consequences of success—a First World frame of reference within Third World structures, and no way within the latter to fulfill the former.

Therein lay the source of the Cuban angst. Vast numbers had learned to negotiate the terms of the dominant paradigms of their time and conduct themselves according to their practical dictates. But the midcentury contradictions between the world idealized in the North American moral order and the world experienced daily as the Cuban reality had become acute. Cubans had fashioned a version of the North in the tropics, one that created high expectations but lacked the capacity to deliver. They went forth into a world for which their training had prepared them, only to find that such a world did not exist in Cuba.

The original North American intent was successful—it did indeed produce the desire among Cubans to emulate. The only problem was that the power of its appeal assumed all-encompassing dimensions. Vast numbers had been formed by the imperative of the North American market, into which they were integrated and from which they derived their bearings. They were conversant with the vernacular of the market and familiar too with its requirements; they had invested themselves in these relationships. Consumption of North American commodities was self-implicating and indeed served as a means of self-definition. Commodity and self converged, and by the mid–twentieth century had emerged as one of the salient characteristics of what Cristina García aptly called "dreaming in Cuban." Whether all people participated all the time—which they did not, of course—mattered less than the ideal that created the condition to inspire all with plausible expectation of access.

These developments cast a shadow that reached into the mid–twentieth century. Prerevolutionary Cuba had reached the limits of economic growth within a context of dependent capitalist structures sustained by sugar exports. Large numbers of Cubans—middle class and working class alike, those seeking individual advancement and those committed to collective mobility—despaired of solutions within existing institutional structures, many of which were derived from and integrated into North American ones. These institutions were no longer capable of resolving mounting tensions, the central element of which was the demand for the primacy of Cuban interests.

The original North American purpose to produce the desire among Cubans to consume implicated Cubans of all social classes in what proved for many to be a futile undertaking. Cubans had indeed become, more or less, "Americanized," but in ways that North Americans could never have foreseen. They acquired sufficiently the values, the methods, and the expectations to allow them to identify and articulate the malaise of dependent capitalism in ways that most directly challenged the premises of North American hegemony in Cuba on its own terms.

NOTES

1. See Philip S. Foner, *The Spanish-Cuban-American War and the Birth of American Imperialism*, 2 vols. (New York: Monthly Review, 1972); Rolando Rodríguez, "El 98: Epifanía del nuevo imperialismo," *Debates Americanos* 4 (July–December 1997): 99–103. For a very useful discussion of the range of the historiography on 1898, see Thomas G. Paterson, "U.S. Intervention in Cuba, 1898: Interpreting the Spanish-American-Cuban-Filipino War," *Magazine of History*, 12 (spring 1998): 5–10.

2. Jorge Quintana, "Lo que costó a Cuba la guerra de 1895," *Bohemia* 52 (11 September 1960): 4–6, 107; George B. Rea, "The Destruction of Sugar Estates in Cuba," *Harper's Weekly* 41 (16 October 1897): 10–34; Gloria García Rodríguez, "La sociedad cubana a fines de siglo," in Instituto de Historia de Cuba, *Cuadernos Cubanos de Historia* 1 (1998): 27–38.

3. United States Department of War, *Report on the Census of Cuba, 1899* (Washington, D.C.: Government Printing Office, 1900), 179.

4. Mrs. W. A. Candler to Brother, 1 December 1898, Warren A. Candler Papers, Special Collections Department, Robert W. Woodruff Library, Emory University, Atlanta, Ga.

5. Fe Iglesias García, "El costo demográfico de la Guerra de Independencia," *Debates Americanos* 5 (July–December 1997): 67–76; María Poumier, "La vida cotidiana en las ciudades en 1898," *Universidad de La Habana* 196–197 (February–March 1972): 170–209.

6. Alejandro Rodríguez to Gonzalo de Quesada, 13 June 1899, in Gonzalo de Quesada, *Archivo de Gonzalo de Quesada*, 2 vols. (Havana: El Siglo XX, 1948–51), 2: 179–80.

7. See Ada Ferrer, *Insurgent Cuba: Race, Nation, and Revolution, 1868–1898* (Chapel Hill: University of North Carolina Press, 1999).

8. Pedro Pablo Rodríguez, "Modernidad y 98 en Cuba: alternativas y contradicciones," *Temas* 12–13 (October 1997): 13–18.

9. For a discussion of postwar reconstruction, see James H. Hitchman, "Unfinished Business: Public Works in Cuba, 1898–1902," *The Americas* 31 (January 1975): 335–59.

10. Herbert G. Squiers to John Hay, 17 September 1904, Despatches from U.S. Ministers to Cuba, 1902–6, General Records of the Department of State, Record Group 59, National Archives, Washington, D.C.

11. Oscar Zanetti, "1898: comercio, reciprocidad, modernización," *Temas* 12–13 (October 1997): 48–61.

12. Wen Gálvez, "Cocas," *El Fígaro* 16 (4 February 1900):53.

13. Llilian Llanes, *1898–1921: la transformación de La Habana a través de la arquitectura* (Havana: Editorial Letras Cubanas, 1993); Ramón Cotarelo, *Matanzas en su arquitectura* (Havana: n.p., 1993). See also Jorge Ibarra Cuesta, *Cuba: 1898–1958. Estructura y procesos sociales* (Havana: Editorial de Ciencias Sociales, 1995).

7

Intervention or Possession?: Puerto Rico, the War of 1898, and the American Colonial Periphery

Francisco A. Scarano

It should be apparent that Puerto Rico's is an odd case for discussion under the heading of "legacies of intervention." If by "intervention" we understand the military occupation and temporary administration of formally constituted nation-states, then Puerto Rico's case clearly stands out as different from the long list of countries, most of them in the broader Caribbean region, in which the United States has intervened during the last century.[1] Like its sister island of Cuba but unlike most other intervened countries, Puerto Rico was not an independent republic at the time of the first appearance of U.S. troops on its soil as part of one of the last campaigns of the Spanish-Cuban-American War. In sharp contrast to Cuba, of course, the "intervention" in the smaller of the Spanish colonies did not result in the establishment of a republic. Rather, owing to a series of decisions that still haunt us today, the landing of U.S. troops at Guánica bay in July 1898 began an indefinite, if constitutionally ambiguous, incorporation of the island and its people into the U.S. sphere. Properly speaking, it was not just an act of "intervention"; it was an act of "possession."[2]

There is something to be said about the value of looking at the Puerto Rican case apart from all other U.S. interventions in the Caribbean basin—as a special case of U.S. nineteenth-century expansionism, perhaps, or as a synthesis of the old empire of continental expansion and the new empire of overseas adventures.[3] This, of course, skirts the issue of its intrinsic worthiness as a national history, a history unto itself, an approach that, although meritorious, would distract us from our present concern with "intervention" and, implicitly, comparative scholarship. In fact, much of the writing on

Puerto Rico's relationship with the United States over the last one hundred years has been of just the kind that views the colony-metropole ties in almost test-tube isolation.[4] Such isolation has been two-sided. Not only has Puerto Rico usually been excluded from consideration within the frameworks of U.S. history and the histories of U.S. expansionism[5] (once authors pay lip service to its acquisition after the Spanish-Cuban-American War), but the United States has also been written out of Puerto Rican history. Such selective treatment has, I would submit, quite damaged our ability to understand U.S. relations with its largest and longest-running colonial possession, while significantly hampering our capacity to grasp major themes of the U.S.-Caribbean and U.S.-Latin American encounter. On the part of Puerto Rican scholarship, this treatment has produced rich, but excessively inward-looking, narratives in history, the social sciences, and literary genres.[6]

In setting Puerto Rico apart, much has been lost. Both metropolitan and island scholarship have missed out on opportunities for deeper comparative insight. The loss of perspective is all the more striking when one considers how some of the main patterns and consequences of U.S. hegemony in Puerto Rico have prefigured and anticipated similar processes and results of intervention in other Caribbean nations.

The register of outcomes for which Puerto Rico stands as a precursor is long and impressive. The list would include, but not be limited to, the following: (a) the formation of corporate plantation economies largely owned by U.S. investors in the early twentieth century; (b) the concomitant appearance of *comprador* bourgeoisies with economic interests closely aligned with (though not infrequently also in competition with) those of U.S. investors; (c) the rapid and thorough transformation of peasant majorities into landless, wage-earning workers; (d) the expression of radical nationalist discourses in opposition to U.S. rule, so radical, in fact, that the struggling nations (or nations-in-the-making) came to be seen by the nationalists in terms of the absolute negation of U.S. influence; (e) the eventual conversion of plantation economies into export-oriented manufacturing economies based on the unhampered movement of goods and capital between metropole and colony; and (f) the displacement of a significant portion of plantation workers toward U.S. cities, a process that paralleled the emergence of a Puerto Rican middle class defined by consumer values and orientations that mimic those of its counterpart in the North. It is fascinating and not the least amusing to observe how, fifty years after the famous "Fomento" experiments in export-led industrialization (known as the Operación Manos a la Obra or Operation Bootstrap program in Puerto Rico), an eerily familiar scenario unfolds in such unlikely places as Mexico and Chile.[7] Just a few years ago, still under the aegis of import-substitution industrialization, this would have seemed almost unimaginable.

That all of the above features seem to have played themselves out in Puerto Rico sooner and more deeply than in the "merely intervened" nations invites a reflection on possible differences between "intervention" and "colonial possession." A full exploration of this difference, of course, would have to recount the special constitutional history of Puerto Rico, but that task falls beyond the scope of this chapter.[8] Two questions suggest themselves at the outset: What happened in Puerto Rico in the aftermath of the 1898 invasion that did not happen elsewhere at points roughly equivalent in their relationship with the United States? Since the most obvious difference between mere intervention and colonial possession is the latter's permanence, this question may be rephrased as: Why did the U.S. government decide to "possess" the Spanish colony when it did so? And the second question we need to ask is: What differences in outcome are attributable to the differences in the nature of U.S. involvement?

In order to assess properly the permanence of the U.S. takeover of Puerto Rico, we need to address an issue of historical accuracy that was hotly debated in Puerto Rico during the centennial year, namely, the motivations for, and character of, the U.S. military takeover in 1898. It is evident that one of the fundamental differences between Puerto Rico in 1898 and Haiti in 1915, the Dominican Republic in 1916, Grenada in 1983, or even Cuba in 1898 is that at the moment of initiating the imperial project, key U.S. policymakers made the controversial decision to invade Puerto Rico for keeps. The military occupation of what Washington euphemistically called at the time the "number two" target did not involve an *imperialismo bobo* ("naïve imperialism"), which sloppily stumbled upon the island and kept it as an afterthought of war. (Remarkable as this may seem, many people have argued over the years for this version of events, in the hope of blunting the negative connotations of the U.S. regime in Puerto Rico.)[9] Nor did it happen simply because some Puerto Rican partisans of independence from Spain had "invited" U.S. troops in in order to facilitate the annexation of Puerto Rico to the United States, as the Commonwealth's Secretary of State, Norma Burgos, proposed during the centennial commemorations in 1998. It happened, rather, as part of a calculated plan to claim and indefinitely possess strategic territory in the eastern Caribbean for use by the U.S. navy and for U.S. investors.[10]

The story of the U.S. possession of Puerto Rico has been told many times and with great authority by some of the leading Puerto Rican and North American scholars of our day.[11] Yet, for the purpose of answering the questions at hand, it is instructive to review briefly the events of the summer of 1898 which lent the Puerto Rican campaign its uniquely purposeful, or classically imperialist, character.

A peculiar, and for the nearly one million residents of Puerto Rico, fateful, set of circumstances presented itself in the conduct of the war which would mark America's rise to global power. For at the outset of this war of all but assured territorial conquest, Congress had declared in the well-known Teller Amendment that the richest prize, Cuba, was off-limits for full incorporation into the U.S. orbit. In the rather frenzied state of public opinion at the outbreak of the war, few people may have realized this paradox and its implications for the actual course of the conflict. But as the various war campaigns progressed in the late spring and early summer and the implications of the Teller Amendment took hold in the minds of policymakers and tacticians, the shape of American intentions vis-à-vis the remaining Spanish colonies, especially Puerto Rico, fell into sharper relief.

Even if at the very outset there had been no plans to pry Puerto Rico loose from Spain in order to possess it—a doubtful claim, as most students of the period would agree—the fact is that as the war evolved, the military politics and geopolitics of the U.S. effort pointed increasingly in that direction. After the first U.S. naval victories in the Pacific, imperialist clamor reached a peak. Public opinion cried for the acquisition of Spanish territory. Gradually but inexorably Puerto Rico came to be regarded as a great prize, desirable unto itself and easily captured to boot. Government officials, such as Under Secretary of the Navy Theodore Roosevelt; senators, including Henry Cabot Lodge; and businessmen from various sections of the country and diverse industries favored this course of action. Already in the first weeks of war, there was talk that Puerto Rico, depicted as a "rich garden" where North American capital would still find fertile and virgin land, should be converted into a permanent possession of the conquering nation. Patriotic fever stifled the protests from anti-imperialists, who opposed the acquisition of territories overseas because they believed that a democratic republic had no moral right to possess colonies.[12]

President McKinley, always watchful of public opinion, responded to the imperialist clamor being raised about Puerto Rico. At the end of May, and under presidential orders, the U.S. military began planning their assault on the island. As soon as they managed to give the Spaniards a definitive blow at Santiago de Cuba—objective "number one"—they would proceed against target "number two": Puerto Rico.

Nowhere in this record of planning for and carrying out an invasion does one find the "naïve imperialism" made so famous in Luis Muñoz Marín's speeches. Secretary Burgos's "imperialism by invitation" also fails the empirical test, because evidence of some nationalist leaders' complicity with the invasion in no way undermines an interpretation that stresses a deliberate acquisition within an indefinite time period. The Puerto Rican campaign was orchestrated with clear political and geopolitical goals in mind: it would satisfy the public's outcry for the material rewards of war and at the same time yield valuable strategic and economic booty. To this end, it bears remembering, Washington placed a shrewd and experienced general, Nelson A. Miles, in command of the preparations for the invasion of Puerto Rico. Miles, a fifty-nine-year-old veteran of the Civil War, had obtained most of his military experience in bloody campaigns against western Indians, for which he had been given the all-too-revealing nickname of "Indian

Fighter."[13] According to his plans for the expedition against target "number two," instead of the troops who had fought in Cuba, fresh soldiers would be given a chance to join the party. Yellow fever had devastated the regular troops in Cuba, and military men feared that the disease would wreak havoc among the invaders of Puerto Rico. But Miles's decision had a potential downside, for it meant that the majority of the troops sent to Puerto Rico would be volunteers or enlisted men with little military training.[14]

The use of volunteer regiments in Puerto Rico fit well with the political objectives of McKinley and the Republican Party. "Mindful of the politics of northern states [like Illinois and Wisconsin], . . ." explains Fernando Picó, "the McKinley administration tried to give the volunteer troops of these states the opportunity to shine."[15] As these soldiers were inexperienced, however, Miles ran the risk that they would be incompetent in battle. Consequently, he needed to insure that the Puerto Rican campaign would present the fewest possible complications—indeed, that it would accomplish its goal of the U.S. occupation of the island without much of a fight. The ideal would be to gain ground from the Spaniards discreetly, doing battle only when necessary. Thus it was that the Puerto Rican phase of the "splendid little war" saw two armies—one all but defeated, the other none too confident—whose main tactical objective was to dance around each other and avoid fighting, in anticipation of a cease-fire that most people suspected could only be days or weeks away.

I discuss some of the geopolitical and military details in order to underscore and give texture to the argument that in no other case of a U.S. "intervention" in the Caribbean region was military power so unequivocally at the service of a classic colonial agenda of territorial acquisition, of pure-and-simple expansionism. Surely one can point to several of the "interventions" in the Caribbean and Central American of the early part of the century—Haiti between 1915 and 1930 especially comes to mind—when U.S. authorities did not appear to be in a hurry to return the government to local control. But in none of those cases does one encounter the kind of resolve to possess the country quite like that found with reference to target "number two" at the time of the Spanish-Cuban-American War. Walter LaFeber has argued that a broad consensus developed in 1896 and 1897 among the U.S. populace in favor of intervening on the side of the Cuban rebels.[16] A similar consensus on taking Puerto Rico had formed by the summer of 1898. The cast of characters in both instances included the president, many of his partisan advisors, not a few congressmen and senators, an influential group of newspapers, and large portions of the public. That this was a potent coalition, capable of drowning the anti-imperialists' protests, few can question.

The story of this act of "possession," of course, cannot end with the deliberate military conquest of July and August 1898, or with the U.S. negotiators' insistence at the Paris peace negotiations a few months later that Spain transfer its sovereignty over the island to the United States. To finish the story here would be not to recognize the critical role played by Puerto Ricans themselves in the consolidation of the new colonialism, especially during the pivotal years between the invasion in 1898 and the formation of a civil government in 1900. One of the features that most stands out across this century of interventions is precisely the extent to which representatives of the "intervening" foreign power and local actors have negotiated the terms of the relationship, albeit from unequal positions of power. Puerto Rico was no exception. There, one hundred years ago, a complex set of circumstances had shaped a political environment receptive to the new colonialism. These circumstances ranged from a broad-based popular resentment to Spanish rule (fueled in part by the sharpening poverty of the rural majority), to the currency of annexationist ideas. Support for annexation flourished among some groups of *hacendados*, especially in the sugar sector, and among some workers, blacks (strange though it might seem), and women, for whom an American Puerto Rico held out the promise of greater legal rights and protections—a promise later fulfilled only partially.[17]

It was this highly contingent alignment of the U.S. colonial project with the hopes and aspirations of a significant portion of the people that gave the United States its hegemonic edge in Puerto Rico. In the short term, the fact that colonizer and colonized could agree on an outcome—the act of possession—for irreconcilable reasons did not much matter. In a classic case of misunderstanding across a huge cultural divide, the players went about reading each other's motives in ways that fit their expectations and goals but had little to do with reality. Many Americans went on thinking that the Puerto Ricans were all too happy with colonial tutelage while many Puerto Ricans read the Americans' intentions to possess as proof that the entire package of democratic prerogatives—including the right to choose between full annexation leading to statehood, independence, or anything in between, as the philosopher Eugenio María de Hostos advocated—would be extended to them. In thinking about the ensuing history of this relationship, it is clear that the misunderstanding contained in this earliest colonial consensus was a determining one.

I have tried to argue that the U.S. thrust to the Caribbean in 1898, during a highly popular war whose military and political logic led inexorably toward the acquisition of territory, was a special kind of "intervention": that of an indefinite, though constitutionally vague, "possession." I have also observed that local collaboration proved critical in establishing the contours of the ensuing relationship, and in laying out the justification for it. But what of the other question with which I began: the extent to which the manner of incorporation affected differences in outcome between the "merely intervened" and the "possessed"?

A full answer to this question would require a close comparative analysis of the U.S. relationship with dependent and subordinate countries of the circum-Caribbean region. The analysis, it seems, would inevitably lead toward two related questions: How deeply embedded in circuits of world trade were the target countries prior to U.S. occupation, and how (or how well) did the preexisting state (whether colonial, as in Puerto Rico and Cuba, or national, as in most other cases) perform the supporting functions called for by this sort of articulation within the world economy? The answer would lie, in short, in political economy.

In glancing over Puerto Rico's situation, one is struck by the extent to which the United States did not have to create structures of political-economic domination after the initial decision to possess. Those structures were already there, either smoothly functioning in the world of business relations in the coffee, sugar, and tobacco trades, or handed down to the new state administrators by their predecessors, the Spaniards. In terms of political economy, and judging by the intimate ties that linked it with the centers of Atlantic capitalism, Puerto Rico was quite modern. Like Cuba, but without the disruptions of continual war and devastation, its preexistent colonial state had evolved over the course of the nineteenth century into a highly centralized apparatus, one that left comparatively little room for local initiative or response.[18] This highly compact colonial state had for decades refined its capacity to influence the lives of even the most remote mountain-dwelling peasants. When the Americans came in, therefore, they found it easy to continue such centralization, as they sought to bring elementary education to the masses, build better roads for the plantation trades, eradicate tropical anemia, or ensure the smooth functioning of labor markets in the export sector.

That combination of a partially subsidized corporate plantation economy and a highly efficient and centralized state apparatus may have ushered in the conditions for Puerto Rico's trail-blazing performance in the periphery of U.S. capitalism. If this island has prefigured so many of the historical patterns of that most intimate of American zones of influence over the last one hundred years, it is because of the eagerness to possess and be possessed—a historical contingency of 1898—combined with the more durable force of a highly favorable political economy hammered out, not without significant pain for the popular majority, by two empires in uninterrupted succession.

NOTES

1. On U.S. interventions, see Ivan Musicant, *The Banana Wars: A History of United States Military Intervention in Latin America from the Spanish-American War to the Invasion of Panama* (New York: Macmillan, 1990); and Lester D. Langley, *The United States and the Caribbean in the Twentieth Century* (Athens: University of Georgia Press, 1982).

2. Despite the increased attention that the U.S. takeover of Puerto Rico in 1898 received on the occasion of its centennial commemoration, the historiography of this event is relatively undeveloped. Some of the more notable works include Carmelo Rosario Natal, *Puerto Rico y la crisis de la Guerra Hispanoamericana*, 1895–1898 (Hato Rey: Brothers Printing Co., 1975); Fernando Picó, *1898: la guerra después de la guerra* (Río Piedras: Ediciones Huracán, 1987); and Edward J. Berbusse, *The United States in Puerto Rico, 1898–1900* (Chapel Hill: University of North Carolina Press, 1966). See also María Eugenia Estades Font, *La presencia militar de Estados Unidos en Puerto Rico, 1898–1918. Intereses estratégicos y dominación colonial* (Río Piedras: Ediciones Huracán, 1988).

3. Walter LaFeber, *The New Empire: An Interpretation of American Expansion, 1860–1898* (Ithaca: Cornell University Press, 1963).

4. María de los Angeles Castro Arroyo, "De Salvador Brau a la "novísima" historia: un replanteamiento y una crítica," *Op. Cit., Boletín del Centro de Investigaciones Históricas*, no. 4 (1988–89): 9–25; Allen Woll, *Puerto Rican Historiography* (New York: Gordon Press, 1978); Laura Náter Vázquez, "El '98 en la historiografía puertorriqueña: del político entusiasta al héroe popular," *Op. Cit., Boletín del Centro de Investigaciones Históricas*, no. 4 (1988–89): 101–22; and Irene Fernández Aponte, *El cambio de soberanía en Puerto Rico: otro '98*, Colección Independencia de Iberoamérica (Madrid: Editorial MAPFRE, 1992).

5. It is quite revealing of the invisibility of Puerto Rico in U.S. historiography that, in a recent book on U.S. imperialism as a cultural phenomenon, there are no references to this most populous and oldest of the American colonies. See Amy Kaplan and Donald E. Pease, eds., *Cultures of United States Imperialism* (Durham and London: Duke University Press, 1993). For a scathing critique of Puerto Rican invisibility in the American academy, see Arcadio Díaz Quiñones, *La memoria rota: ensayos sobre cultura y política* (Río Piedras: Ediciones Huracán, 1993), 78–82.

6. This is a point raised by Raymond Carr, *Puerto Rico: A Colonial Experiment* (New York: Vintage Books, 1984), but his account of the resulting "isolation" is, unfortunately, disdainful of island intellectuals.

7. For a discussion of Fomento and its importance in the Puerto Rican industrial development program, see James L. Dietz, *Economic History of Puerto Rico: Institutional Change and Capitalist Development* (Princeton: Princeton University Press, 1986). Also see Richard Weisskoff, *Factories and Food Stamps: The Puerto Rico Model of Development*, Johns Hopkins Studies in Development (Baltimore: Johns Hopkins University Press, 1985).

8. José Trías Monge, *Puerto Rico: The Trials of the Oldest Colony in the World* (New Haven: Yale University Press, 1997).

9. Some of the earliest formulations of how the United States became Puerto Rico's colonial master without really wanting to ironically came from the critical pen of Luis Muñoz Marín. See his "The Sad Case of Porto Rico," *The American Mercury* 16, no. 62 (February 1929): 136–41.

10. Francisco A. Scarano, *Puerto Rico: cinco siglos de historia* (Bogotá: McGraw-Hill, 1993), 551–55.

11. For the most authoritative review of the decisions leading to the U.S. invasion and the decision to keep Puerto Rico, see Rosario Natal, *Puerto Rico.*

12. On the anti-imperialist campaigns of 1898, see E. Berkeley Tompkins, *Anti-*

Imperialism in the United States: The Great Debate (Philadelphia: University of Pennsylvania Press, 1970).

13. Robert M. Utley, "Nelson A. Miles," in *Soldiers West: Biographies from the Military Frontier*, ed. Paul Andrew Hutton, with an intro. by Robert M. Utley (Lincoln: University of Nebraska Press, 1987), 213–27.

14. Picó, *1898*, 54–55.

15. Ibid., 53.

16. LaFeber, *The New Empire*, passim.

17. Mariano Negrón Portillo, "Puerto Rico ante la invasión norteamericana de 1898," *La Toga* 10, no. 2 (1978): 18–21; and Carmelo Rosario Natal, *El 1898 puertorriqueño en la historiografía: ensayo y bibliografía crítica* (San Juan: Academia Puertorriqueña de la Historia, 1997).

18. Jesús Lalinde Abadía, *La administración española en el siglo XIX puertorriqueño (pervivencia de la variante indiana del decisionismo castellano en Puerto Rico)*, Publicaciones de la Escuela de Estudios Hispano-Americanos de Sevilla (Sevilla: Escuela de Estudios Hispano-Americanos, 1980); Teresita Martínez Vergne, "Politics and Society in the Spanish Caribbean in the Nineteenth Century," in *The Modern Caribbean*, ed. Franklin W. Knight and Colin A. Palmer (Chapel Hill: University of North Carolina Press, 1989), 185–202.

8

The Anti-Imperialist Movement, 1898–1921

Jim Zwick

On 3 May 1902, the *New York Evening Post* published an editorial entitled "The Pesky Anti-Imperialist" that highlighted the number of times the anti-imperialist movement had been declared "dead" in the five years since the formation of the Anti-Imperialist League in 1898:

> It is most provoking, we know, for Anti-Imperialists to pretend that they are still alive. They have been killed so often. After 1899 we were to hear no more of them. In 1900 they were again pronounced dead, although, like the obstinate Irishman, they continued to protest that, if they were dead, they were not conscious of it. Last year the slain were slaughtered once more, and that time buried as well, with all due ceremony. Yet the impudent creatures have resumed activity during the past few months just as if their epitaphs had not been composed again and again.[1]

With different dates, a statement like that could have been published during almost any other decade of the twentieth century. The Anti-Imperialist League itself survived until 1921, and it was followed by a succession of other anti-imperialist, noninterventionist, and solidarity organizations from that year to the present.

Created in November 1898 to oppose the annexation of Cuba, Puerto Rico, Guam, and the Philippines at the end of the Spanish-American War, the Anti-Imperialist League was the first national anti-imperialist organization formed in the United States. Although it operated for more than two decades and influenced numerous later anti-imperialist organizations, most historical studies of the anti-imperialist movement in the United States have repeated contemporary claims about the anti-imperialists' demise. Focusing on either the presidential election of 1900 or Theodore Roosevelt's 4 July 1902 declaration that the Philippine-American War was over, most studies have argued that anti-imperialism became a "dead issue" in 1900 or 1902. The few studies that have paid attention to the League's later years have argued that there was a clear disjuncture between the League's initial opposition to territorial imperialism and the later organizations formed to oppose economic imperialism.[2] There was, however, considerable continuity in personnel between the League and the later anti-imperialist organizations formed in the 1920s and 1930s. Officers of the League formed or served as officers of nearly every major anti-imperialist organization formed in the next two decades, including the Haiti-Santo Domingo Independence Committee formed in 1921, the American Fund for Public Service Committee on American Imperialism formed in 1924, the All-America Anti-Imperialist League formed in 1925 by the Workers (Communist) party, and the Fair Play for Puerto Rico Committee created by the American Civil Liberties Union in the late 1930s. They also chaired ad-hoc "hands-off" committees, and several of the League's female officers opposed imperialism during the 1920s through the Women's International League for Peace and Freedom, cofounded by League vice president Jane Addams.

Although the Anti-Imperialist League has been the subject of numerous historical studies, it has never been examined as a social movement. This omission is probably due to the fact that its leadership included many of the most prominent politicians, educators, literary figures, and business and labor leaders of the time. It had a mass following for at least a few years, but its leadership was drawn primarily from elite circles and it had extraordinary access to both financial resources and to government leaders. For these reasons it does not fit easily within a typical social movement research framework. William Gamson's historical survey of social movements in the United States probably excluded the League because it was "rich in resources from the start" and "hoped to rely on the persuasiveness of their arguments or the prestige of the names on their letterhead" rather than mobilization of mass support as an important first step in organizing the movement.[3] Although he does not mention the League in his book, it is easy to see how that criteria for rejection from his study could apply to the organization. George S. Boutwell, an aging but highly regarded cofounder of the Republican party, was its first president, and Andrew Carnegie and former president Grover Cleveland were among its vice presidents. Its national slate of officers included many prominent names, but most of its local branches were formed by radical reformers affiliated with the single-tax movement inspired by Henry George's 1879 book, *Progress and Poverty*. Single-taxers founded and served as president and/or secretary of the branches in New York, Philadelphia, Cincinnati, and Minneapolis, and played a prominent role in the creation of both the Central Anti-Imperialist League and the national American Anti-Imperialist League based in Chicago.

Despite the prestige and financial wealth of some of its officers, the League deserves recognition as the social movement organization that started what has become a long tradition of opposition to foreign interventions by the United States. Because the League was the first such organization formed in the United States, it represents the beginning of the anti-imperialist social movement sector that would later include organizations formed by or allied with the Communist Party USA as well as many of today's numerous country- or region-specific solidarity organizations.[4] With significantly less access to financial resources and mainstream political leaders, these later organizations fit more closely with what scholars generally define as social movements. The League was formed during a dramatic and unusual split within the country's elite over the annexations of 1898 and 1899, and it could immediately count upon the support of many of the country's leading politicians and some of its wealthiest men and women. All later organizations have had to start further from the halls of power but can be viewed as part of a continuum of anti-imperialist organizing that has spanned the twentieth century. This is a common sense approach that is routinely applied in historical discussions of organizing on women's rights, civil rights, peace, labor, etc., but which is rarely applied in studies of anti-imperialists from the 1890s to the present.[5] In particular, the marginalization of more recent anti-imperialist organizations within the United States cannot be fully understood without looking at the processes involved in the marginalization of the Anti-Imperialist League from 1898 to its demise in 1921.

Three periods in the League's history during which the anti-imperialist movement experienced splits that diminished the power of the movement and ultimately led to its dissolution are examined here. They are the election of 1900, during which the strategy of partisan political endorsement was the primary issue; the period from 1904 to 1905, when a split occurred over definitions of imperialism and some members' attempts to gain influence with the Republican party; and the period from 1912 to 1921, when a split that erupted between the Anti-Imperialist League and the Filipino independence movement ended in the dissolution of the former. I examine how the Anti-Imperialist League positioned itself in relation to macropolitical changes, including the formation of rival organizations, and in relation to its individual members. This approach illuminates why it is useful to view the League within the context of the broader anti-imperialist social movement sector, and highlights the influence of specific individuals within the organizations. Changes in political conditions certainly influenced the League's history but its longevity and enduring influence can only be explained by the tenacity of some of its individual officers and members.

THE ANTI-IMPERIALIST LEAGUE IN THE 1900 PRESIDENTIAL ELECTION

When it was formed in November 1898, the Anti-Imperialist League described its purpose of opposing the annexation of the former Spanish colonies solely in terms of the debate within the Senate over the Treaty of Paris that concluded the Spanish-American War. Only Cuba, for whose independence the war was ostensibly fought, was explicitly promised independence under the terms of the treaty; Puerto Rico, Guam, and the Philippines were to become colonies of the United States. The requirement that the treaty be ratified by the Senate provided the League with a concrete goal and an opportunity to stop the emerging imperialist policy before formal annexation could be accomplished. The League's first action was to circulate a petition to the Senate to "protest against any extension of the sovereignty of the United States over the Philippine Islands, in any event, or other foreign territory, without the free consent of the people thereof, believing such action would be dangerous to the Republic, wasteful of its resources, in violation of constitutional principles, and fraught with moral and physical evils to our people."[6] By February 1899, more than fifty thousand signatures to this petition were delivered to the Senate, and the League considered each signatory as a member of its organization.

The treaty was ratified on 6 February 1899, but it passed by only one vote, and all sides considered the start of the Philippine-American War two days before as the deciding factor in its ratification.[7] The opposition to the treaty revolved exclusively around the issue of imperialism. Although the anti-imperialists lost the vote, the rapid growth of the movement in the preceding months and the narrow margin of their defeat are good indications of the strength of anti-imperialist thought in the United States at that time. The Anti-Imperialist League was very much within the mainstream of contemporary political thought, and its reliance on such texts as the Declaration of Independence, Washington's Farewell Address, and Lincoln's antislavery statements underscored its adherence to deeply rooted anticolonial and democratic political traditions.

After the Treaty of Paris was ratified, the League turned its attention to the upcoming presidential election of 1900 as its next chance to overturn the "new un-American policy of imperialism."[8] In October 1899, the League broadened its national reach by creating the American Anti-Imperialist League in Chicago. During the debate about the treaty, it had operated primarily as a lobbying organization. Its Boston headquarters were supplemented by a Washington, D.C. office provided by Jackson H. Ralston, the U.S. legal counsel for the Philippine Republic during its 1898–99 attempt to gain recognition from the U.S. government. Once the intention to move the national headquarters to Chicago was announced, local organizing efforts were accelerated throughout the country and numerous local branches were created. The platform of the American Anti-Imperialist League described imperialism as the "paramount issue" of the time and called upon all anti-imperialists to oppose the election of any candidate who supported the policy. There was apparently widespread, though not total, agreement that imperialist candidates should be opposed, but the precise method of doing so became a significant source of conflict within the movement.

In August 1900, after the Republicans nominated William McKinley and Theodore Roosevelt and the Democrats nominated William Jennings Bryan, the Anti-Imperialist League held a National Liberty Congress in Indianapolis to decide upon its strategy for the presidential campaign. A few days before, a group of anti-imperialists in New York had formed a Third Party Movement that opposed William McKinley on the issue of imperialism but was equally opposed to William Jennings Bryan on the issue of Free Silver. A number of influential officers of the Anti-Imperialist League, including Carl Schurz, Moorfield Storey, and Louis Ehrich, supported the creation of a third party at this time but felt that it would need to have a prominent Republican at its head to be an effective force in the campaign. Few, if any, of the League's officers gave unqualified support to the Third Party Movement. At the Liberty Congress, the Third Party Movement was given a chance to present its case but was voted down by the majority of participants in favor of an endorsement of Bryan. Supporting Bryan was seen as the most effective means of preventing McKinley's reelection and overturning the policy of imperialism. The leadership of the Third Party Movement was alienated from the League for many years afterward. Two of its officers, Thomas Mott Osborne and Oswald Garrison Villard, joined the League only after eight to ten years had passed; others in the movement never joined.

An immediate impact of the League's endorsement of William Jennings Bryan was to alienate many anti-imperialists who objected to making a presidential endorsement because they believed that the issue superseded party politics. This division provided an opening for another new organization to be formed in the anti-imperialist social movement sector. The National Association of Anti-Imperialist Clubs was formed in New York to rally opposition to imperialism without taking an overt partisan stance in the election. It gained support from most of the officers of the Washington [D.C.] Anti-Imperialist League and many officers of other League branches. Gamaliel Bradford, whose "Call for Help" against imperialism led to the first anti-imperialist mass meeting in Boston in June 1898, campaigned for the Association in 1900 as did Herbert Welsh, an influential officer of the League's Philadelphia branch. Recognizing that the Association was playing a leading role in grass-roots organizing within New York City, the Anti-Imperialist League of New York decided to cooperate with the Association and the two organizations cosponsored an anti-imperialist rally in Carnegie Hall shortly before the election.

The organizations that were formed during the campaign did not have a significant impact on the Anti-Imperialist League. The Third Party Movement never got off the ground and was disbanded or drifted apart in early 1901. In late November 1900, the National Association of Anti-Imperialist Clubs was taken over by William Randolph Hearst. He unsuccessfully tried to transform it into a National Liberty League intended to supplant the American Anti-Imperialist League. Several of the New York officers of the old association bolted to the Anti-Imperialist League of New York, and the National Liberty League never took off.[9] Short-lived Liberty Leagues were also created in Chicago and New England. The thought behind these groups was that the Anti-Imperialist League had become too closely tied to the Democratic party during the campaign to be effective in advocating independence for the Philippines under the newly reelected Republican administration of William McKinley.

The Anti-Imperialist League itself was also in an awkward position because its efforts had been so thoroughly focused on the presidential election. Although some public meetings were held, and individual officers continued to make public statements against imperialism and to argue against McKinley's claim of an "electoral mandate" on imperialism, the League did not issue another national appeal against imperialism until 4 July 1901, after a long period of reassessment that included numerous private meetings to develop a postelection strategy.

During this period, a significant group split off from the Boston-based New England Anti-Imperialist League to form the new, nonpartisan Philippine Information Society. It would become the most important rival organization formed after the election. Among its organizers were two of the League's more important officers: Fiske Warren and Charles Francis Adams. Adams had tremendous local influence as well as a national reputation and access to the leadership of the Republican party. His initial support for the new organization was perhaps consistent with his conservative politics. But Warren's participation can only be explained with reference to the divisions that occurred within the League over strategy after the election. Warren was the League's foremost advocate of creating direct ties between the Anti-Imperialist League and the Philippine independence movement. At that time he was hosting in his home Sixto Lopez, a Filipino with close but unofficial ties to the leadership of the Philippine Revolution; he would later escort Lopez back to the Philippines only to be threatened with arrest and deportation for giving "aid and comfort to the enemy."[10] Warren's continued involvement with the anti-imperialist movement led him to join the single-tax movement a few years later, and he created numerous single-tax enclaves throughout New England.

Many of Warren's reasons for supporting the new organization were similar to the objections to the Anti-Imperialist League that were raised by people who formed the Liberty Leagues. In letters to Carl Schurz in New

York, Warren stated that many people thought the "anti-" in the League's name was too negative, and he suggested that the League should be reorganized with a new name, constitution, and personnel to obscure any connection between the new and the old organizations. He wrote that in Boston, the very word "anti-imperialist" had become associated with "extravagant acts of enthusiasts connected with the movement, [and] has hardened the hearts of numbers of people who would otherwise have been fit subjects of persuasion that our foreign policy should be changed."[11] This undoubtedly reflected the bitterness produced during the hard-fought presidential campaign, but Warren would raise similar objections to the League several years later that would lead to yet another split within the organization. Although he resigned from his position on the League's executive committee at this time and worked with the Philippine Information Society, his position remained ambiguous and he later rejoined the League as a vice president.

The Philippine Information Society produced an extensive series of publications between 1900 and 1902 that primarily supported the administration's views on the Philippines. With the exception of one pamphlet of the speeches and letters of Sixto Lopez that Warren arranged, the Society's publications were drawn from official government documents, and the imperialist press endorsed them as "unpartisan and trust-worthy."[12] Although the Society was never a mass-based membership organization and did not recruit many of its officers from the League, its widely distributed publications undoubtedly added to the difficulties the League faced in getting its positions across after the election. The Society was disbanded in mid-1902, shortly before Theodore Roosevelt declared that the war in the Philippines was over.

The various splits that took place during 1900 were similar in the sense that none involved direct criticism of the League's positions on imperialism or the continuing war in the Philippines. The issues raised concerned differences in strategy and assessment of the League's ability to influence Republican policy after the election. The Philippine Information Society, its most serious rival, distributed information that originated from the McKinley and Roosevelt administrations, but it made no policy prescriptions in an effort to maintain its nonpartisan position. Because there was no other political opening on the horizon—such as those the League had used to oppose the Treaty of Paris and McKinley's reelection—the movement was faced with few options. Combined with the perception that the League had diminished its own political force by endorsing the losing presidential candidate, this led to various openings for new organizations to be formed with different oppositional strategies. The continuing struggle to change the administration's policy led to more significant splits within the movement a few years later.

THE SPLIT OF 1904–5

None of the divisions that occurred within the anti-imperialist movement during and after the presidential campaign of 1900 were as significant as the split that developed in 1904 and 1905. The League's increasing isolation after the presidential election led at least several of its branches to disband by the end of 1901, and the leaders of the League's surviving branches began to seek new ways of gaining influence with the Roosevelt administration and the Republican party as a whole. This led to further, more serious divisions within the movement. The split eventually led to the formation of two organizations that were willing to compromise with the Roosevelt administration in support of a limited grant of independence for the Philippines modeled after the protectorate established for Cuba—a compromise the League had consistently rejected for either Cuba or the Philippines. Although "Cuban freedom" was a rallying cry during the Spanish-American War, the autonomy Cuba actually received after the war was severely limited. Its constitution had to meet U.S. congressional approval, it was not allowed to form international alliances, and the United States reserved the right to intervene militarily at times of political unrest or whenever Cuba could not pay its international debts, including those to U.S. corporations. By making this compromise, the new organizations adopted what has since come to be known as a neocolonial position—acceptance of the political and economic domination of Cuba and the Philippines so long as it did not entail territorial acquisition and direct governance.

Initial steps towards the split were taken as early as January 1903, when Edward Ordway and Josephine Shaw Lowell of the Anti-Imperialist League of New York began to consider alternatives to the Anti-Imperialist League that would elicit more support from members of the Republican party. After Cornell University president Jacob Gould Schurman declined to speak in New York under the auspices of the League, they considered renaming the organization in response to his objections.[13] Although Schurman presided over the first Philippine Commission in 1899 and wrote the Philippine plank of the Republican party's 1900 campaign platform, he was well-known as an opponent of imperialism and many members of the Anti-Imperialist League hoped to recruit him into their organization. The 29 January 1903 meeting in Cooper Union, at which Schurman eventually spoke, was organized by the Anti-Imperialist League of New York and addressed by two of its officers, but its chairman declared that "This gathering has not been called together by any organization."[14]

Less than two months later, Fiske Warren attended a meeting of the executive committee of the American Anti-Imperialist League in Chicago and proposed that a new organization should be formed that would not be associated with the old Anti Imperialist League, would not have adherence to the Declaration of Independence as a requisite of membership (as the League's constitution required), and would seek to gain support from members of the Republican party. Immediately after this meeting, Edwin Burritt Smith, chairman of the executive committee of the American Anti-Imperialist League, circulated a proposal for a new organization along the lines Warren suggested. Jacob Gould Schurman was proposed as a potential president for the new organization. Responding to Smith's suggestion, Erving Winslow, secretary of the New England Anti-Imperialist League, issued a letter stating that he and others in both Boston and Philadelphia were "absolutely opposed" to the suggestion that a new organization be formed that would "allow our forces . . . to be annexed to the Republican Party." "If the tide is setting our way," he argued, "it is time to expect recruits and maintain our position and not to desert it which would be a sign of weakness at a critical moment."[15] In January of the following year, Ordway and Lowell nevertheless formed the Philippine Independence Committee to obtain signatures on a petition to the national conventions of the Democratic and Republican parties. The petition called for the "ultimate" independence of the Philippines "upon terms similar to those offered to Cuba."[16]

Many anti-imperialists from throughout the country gave Ordway and Lowell advice on the composition of the new organization. All agreed that it should be distanced as far as possible from the Anti-Imperialist League. "The less that appeal may appear to proceed from men already noted as anti-imperialists, the better," Charles Eliot Norton wrote to Ordway. He warned that newspapers would carefully examine the list "and if they find a number of prominent anti-imperialists upon it, they will be sure to dwell upon that fact, in order to weaken its force with the public and with the conventions." Although he was not consulted about the new organization, Edwin Burritt Smith relayed the suggestion of Samuel Bowles, editor of the *Springfield Republican*, that Ordway should "obtain fifty good names, if practicable, of persons who have not been active in our movement." Smith specifically suggested that William J. Palmer, an officer and financial supporter of the American Anti-Imperialist League, be included in this group because "he has not become known as an offensive Anti-Imperialist."[17] The final list of the Philippine Independence Committee's members included only a few individuals—like William James, William Graham Sumner, and Rufus B. Smith—who might have been considered "offensive anti-imperialists." Many had no previous connection with the Anti-Imperialist League and at least two, Jacob Gould Schurman and Bishop Henry Codman Potter, had previously distanced themselves from the movement.

As intended, the Philippine Independence Committee's petition obtained wide acceptance beyond the older anti-imperialist ranks, gaining more than five thousand signatories before being printed for submission to the national conventions of the Democratic and Republican parties. The extent to which it was viewed as conforming with government policy can be seen in General

Roeliff Brinkerhoff's response to Ordway's request for his signature. "I am not an anti-imperialist," Brinkerhoff declared when he returned his signed petition form. "On the contrary I have been in hearty accord with our government in its action in the Philippines, but I certainly am in favor of 'the ultimate independence of the islands' when they are sufficiently developed and ask for it." Brinkerhoff added, "I presume President Roosevelt himself would not object to that proposition."[18]

Many prominent anti-imperialists either refused to sign the petition because it undermined the League's call for the immediate and unconditional independence of the Philippines or were excluded because they were widely known as ardent anti-imperialists. Endorsements came from roughly half of the officers of the New York and New England branches of the Anti-Imperialist League and from about one-third each of the national American Anti-Imperialist League and its Philadelphia and Cincinnati branches. Although it received numerous endorsements in both cities, the names of only one person each from the Minneapolis and Washington, D.C. branches appear among the list of signatories. Although the "unoffensive" anti-imperialist William J. Palmer did sign the petition, his letter to Ordway criticizing its approach undoubtedly expressed the thoughts of many anti-imperialists who refused to endorse it. "I should prefer that we should get out of the Philippine Islands at once," he wrote. "When a tramp has broken into your house you do not ask him to give a pledge of 'ultimate' departure." The thoughts of other anti-imperialists were represented by the response of Judge N. H. Conklin of San Diego, California. He signed the petition but with the proviso noted that he was "for absolute independence."[19]

By November 1904, the Anti-Imperialist League's national organization had collapsed. The New England branch, which had founded the movement, was then reconstituted as a national organization with a new slate of officers. Erving Winslow, who remained the League's secretary, obviously felt that widespread support for the organization could only be obtained by implying a compromise on the issue of Philippine independence like that made by the Philippine Independence Committee. He cast his letters recruiting new officers to appeal to the Committee's members and signatories. In February 1905, when he solicited Mark Twain's support of the reorganized Anti-Imperialist League, Winslow wrote: "Our organization is a nonpartisan one and may be said to be working on lines suggested by the highest official authorities which have held up the ideal of a future relation between the United States and the Philippine Islands similar to that which exists between this country and Cuba, though we believe that this policy to be effectual should be officially declared at the earliest opportunity." Winslow included with this letter an article from the League's constitution that condemned the forcible extension of U.S. sovereignty and specified the League's objective "to work constantly for the early and complete independence of the Philippine Islands."[20] Although the League's official program remained intact in its constitution, Winslow's letter to Twain clearly implied a compromise like that made by the Philippine Independence Committee. Winslow tried unsuccessfully to recruit Jacob Gould Schurman using similar statements.[21]

In New York, Edward Ordway and Josephine Shaw Lowell were also busy reorganizing the intentionally short-lived Philippine Independence Committee. By February 1905, they had formed the Filipino Progress Association to continue its work on the goal of "ultimate" independence. The Association also proposed a program of reforms to be carried out under continued U.S. rule. Jacob Gould Schurman agreed to serve as the Association's president. Several of the Anti-Imperialist League's New York-based officers resigned at this time to join the Filipino Progress Association's slate of officers.

The Anti-Imperialist League responded to the formation of this organization and an almost simultaneous statement by Secretary of War William H. Taft that the government planned to stay in the Philippines indefinitely, by clarifying its own position on Philippine independence and by publicly dissociating itself from the Association's program. "It is no part of the policy of the League," it stated in April through *The Public*, a Chicago-based weekly, "to bind itself or to give any countenance to the policy of the Administration in the Philippine Islands, so long as the Administration contemplates and aims at securing an 'indefinite retention of the islands.' " Alluding to the Filipino Progress Association, the formation of which had been announced in *The Public* one month earlier, the statement continued by highlighting the differences between the two organizations: "In this attitude the Anti-Imperialist League is differentiated from every organization which has in view the amelioration of existing conditions, while trustfully confiding in the 'hope' expressed by President Roosevelt . . . that the Philippine Islands may be in the future 'in some such relation to the United States as Cuba now stands.' "[22]

During the next two years, this difference in the organizations' positions would lead to heated conflicts between their core officers. Although most of these were kept private between the organizations, two spilled over into public venues that affected their ability to influence policy. The first of these arose when they took opposing sides on the issue of Philippine independence. The League proposed the immediate and complete independence of the Philippines backed up by an international treaty for the neutralization of the country. The Filipino Progress Association initially agreed to support this position, and its representative was scheduled to testify before Congress along with the president of the Anti-Imperialist League. At the last minute, however, the Association reversed its position and refused to send a representative to the hearings, leaving the League unable to explain the absence without disclosing the division between the organizations.[23] Later that year, the Filipino Progress Association sent a representative to the Philippines with a letter stating that he was there as a representative of the Anti-Imperialist League (the League had close ties with many Filipino leaders but the Association was unknown there). When the League learned of this, it sent notices to the Philippines describing the differences between the organizations and warning against cooperation with the Association, which it portrayed as not being in favor of Philippine independence.[24]

The final conflict between the organizations took place in 1907, when a joint committee was formed between them to draft a plan for independence that would be acceptable to the U.S. government. The Boston-based anti-imperialists were so inflexible on the issue of absolute independence that Horace White, then president of the Filipino Progress Association, finally accepted their position for the plan but refused to have anything more to do with any of the people involved and disbanded the Association before a reply to the proposal had been received from the government.[25]

Both the Philippine Independence Committee and the Filipino Progress Association promulgated programs that were different from and represented direct challenges to those of the League. The anti-imperialists who supported the new organizations were motivated by the same desire to gain influence with the Republican party that had motivated the splits of 1900. The compromises made in 1904 and 1905 were new, however, and represented a significant break from the unity of purpose that had prevailed within the movement until then. Both the initial successes of the new organizations and the nature of the compromises they made indicate the extent to which both the Anti-Imperialist League and the movement as a whole had declined in influence by this time. If the League's strength outside of Boston had not declined significantly, there would have been little incentive to create the new organizations. If the movement as a whole was not weak, the people who organized the new groups would not have felt compelled to make such significant compromises. The League's overall chances of influencing government policy did not change significantly after this until Woodrow Wilson was elected in 1912.

THE WILSON ADMINISTRATION AND THE FILIPINO INDEPENDENCE MOVEMENT

From 1898 until Woodrow Wilson was elected president, the Anti-Imperialist League was in an oppositional position because the dominant political party supported imperialism. This led to the earlier splits within the organization as factions broke off to work in either a nonpartisan manner or explicitly to support Republican goals. With the election of a Democratic president, the League expected quick action towards Philippine independence. The Democratic party had, since 1900, included an anti-imperialist plank in its campaign platforms, and a number of prominent anti-imperialists—William Jennings Bryan, Charles Warren, Louis F. Post, and Josephus Daniels—were given influential positions within the new administration. No longer needing to appease the Republican party, the League was also able to recruit numerous members of the Democratic National Committee to fill positions in its slate of vice-presidents.[26] But new organizing by domestic proponents of imperialism, international events, and changes in the aspirations of Filipino leaders combined to inhibit progress towards independence.

The new domestic opposition to the League came from the American-Philippine Company, a corporation formed in 1912 to facilitate U.S. investments in the Philippines. While the Republicans controlled the White House, there had never been a need for national countermovements against the anti-imperialists. But after Wilson was elected, the American-Philippine Company mounted a vigorous campaign to portray the Filipinos as a primitive people who still needed U.S. control and tutelage. It was able to employ Dean C. Worcester, former secretary of the interior for the Philippines (1901–13), to campaign on its behalf. Worcester made a national speaking tour that ostensibly had an educational focus but which was funded by the American-Philippine Company and was clearly directed towards establishing the need for continued U.S. occupation of the Philippines. Henry Parker Willis, a longtime officer of the league who attended one of Worcester's lectures in 1914, described it in this way:

> It was the usual series of photographs and motion pictures of savage tribes, men engaged in barbarous practices, etc., and the athletic sports substituted under American influence. Just at the beginning, Mr. Worcester said: "Lest I be misunderstood, I wish to say that these savages are at one end of the scale while at the other are men like General Aguinaldo and Speaker Osmena"—then showed pictures of these two men. He then passed on to the savages and ended by saying that with American influence withdrawn the work of civilizing the natives would "collapse like a house of cards."[27]

This campaign by the American-Philippine Company caused the League to divert its attention once again to old claims made early in the debate about imperialism that the Filipinos were incapable of self-government. With the Philippines having already been granted a Resident Commissioner's Office in Washington, this was an issue that had not been seriously debated for nearly a decade. The campaign waged by the American-Philippine Company is more significant, however, as an indication of how the Anti-Imperialist League and its position on Philippine independence were seen at the time. The roles had been reversed, with the League now representing an "inside" organization while the corporate interests that benefitted from continued U.S. control of the Philippines were on the defensive, needing for the first time to wage a national propaganda campaign against independence.

Over the next few years, from 1912 to 1916, the League worked closely with Philippine Resident Commissioner Manuel L. Quezon as the two Jones Bills for Philippine independence were drafted and brought before Congress. But unknown to the League's leaders, Quezon and other Filipino leaders in the U.S.-sponsored Philippine Assembly were having second thoughts about gaining an independence that would threaten their own U.S.-sponsored political positions.[28] Because the Filipinos were confronted with a political climate in the Philippines that required them to make strong statements in favor of immediate independence in order to retain their offices, they could not publicly abandon their efforts for independence. Instead, while drafting the second Jones Bill, Quezon eliminated the sections from the 1912 version that promised immediate independence, telling the leaders of the Anti-Imperialist League and the opposition in the Philippines that those provisions would be impossible to pass. Quezon at this time had the confidence of the League's leaders, and no one in the Philippines had information with which to challenge him.[29] Because the version finally passed in 1916 did not contain any specific statement of when the Philippines should be granted independence, it essentially institutionalized a pledge of "ultimate" independence like that sought a decade earlier by the Philippine Independence Committee and the Filipino Progress Association. Shortly after passage of the Jones Bill, U.S. entrance into World War I impeded any further progress toward Philippine independence.

After the war, the Anti-Imperialist League grew impatient waiting for the Filipinos to organize a mission to the United States to petition Congress for independence and began to doubt the sincerity of their motives. In 1918 Erving Winslow and Fiske Warren began to correspond with their other contacts in the Philippines to ascertain the intentions of the majority party that Quezon represented. When the independence mission finally arrived, the League learned that it had been instructed to request both independence and additional U.S. economic investments in the Philippines, and that the request for investments was to take equal precedence with the request for independence.[30] The League's officers conferred by mail about what position to take in regard to the independence mission. None were happy with the course the mission had taken and Winslow, especially, thought it represented a great betrayal of the cause. In an unpublished draft of a report to the League, he criticized the mission for coming so late that its requests could only be dealt with by a new Republican administration that was hostile to independence and for expecting to receive both independence and continued economic investments. Winslow represented the Filipino politicians as having taken a volte-face in the struggle for independence. His bitterness and disillusionment were especially evident in the concluding paragraph, in which he claimed that "few men who 'run things' have been so successful 'to have their cake, and to eat it!' as the Filipino patriot 'independence shouter' so far. But are their people 'at home' satisfied with the programme? Are there no worthy heritors of the patriots of 1898? Is this the end?"[31]

Winslow's views were shared by the majority of the League's executive committee. Although some of them, like Winslow and Warren, clearly recognized that the position taken by the independence mission was inconsistent with the demands of the Filipino people as a whole for independence, they were not in a position to argue for independence if the Filipino leadership they had supported for more than a decade refused to ask for it. "It would be devil's work," Winslow wrote to Herbert Welsh the following year, "to stir up if we could the old animosities of the war for independence of 1898–1899 to demand actual immediate independence not now wanted" by the Filipino leaders themselves.[32] The League's annual meeting of November 1920 would prove to be its last. The organization was dissolved after further correspondence and discussions among the executive committee the following year.

The events of 1912 to 1921 are interesting at several levels. First, the election of a Democratic president inspired the first significant countermovement by supporters of imperialism. This is a clear indication of a shift in political conditions leading to both increased influence and a new opposition. But the broader political situation, including the war in Europe, led to increased tensions between the United States and neighboring countries throughout Central America and the Caribbean and to a postponement of any concrete action on Philippine independence until after the war. The League was effectively undermined after the war by the Filipino elite whose own priorities had shifted from demanding immediate independence to not wanting to do anything that would jeopardize continued U.S. investments. The League was finally dissolved only after its leadership gave up on its longstanding alliance with the Filipinos.

The events that led to the dissolution of the League also shed light on why it focused so much of its attention on the Philippines, apparently ignoring Guam altogether and giving relatively little attention to Cuba and Puerto Rico. In fact, the League did not ignore Cuba or Puerto Rico. In March 1901, while the Platt Amendment was being debated in the U.S. Senate, it held a mass meeting in Boston to denounce both the amendment and the continuing warfare in the Philippines. The following month, Erving Winslow contacted Cuban representatives to offer the League's assistance in defeating the U.S. government's plan to force the Cuban Constitutional Convention to accept the Platt Amendment. He received warm responses, but the representatives to the convention thought it would be unwise to associate themselves with the League and declined its offer of assistance.[33] The League's opposition to the limited independence imposed upon Cuba never changed, but it shifted its focus to the Philippines, where warfare continued and where they were able to develop close ties with the leaders of the Philippine Revolution. When the Philippine Independence Mission arrived in 1919, the League's leadership compared its dual goals of independence and economic investments with the compromises Cuban politicians had made when they accepted the Platt Amendment. "If they want a Cuban protectorate," Moorfield Storey wrote in a letter assessing the Independence Mission, "I should not be disposed to help them."[34] The League learned from the Cuban experience and it became a touchstone representing the opposite of what it wanted to achieve in the Philippines.

CONCLUSION

The history of the anti-imperialist movement from 1898 to 1921 highlights both the obstacles faced by oppositional movements trying to change foreign policy and the ways those obstacles have tended to marginalize the movements, reducing their political influence and ability to mobilize when they have no clear opportunities to change a policy. In its first few years, from 1898 through most of 1900, the League had at least two clear opportunities to stop or reverse the policy of imperialism—the requirement of Senate ratification of the Treaty of Paris and the presidential election of 1900. During those years its strength was at its height, and it would never be able to gain the same degree of mass mobilization or influence afterward. That the League had such limited means of reversing the policy after 1900 has to be seen as a product of political institutions within the United States. Once the treaty had been ratified and McKinley was reelected, the League had no other clear opportunity to reverse the policy until the next presidential election. By that time, however, the war had already been declared over (though warfare continued through 1913), both the League and the movement as a whole had been effectively reduced in influence, and the United States had gained firm control over its new colonies. The League could assert that imperialism was the "paramount issue" of the presidential election of 1900, but it was never able to elevate the issue to that stature again.

The individual anti-imperialists who actually made decisions about the direction the movement should take responded to changes in the political situation in different ways depending on how severely weakened they thought the movement was at different times. In 1900, the National Association of Anti-Imperialist Clubs used the League's endorsement of Bryan to mount its own campaign against imperialism but did not challenge the Anti-Imperialist League's leadership of the movement. After the election, people who believed the League could no longer function as an effective opponent of imperialism formed the Liberty Leagues and the Philippine Information Society, but they did not directly challenge the League's program. That was left to the Philippine Independence Committee and the Filipino Progress Association, formed in 1904 and 1905 respectively. With the Anti-Imperialist League's offices in New York and Chicago isolated, and its local organizations in Cincinnati and Minneapolis already disbanded, the organizers of the Philippine Independence Committee and the Filipino Progress Association made significant compromises that were not considered by the anti-imperialists several years earlier. Theirs was, in effect, a position akin to "if you can't beat 'em, join 'em." Like the earlier splits, it was motivated by assessments of the likelihood of gaining influence with the dominant Republican party, but it also reflected the diminished power of the movement and its inability to make imperialism a major issue in the 1904 presidential campaign. In both 1900 and 1904–1905, there was clearly an interaction between changes in the political situation and the assessments made by individual organizers of the potential for successful anti-imperialist organizing. Those assessments led to the formation of the new organizations.

The nature of the changes that took place after 1912 show both the influence of the shift from Republican to Democratic party ascendancy and the nature of the obstacles faced by an oppositional movement when confronting a well-established policy. Although it had significantly more access to government circles and a comparatively friendly politician in the White House, the League was confronted by both domestic groups with significant financial interests in the Philippines and by a Filipino elite that had come to enjoy its position within the U.S.-controlled Philippine Assembly.

Although the many divisions within the movement can be attributed to changes in political contexts and the responses to them by individual activists, those factors do not explain why the Anti-Imperialist League was able to keep going for more than two decades through periods of both extreme isolation and considerable influence. For that, the League's Boston leadership, including Moorfield Storey, Erving Winslow, Fiske Warren, Albert S. Parsons, and David Green Haskins, must be given credit. The core leadership in Boston included the first organized opponents of imperialism, and it remained relatively stable throughout the League's history. Its leaders were undoubtedly among the staunchest and most principled anti-imperialists of the time and were both unwilling to make significant compromises to gain short-term political influence and committed enough to endure long periods of organizational decline. None of the rival organizations formed during these years lasted more than three years, and all were long gone before the League regained some of its earlier influence with Wilson's election in 1912. There is undoubtedly a range of possible responses to broad political changes that different individuals can make. Those, along with the changes in the political environment, shaped the movement's prospects for success.

The demise of the Anti-Imperialist League in 1921 marked the end of an era within the history of the anti-imperialist social movement sector and opened opportunities for new organizations to be formed and new tactics to be deployed. From 1921 to the late 1930s, organizations such as the Haiti-Santo Domingo Independence Committee, the American Fund for Public Service Committee on American Imperialism, the All-America Anti-Imperialist League, and the Fair Play for Puerto Rico Committee were formed within the anti-imperialist social movement sector previously dominated by the Anti-Imperialist League.[35] Although they represented a new generation of anti-imperialist organizations, all were formed by or included people who had previously served as officers of the Anti-Imperialist League.[36] The Women's International League for Peace and Freedom, whose leadership included former League vice-presidents Jane Addams, Alice Thatcher Post, and Lucia Ames Mead, also focused much of its attention on imperialism during the 1920s.[37] Educational and legislative initiatives were still the primary organizing tools of the less radical organizations, but the All-America Anti-Imperialist League founded by the Workers (Communist) party in 1925 introduced mass public demonstrations, civil disobedience, and other disruptive tactics most commonly associated with social movement organizations that operate at a distance from political power. Such tactics were new within this social movement sector in the 1920s but would be repeated by later organizations such as the Fair Play for Cuba Committee of the early 1960s, opponents of the war in Vietnam, and the solidarity organizations formed in the 1970s and 1980s. Beyond borrowed tactics and shared ideological roots in the Declaration of Independence's assertion of both individual human rights and the collective right to self-determination, these later organizations also share the earlier anti-imperialist organizations' marginalization within U.S. politics.

NOTES

1. "The Pesky Anti-Imperialist," *New York Evening Post*, 3 May 1902, p. 4. This editorial can also be found, as reprinted in *The Nation* 74 (18 May 1902): 360–361, in Roger J. Bresnahan, ed., *In Time of Hesitation: American Anti-Imperialists and the Philippine-American War* (Quezon City: New Day Publishers, 1981), 154–156. The references to specific years are to the ratification of the Treaty of Paris in 1899, the presidential election of 1900, and the capture of Philippine independence leader General Emilio Aguinaldo in 1901.

2. For examples of these arguments, see Fred H. Harrington, "The Anti-Imperialist Movement in the United States, 1898–1900," *Mississippi Valley Historical Review* 22 (September 1935): 211–30; Robert L. Beisner, *Twelve against Empire: The Anti-Imperialists, 1898–1900* (1968; Chicago: University of Chicago Press, 1985); Richard E. Welch, *Response to Imperialism: The United States and the Philippine-American War, 1899–1902* (Chapel Hill: University of North Carolina Press, 1979); and E. Berkeley Tompkins, *Anti-Imperialism in the United States: The Great Debate, 1890–1920* (Philadelphia: University of Pennsylvania Press, 1970).

3. William Gamson, *The Strategy of Social Protest* (Belmont, Calif.: Wadsworth Publishing, 1990), 17.

4. The Anti-Imperialist League was not the first solidarity organization formed in the United States. The Society of American Friends of Russian Freedom was formed in 1891, and a similar society, Friends of Armenia, was created a few years later. Both organizations included people who would later become prominent anti-imperialists. The distinction made here in crediting the Anti-Imperialist League as the first organization formed in the anti-imperialist social movement sector is that it was formed specifically to oppose U.S. foreign policy while the other organizations were critical of the policies of other governments. Anti-imperialist organizations have also historically had strained relations with many peace movement organizations, from the Lake Mohonk Conference on International Arbitration's exclusion of discussion of imperialism in 1899 to the Nuclear Freeze movement's refusal to ally itself with Central America solidarity organizations in the early 1980s. Anti-imperialists are not necessarily opposed to war while advocates of peace are not necessarily committed to supporting the right to self-determination.

5. Among the few exceptions are Merle Curti, *Peace or War: The American Struggle, 1636–1936* (New York: W. W. Norton, 1936), 182–183, which argues that the League "applied all that they said regarding the Philippines to our imperialism in the Caribbean"; and Julius W. Pratt, *America's Colonial Experiment: How the United States Gained, Governed, and in Part Gave away a Colonial Empire* (New York: Prentice-Hall, 1950), 312, which notes that in the early 1920s, "though the Anti-Imperialist League might be moribund, there was no lack of anti-imperialists."

6. Anti-Imperialist League, *Address to the People of the United States* (Boston: Anti-Imperialist League, 19 November 1898).

7. Daniel B. Schirmer, *Republic or Empire: American Opposition to the Philippine-American War* (Cambridge, Mass.: Schenkman, 1972), 130.

8. American Anti-Imperialist League, "Platform of the American Anti-Imperialist League," in Carl Schurz, *The Policy of Imperialism*, Liberty Tract No. 4 (Chicago: American Anti-Imperialist League, 1899), inside front cover.

9. C. C. Hughes to Carl Schurz, 20 November 1900, Carl Schurz Papers, Library of Congress. For reactions to Hearst's move by anti-imperialists in New York, see "Repudiate Liberty League," *New York Times*, 11 December 1900, p. 7; "Mr. Hughes Explains," *New York Times*, 12 December 1900, p. 10; "Names Used without Authorization," *New York Times*, 19 December 1900, p. 16.

10. Fiske Warren, Typescript of Diary of Travels in the Philippines, 1901–1902, Joseph Ralston Hayden Papers, Michigan Historical Collections, Bentley Historical Library, University of Michigan, Ann Arbor. On Warren's activities, see also Martin Green, *The Mount Vernon Street Warrens: A Boston Story, 1860–1910* (New York: Charles Scribner's Sons, 1989), 153–158; and Jim Zwick, "The Anti-Imperialist League and the Origins of Filipino-American Oppositional Solidarity," *Amerasia Journal* 24 (Summer 1998): 69, 72–76, 79.

11. Fiske Warren to Carl Schurz, 23 November 1900, Schurz Papers.

12. Elizabeth Evans to Carl Schurz, 9 April 1901, Schurz Papers. The Philippine Information Society published Sixto Lopez to the American People (1900); a ten-volume series of pamphlets called *The Story of the Filipinos* (1900); a revised and expanded version of the series, *Facts about the Filipinos* (1900–1901); and two volumes of a monthly journal, *The Philippine Review* (1901–1902).

13. As the following discussion will show, Schurman was a particular target of league recruitment efforts during this period. On 20 January 1902, he spoke before

the Massachusetts Reform Club in favor of "the ultimate goal of independence for the Philippines." His speech received considerable national attention and raised the anti-imperialists' hopes of formally recruiting him to their cause. See "Independence / Pres. Schurman Speaks in Behalf of Filipinos," *Boston Globe*, 21 January 1902, p. 5; and Jacob G. Schurman, *Philippine Fundamentals* (New York: Anti-Imperialist League of New York, 1902).

14. "Discussion on Affairs in the Philippines," *New York Times*, 30 January 1903, p. 2. See also J. G. Schurman to J. S. Lowell, 26 December 1902, Edward Ordway Papers, Rare Books and Manuscripts Division, New York Public Library, Astor, Lenox and Tilden Foundation; E. W. Ordway to E. M. Shepard, 9 January 1903, Edward Morse Shepard Papers, Rare Books and Manuscripts Library, Columbia University; and J. S. Lowell to J. G. Schurman, 30 January 1903, Jacob Gould Schurman Papers, Rare Book and Manuscript Collections, Kroch Library, Cornell University.

15. Erving Winslow to Dear Sir, 14 March 1903, Ordway Papers.

16. Philippine Independence Committee, *Address and Petition with List of Signatures to the Republican and Democratic National Conventions*, Chicago and St. Louis (New York: Philippine Independence Committee, 1904), 4.

17. Carl Schurz to E. W. Ordway, 24 November 1903, Ordway Papers; and E. B. Smith to Charles Eliot Norton, 28 January 1904, Ordway Papers.

18. Roeliff Brinkerhoff to E. W. Ordway, 27 January 1904, Ordway Papers.

19. William J. Palmer to E. W. Ordway, 30 January 1904, Ordway Papers; and Philippine Independence Committee, Address and Petition, 5.

20. Erving Winslow to Mark Twain [Samuel Clemens], 21 February 1905, Mark Twain Papers, The Bancroft Library, University of California, Berkeley. Twain was an outspoken vice-president of the Anti-Imperialist League of New York from 1901 until its formal dissolution in 1905, and of the national Anti-Imperialist League from 1905 until his death in 1910.

21. See Erving Winslow to Jacob Gould Schurman, 17 November 1904; J. G. Schurman to Erving Winslow, 26 November 1904; and Erving Winslow to J. G. Schurman, 29 November 1904, all in the Schurman Papers.

22. *The Public* 8 (15 April 1905): 21. For the announcement about the Filipino Progress Association, see *The Public* 7 (18 March 1905): 794. See also "To Hold the Philippines," Boston Transcript, 17 March 1905, p. 4; and *Philippine Independence: Discussion of the Hon. W. H. Taft's Letter*, March 16, 1905 (Boston: Anti-Imperialist League, [1905]).

23. Erving Winslow to Edward Ordway, 17 March 1906 and 11 April 1906, Ordway Papers.

24. Erving Winslow to Moorfield Storey, 20 September 1906, Moorfield Storey Papers, Library of Congress.

25. Correspondence of Horace White and Edward Ordway, April 1907 to February 1908, Ordway Papers; Correspondence of Moorfield Storey, Charles W. Eliot, and Erving Winslow, April–November 1907, in the Storey Papers, Library of Congress and Massachusetts Historical Society.

26. The changes over time in the composition of the League's national slate of officers deserve more attention than they have received. Although a number of its officers remained throughout its history, there was considerable turnover. The effort to recruit prominent Democrats after Wilson's election produced a significant change in the organization's political composition that has relevancy for studies of later for-

eign policy debates. In particular, many of the Democrats who have typically been labeled "isolationist" for their positions on foreign policy issues in the 1920s and 1930s served as officers of the Anti-Imperialist League from 1912 to 1921. Robert David Johnson, *The Peace Progressives and American Foreign Relations* (Cambridge: Harvard University Press, 1995) provides a correction of earlier studies of senate opposition to foreign interventions in the 1920s by identifying it as an anti-imperialist position, but he does not adequately recognize its roots in the Anti-Imperialist League.

27. Henry Parker Willis to Moorfield Storey, 2 January 1914, Storey Papers, Massachusetts Historical Society. See also Oswald Garrison Villard to Moorfield Storey, 30 December 1913, Oswald Garrison Villard Papers, Houghton Library, Harvard University; and "Dean C. Worcester's Job/In Connection with the American-Philippine Company," *New York Evening Post*, 21 January 1914, pp. 1–2.

28. The Philippine Assembly was the legislative body created in the Philippines in 1907 by the U.S. colonial government.

29. The best sources on the interaction among the contending parties in the Philippines and Quezon's relations with the Anti-Imperialist League are Peter W. Stanley, *A Nation in the Making: The Philippines and the United States, 1899–1921* (Cambridge: Harvard University Press, 1974), 212–25; Rolando M. Gripaldo, "The Quezon-Winslow Correspondence: A Friendship Turned Sour," *Philippine Studies* 32 (1984): 129–162; and Reynaldo C. Ileto, "Orators and the Crowd: Philippine Independence Politics, 1910–1914," in Peter W. Stanley, ed., *Reappraising an Empire: New Perspectives on Philippine-American History* (Cambridge: Harvard University Press, 1984), 85–113.

30. James L. Slayden to Erving Winslow, 12 November 1918, Winslow Papers, University of Michigan. The same collection contains most of the other correspondence on this period referred to in this section.

31. Untitled and undated draft, Winslow Papers, University of Michigan.

32. Winslow to Herbert Welsh, 15 December 1920, Herbert Welsh Papers, Historical Society of Pennsylvania, Philadelphia. The League's long relationship with the Filipino independence movement and the split that led to the League's demise are described in more detail in Zwick, "The Anti-Imperialist League and the Origins of Filipino-American Oppositional Solidarity," 65–85.

33. See the correspondence quoted in Erving Winslow, "The Anti-Imperialist Faith," *North American Review* 175 (December 1902): 816–18. Additional assessments of the Cuban representatives to the convention can be found in Winslow's correspondence with W. A. Croffut of the Washington Anti-Imperialist League, 25 April 1901, 30 April 1901, 2 May 1901, and 27 June 1901, all in the William Augustus Croffut Papers, Library of Congress. After this, the League's efforts regarding both Cuba and Puerto Rico primarily focused on tariff reform and humanitarian issues like famine relief.

34. Moorfield Storey to Erving Winslow, 26 May 1919, Winslow Papers, University of Michigan.

35. Information about the anti-imperialist organizations discussed in this paragraph is drawn primarily from the Storey Papers, Library of Congress; Villard Papers; *New York Times* accounts of the activities of the All-America Anti-Imperialist League; Charles Shipman, *It Had to Be Revolution: Memoirs of an American Radical* (Ithaca: Cornell University Press, 1993), 153–69; Elizabeth Dilling, *The Red Network: A*

"Who's Who" and *Handbook of Radicalism for Patriots* (Chicago: published by the author, 1935), 102–4, 168; Johnson, *Peace Progressives*; and Van Gosse, *Where the Boys Are: Cuba, Cold War America and the Making of a New Left* (London: Verso, 1993), 13–34.

36. Some of the personal and symbolic continuities can be seen by looking briefly at the career and influence of Oswald Garrison Villard. Villard was an organizer of the Third Party Movement in 1900 and an officer of the Anti-Imperialist League for more than ten years. In the early 1920s, he became one of the primary organizers of the Haiti-Santo Domingo Independence Society and the American Fund for Public Service Committee on American Imperialism. The latter organization provided editorial direction and financial support for an important series of books on economic imperialism that began with Scott Nearing and Joseph Freeman's *Dollar Diplomacy* (New York: The Viking Press, 1925). In the late 1930s, Villard chaired the Fair Play for Puerto Rico Committee created by the American Civil Liberties Union. In 1928, as owner and editor of *The Nation*, Villard sent Carleton Beals to find and interview General Augusto Sandino in the mountains of Nicaragua during the U.S. intervention there. That history was recognized decades later when Beals was chosen to cochair the Fair Play for Cuba Committee in 1960. In 1964 Ernest Gruening, who had worked on Haitian issues under Villard as a young journalist at *The Nation* in the 1920s, was one of only two U.S. senators who voted against the Tonkin Gulf Resolution that escalated U.S. military involvement in Vietnam. Gruening was a frequent speaker at peace marches and campus teach-ins about the war until his death in 1974. For a more thorough examination of continuities between the Anti-Imperialist League and the later anti-imperialist organizations, see my essay, "Oswald Garrison Villard and American Anti-Imperialism: A Biographical Excursion from 1900 to the 1960s," http://www.boondocksnet.com/ail/villard.html, in Jim Zwick, ed., *Anti-Imperialism in the United States, 1898–1935*, http://www.boondocksnet.com/ail98-35.html (29 April 2000).

37. See Carrie A. Foster, *The Women and the Warriors: The U.S. Section of the Women's International League for Peace and Freedom, 1915–1946* (Syracuse, N.Y.: Syracuse University Press, 1995), 58–73.

Conclusions

Virginia M. Bouvier

What the authors in this volume suggest is that one hundred years ago, the concept of nation was evolving. Each nation contained within it pluralities that make it difficult to speak of a single national perspective in the period surrounding the War of 1898 and the Philippine-American War. In the United States, in Spain, in Cuba, in Puerto Rico, in the Philippines, and in Guam, multiple struggles were under way to define national identities. Among the latter countries, each nation was also seeking to define its relationship to America and the Americas. These struggles continue today.

In the dialogue established between the authors of the individual chapters of this book, a number of themes emerge that suggest new avenues for research and that shed light on the challenges unfolding in the next century. We find first of all that concepts such as America, Monroeism (the interpretation or application of the Monroe Doctrine), manhood, nationalism, and human rights are in fact highly unstable and contingent upon the particulars of place and time for their meaning. Several of the authors thus underscore the importance of analyzing discourse within the particular political and historical context from which it issued.

Both Langley and Hilton discuss the Monroe Doctrine and its interpretations as a function of domestic discourses. Langley notes the variations in U.S. interpretations of the Monroe Doctrine over time and describes how the doctrine moved from one that initially protected the newly established Latin American republics from European intervention to one that supported U.S. hegemony in the Western Hemisphere.[1] In Langley's view, U.S.-Latin American relations and, one presumes, the discourse that flows from those relations have historically been related to domestic political considerations. Hilton, for her part, analyzes the debates among Spanish politicians across the political spectrum and concurs with Langley that political discourse on the colonial crisis must be understood within the context of national politics. Hilton focuses particularly on the last five years of the nineteenth century, when similarities and differences in approaches to the Monroe Doctrine reflected largely domestic political agendas relating to the war and, we might add in hindsight, to Spain's slipping prestige in a new world order. In both Spain and Europe, Hilton notes, the U.S. intervention in the Cuban-Spanish War was seen as a function of the Monroe Doctrine; in the United States, the Monroe Doctrine was barely mentioned. Within Spain, the Monroe Doctrine provided the spark that ignited the fuel of national sovereignty, non-intervention, and international law and was used to set aflame the Spanish population's desire for war. Likewise, the Monroe Doctrine also provided the flint for protesting the war on human rights grounds. None of the essayists in this volume address the shifting understandings of the Monroe Doctrine within Latin America itself, the use of rhetorical strategies by Latin American political leaders to counter the imperial uses of the doctrine, or the invocation of human rights as part of the U.S. national discourse to rally the population to war. Such perspectives merit further investigation.

The authors in this volume diverge in the weight they give to international, national, regional, or local factors. Where Langley contends that regional attitudes were key obstacles to partnership with Latin America one century ago, and that local circumstances are becoming increasingly important as economic globalization deepens at the beginning of the twenty-first century, both Louis A. Pérez, Jr. and Lillian Guerra give greater weight to global factors. They underscore the difficulties of defining Cuban nationalism without first situating Cuba within a hemispheric, if not global, context. Guerra offers a vision of the Cuban émigré community living in the United States as one whose cultural values and aspirations often had more in common with its U.S. counterparts than with its revolutionary allies in Cuba. Both Guerra and Pérez concur that the U.S. cultural influence on Cubans living on the island and on the mainland was substantial. Guerra attributes this influence to the shared values acquired in the course of living in the United States. Pérez suggests that it was the U.S. economic, military, political, and social penetration of the island that altered Cuban mores, lifestyles, and yearnings. Pérez, on the one hand, argues that the United States reconfigured Cuban institutions to accommodate U.S. interests and that there was a realigning of social relationships that would "guarantee that success would come easiest to those most conversant with and adept at North American ways." Guerra argues, on the other hand, that by defining the Cuban nation to include the émigré community more explicitly, one could conclude that the Cuban émigré imperialist nationalists were in fact ultimately successful in securing U.S. intervention and a closer relationship with the United States. Guerra's essay contends that nationalist discourses themselves are multiple and that claims to represent the nation must be analyzed with this multiplicity in mind. Taken together, the chapters by Guerra and Pérez underscore the fundamental conflicts over defining the Cuban nation, and the persisting schisms between and within Cubans on the island and the Cuban émigré community in the United States. Such tensions gained national attention in the recent debates about the fate of six-year-old Elián González and his "right" to remain with his Cuban family in Florida or to return to his family in Cuba.

Francisco A. Scarano's chapter raises similar questions about Puerto Rican "national" identity, about who speaks for the Puerto Rican people, and about how the relationship of Puerto Ricans to the U.S. mainland and the island of Puerto Rico will be defined in the twenty-first century. In Puerto Rico, Scarano documents among the legacies of the war the development of nationalist discourses in opposition to U.S. rule, the marginalization of peasant majorities, and the displacement of workers. As in Cuba, he notes the emergence in Puerto Rico of a middle class "defined by consumer values and orientations that mimic those of its counterpart in the North." He analyzes the nature and timing of U.S. intervention in Puerto Rico and the extent to which representatives of the United States and local actors have "negotiated the terms of the relationship; albeit from unequal positions of power." Scarano underscores that local collaboration was critical during and after the war in establishing the contours of Puerto Rico's ensuing relationship with the United States and in laying out the justification for it. He notes that the political economy of Puerto Rico was similar to that of Cuba, but without the devastation of a war. In both cases, we see the U.S. empire easily assumed the highly centralized role of the colonial Spanish state.

The chapters on the Cuban and Puerto Rican cases raise a series of questions regarding the legacies of the war on U.S. culture and U.S. attitudes toward Cubans and Puerto Ricans. To what extent did the presence and incorporation of these groups into the U.S. sphere of influence contribute to the redefining of the U.S. nation? And what was the role of the War of 1898 in this process of what the Cuban ethnologist Fernando Ortiz might have described as "transculturation"?[2] Analysis of such themes suggests that the legacies of the War of 1898 have had profound effects on the relationship between dominant U.S. populations and Hispanic populations both within and outside of the shifting U.S. borders.[3] A study of the debates regarding U.S. intervention in the Asian Pacific also has much to tell us about American identities one hundred years ago.

Jim Zwick's chapter speaks to the multiple nationalist discourses both in the Philippines and in the United States. He discusses how the Filipino leadership, dependent on U.S. political support and interested in continued U.S. investments, retreated from a position favoring full independence demanded by other Filipino nationalists. Zwick documents the emergence of the Anti-Imperialist League, a group that articulated a different vision for the U.S. nation than that expressed by the jingoes of the time. He does not simply pit the imperialists against the anti-imperialists, however, but explores the divisions among the anti-imperialists and their allies over issues of strategy. Zwick notes, for example, that during and after the presidential campaign of 1904–5, divisions among the anti-imperialists were related to conflicting assessments of their potential to influence Republican policy. By endorsing the losing presidential candidate, the League effectively lost political clout. Subsequent efforts to curry favor with the Roosevelt administration resulted in compromises that were unacceptable to sectors of the League. Zwick's analysis of the goals, strategies, and divisions of anti-imperialists at the end of the nineteenth and beginning of the twentieth century have relevance to the debates and operations of an increasingly vibrant nongovernmental sector seeking to wield influence in the foreign policy arena of U.S. politics today.

The authors of this volume concur that the creation of images was important in setting the stage for intervention and its outcomes. Images of the war, often varying widely by nationality and political stripe, convey the essence of nationalistic fervor and reveal starkly the vast gulfs between diverse national perceptions of realities. Kristin Hoganson discusses the ways that gendered images were critical in the debates to go to war. Both Virginia M. Bouvier and Jim Zwick document ideologically motivated projects to promote images of Cubans, Puerto Ricans, and Filipinos (and inhabitants of Hawaii and Guam as well) as primitive people in need of U.S. control and tutelage. Such images nourished a domestic political agenda that supported the exclusion of Philippine and Cuban nationals from the negotiations for peace and, at least until 1902, from direct participation in governing the postwar societies. These images also fostered a mythic understanding of the war which sanctioned a benevolent role for the United States in "liberating" the oppressed Spanish colonies, and promoted U.S. national myths of social progress and democratic values.

Some of these images were clearly related to gender ideologies and concepts of honor. Several of the authors address the myriad ways that honor acted as a prism for national identity. Hoganson's chapter most explicitly focuses on the ways that national honor (linked to gendered notions of chivalry) was a motivating force in the ideological struggle among U.S. policymakers. Her study underscores the power of honor as an idiom that explains a vast range of contradictory causes generally cited as motivations for engagement in the War of 1898 and the Philippine-American War. In the United States, Hoganson argues, honor was seen as an attribute of male courage, bravery, liberty, glory, and manhood. Political discourse relied heavily on such concepts of honor and underscored the applicability of individual standards of honor to the nation. Hoganson's analysis of the discourse in the U.S. congressional debates documents the emergence of new standards of passionate manhood, exalted aggression, toughness, and physical prowess. These new standards conflicted with the notions of self-denial, the tragic hero, the pursuit of liberty, and other ideals of the "standard of Victorian-age masculinity" expressed, as Guerra notes in her essay, in the persona of José Martí.

The rhetorical currency of honor and gender ideologies was not limited to U.S. jingoes eager for war. We see from Hilton's chapter that Spanish politicians across the political spectrum also relied on gendered images and concepts of honor to rouse the Spanish population to war. Bouvier suggests that cartoonist Charles Nelan borrowed from the ideologies about honor and manhood with a different purpose—he portrayed notions of honor and manhood as antiquated symbols of a Spanish empire in decline. The vocabulary of honor, in the cartoonist's mind, belonged more to Spanish rhetorical images than to the U.S. discursive repertoire. It merits pointing out here that Nelan also declined to use the more provocative images used by cartoonists of other newspapers that represented Cuba as the damsel in distress to stir up jingoistic fervor. Nelan studiously avoided the images that seemed most likely to fan the desire to go to war and he poked fun at the discourse of honor via his criticisms of Spanish honor. Guerra suggests that Cuban émigrés engaged in their own mythmaking in their efforts to garner U.S. support for their cause, but we do not have a sense of the degree to which codes of honor or gender formed part of their vocabulary. The role of gender in image-making and the war seems a particularly rich field for future scholarship. Yet to be analyzed is the extent to which the anti-imperialists, Cubans, Puerto Ricans, Filipinos, and other non-U.S. actors engaged in the conflict also manipulated the discourse of honor as a standard for individual and national behavior and how these codes differed across time, place, and region.

On another front, Guerra and Hoganson make a valuable contribution in beginning to elucidate the role of women in the struggle to define a more inclusive Cuban and U.S. nation. Guerra documents the role of elite Cuban émigré women in contributing to the imperialist-nationalist construction of *Cuba Libre*, and incidentally, the role of a few Cuban women within Cuba.[4] Hoganson asserts that middle-class U.S. women were active in anti-interventionism in the United States, but that the framing of the debates over issues of honor left relatively little room for women to participate on the side of the jingoes. Both of these chapters open wide the doors for further exploration of the roles of U.S. women (which might be further articulated by race and class) and their relationship to the foreign policy debates and to domestic and international nongovernmental organizations. Likewise, Scarano's note that workers, blacks, and women were among the supporters of the U.S. annexation of Puerto Rico, in part because they anticipated the promise of greater legal rights and protections than those that they experienced under Spanish rule, is indicative of the importance of examining factors related to race and ethnicity, gender, and class, not only among the interventionists, but also among those whose nations come into the orbit of colonial and neocolonial powers.

The authors of this volume (particularly Zwick and Guerra) speak powerfully to the sometimes-uneasy relationship between émigrés, nationals, internationalists, and policymakers, and the particular difficulties inherent in transnational relationships based on loosely defined or multiple "national interests." They raise important questions about representation, legitimacy, and nationalism. They show how, in the context of multiple nationalisms, a single individual or group of individuals can wield tremendous power to influence the shape of national identities. Finally, several of the authors address the complexities of inter-American visions of the "other." Langley, Guerra, Pérez, and Scarano underscore the paradox of concurrent Latin American hostility toward U.S. governmental practices that undermine self-determination and identification with U.S. cultural preferences and political values. Such attitudes may be traced to the War of 1898.

The War of 1898 marked both the culmination and the initiation of a series of ideological battles within the United States to define America, as diverse groups lay claim to the rights, protections, and "imagined community" that America offered.[5] The formation of empire had its repercussions in every sphere of a broader American identity. As the literary scholar Edward Said reminds us, "Partly because of empire, all cultures are involved in one another; none is single and pure, all are hybrid, heterogeneous, extraordinarily differentiated, and unmonolothic."[6] The authors of this book address this relationship between culture and empire. They testify to the plurality of voices and viewpoints within and between nations in relationship to the U.S. interventions in the Spanish-Cuban and Philippine-American wars. These multiple perspectives of the past continue to serve as the palimpsest upon which current relations between and within the Americas are inscribed.

NOTES

1. For discussions of the relationship between Cuban culture in Cuba and in the United States, see Louis A. Pérez, Jr., *On Becoming Cuban: Identity, Nationality, and Culture* (Chapel Hill: University of North Carolina Press, 1999); and Gustav Pérez Firmat, *Life on the Hyphen: The Cuban-American Way* (Austin: University of Texas Press, 1994).

2. See his discussion of the term in Fernando Ortiz, "El fenómeno social de la transculturación y su importancia en Cuba," *Revista Bimestre Cubana* 46, no. 2 (1940): 273–78.

3. See Edna Acosta-Belén and Carlos E. Santiago, "Merging Borders: The Remapping of America," *The Latino Review of Books* 1, no. 1 (spring 1995).

4. On this topic see Raquel Vinat de la Mata, "A cien años de una experiencia: Participación femenina en la lucha independentista cubana, 1895–1898," in Manuel

López Díaz, comp., *Cuba: La guerra de 1898* (San José, Costa Rica: FLACSO and SSRC, 1999), 151–70.

5. On the idea of "imagined communities," see Benedict R. Anderson, *Imagined Communities: Reflections on the Origin and Spread of Nationalism* (New York: Verso, 1991).

6. Edward W. Said, *Culture and Imperialism* (New York: Vintage Books, 1994), xxv.

Bibliographic Essay

The centennial of the War of 1898, which effectively ended Spanish colonial rule in the Americas, like the quincentennial of Columbus's "discovery," which initiated the Spanish colonial era in America in 1992, produced a tremendous amount of new scholarship. This annotated bibliography is meant to supplement the notes given at the end of each chapter with mention of some of the conferences, websites, film productions, books, special issues of scholarly journals, articles, multiauthored volumes of essays, and published conference proceedings that have become available in the years surrounding the centennial. It aims to assist both the general reader and the specialist by identifying some of the key publications produced in the 1990s and situating them within the current historiographical debates. I also include references to classic works on particular themes, including U.S.-Latin American relations, the war and the role of McKinley and Roosevelt, diplomacy, economic and military aspects of the war, the debates on imperialism, and the role of the press and public opinion. A useful guide to the literature is *Bibliografías de Historia de España, número 8: La crisis del 98* (Madrid: Consejo Superior de Investigaciones Científicas, CINDOC, 1998). For works in English prior to 1990, readers are urged to consult Anne Cipriano Venzon, *The Spanish-American War: An Annotated Bibliography* (New York: Garland, 1990); for earlier references in Spanish, see Araceli García-Carranza, *Bibliografía de la guerra de independencia (1895–1898)* (Havana: Editorial Orbe, 1976). Joseph Smith, "The 'Splendid Little War' of 1898: A Reappraisal," *History* [Great Britain] 80, no. 258 (1995): 22–37; Thomas G. Paterson, "United States Intervention in Cuba, 1898:

Interpretations of the Spanish-American-Cuban-Filipino War," *History Teacher* 29, no. 3 (1996): 341–61; and Louis A. Pérez, Jr., "1898 and Beyond: Historiographical Variations on War and Empire," *Pacific Historical Review* 65, no. 2 (1996): 313–15 provide concise assessments of the historiography of the war. An overview of the twentieth-century historiography of U.S.-Cuban relations may be found in Louis A. Pérez, Jr., *Essays on Cuban History: Historiography and Research* (Miami: University Press of Florida, 1994), 115–43. For an extensive review of Spanish and British historiography of the war, see Sylvia L. Hilton and Steve J. S. Ickringill, "William McKinley and the Pacific: Spanish and British Interpretations. An Essay in Comparative History," in *Las relaciones internacionales en el Pacífico (siglos XVIII–XX): Colonización, descolonización y encuentro cultural*, ed. María Dolores Elizalde (Madrid: Consejo Superior de Investigaciones Científicas, 1997), 317–57. The authors show how historiography is a function not only of national perspectives and different views within each nation, but of academic definitions of fields of specialization. Such compartmentalization has meant that until recently Spanish scholars of the Philippines, the Caroline Islands, and the Pacific in general tended to work from and on the fringes of colonial Hispanic Americanism, while the scholarship of British Americanists interested in the War of 1898 and U.S. expansionism in the Pacific rarely showed any influence of the work of British specialists in the history of the Far East. This is also true for Latin Americanists and Asian specialists who generally have treated the War of 1898 and Spanish colonialism in the Pacific as unrelated phenomena.

GENERAL OVERVIEWS OF THE WAR

Scholarly production has flourished in all of the countries touched by the war. Two trends have recently emerged—historians appear to be moving beyond the limits of their own national historiography and seeking to incorporate perspectives from outside their borders, on the one hand, and elucidating the previously hidden patterns of engagement within the nation, on the other. In both cases, historians are bringing into relief perspectives and trends previously overshadowed by dominant national discourses.

U.S. Scholarship

Representative of the first trend is Louis A. Pérez, Jr., *The War of 1898: The United States and Cuba in History and Historiography* (Chapel Hill: University of North Carolina Press, 1998). This slender and elegantly written volume pierces the shrouds of national historiography. Each of the five chapters begins with a series of pointedly contradictory quotes from U.S., Cuban, and occasionally Spanish sources. Pérez's book is in effect an extended bibliographical essay that treats historiography as "an artifact of the war" (p. xi) worthy of being placed under the scholar's microscope. The author provides a useful review of both contemporary and subsequent representations of the war and uses material from the Cuban archives (although perhaps not as much as more specialized scholars would like) to challenge the historiography relating to the nature and representation of U.S. engagement (which has been depicted simultaneously as accidental, inevitable, unnecessary, generous, ingenuous, deliberate, and well-meaning). The author also examines the role and representation of the Cubans before, during, and after the war and the role of myths and memory in the formation of national identity. Pérez argues convincingly that despite their absence from the U.S. historiography (which generally attributes the U.S. victory to either U.S. bravery or Spanish blundering), the Cubans "played a decisive if largely unacknowledged role in the U.S. victory" (p. 86).

Many new centennial books continue to address the role of 1898 in the U.S. national consciousness and in the emergence of the United States as a global power in the twentieth century. Ivan Musicant's *Empire by Default: The Spanish-American War and the Dawn of the American Century* (New York: A Marian Wood Book, Henry Holt and Company, 1998) and David Traxel's *1898: The Birth of the American Century* (New York: Knopf, 1998) treat the war as an epic that defined U.S. national character in the same way that the frontier had; both contain lengthy descriptions of the military battles of the war. Despite the somewhat misleading title of his book, Musicant argues that there was a decisive plan behind U.S. expansionism one hundred years ago. Traxel's well-written tome provides the reader with a rich sense of U.S. culture at the end of the nineteenth century. Both books are more successful at portraying U.S. debates over the war than in placing those debates within a broader international context. (A book which is more successful at this is Angel Smith and Emma Dávila-Cox, eds., *The Crisis of 1898: Colonial Redistribution and Nationalist Mobilization* [New York: St. Martin's Press, 1999], which contains chapters by the editors, John Offner, John Oldfield, Alistair Hennessy, María Dolores Elizalde, Sebastian Balfour, and Joseph Smith on the relationship of the nationalist mobilizations in the period prior to the war and their impact on the colonial balance of power.)

Other recent books on 1898 include Harvey Rosenfeld, *Diary of a Dirty Little War: The Spanish-American War of 1898* (Westport, Conn.: Praeger, 2000), which recreates the war through the eyes of the *New York Times* and concludes that "partisan politics and economic interests" dictated the need to end Spain's influence over Cuba; John A. Corry, *1898: Prelude to a Century* (New York: John A. Corry, distributed by Fordham University Press, 1998), which places the war within the wider context of European politics and government; Elmore Leonard's *Cuba Libre* (New York: Delacorte Press, 1998), a fast-paced historical novel of illegal arms transfers set against the backdrop of the war; H. Wayne Morgan's *1898–1998 Echoes and Lessons from the Spanish-American War* (Greenville, N.C.: East Carolina University, 1998); and two useful reference works on the war—Brad K. Berner's *The Spanish-American War: A Historical Dictionary* (Lanham, Md.: Scarecrow Press, 1998) and Benjamin Beede's *The War of 1898 and U.S. Interventions, 1898–1934: An Encyclopedia* (New York: Garland, 1994).

Written for high school students, Deborah Wei and Rachael Kame's *Resistance in Paradise: Rethinking 100 Years of U.S. Involvement in the Caribbean and the Pacific* (Philadelphia: American Friend Service Committee, 1998) provides innovative ideas and useful documents for educators at both the high school and undergraduate levels. Like Pérez's book, it is indicative of the trend which critiques the myths fostered in the U.S. historiography. Its scope is broader than Pérez's and it includes chapters on Cuba, Puerto Rico, American Samoa, Guam, the Mariana Islands, Hawaii, and the Philippines, with particular attention to resistance movements and the impact of U.S. intervention in each of these former Spanish colonies. Each section provides an overview, primary documents (including poetry, songs, letters, laws, treaties, and political cartoons), and recommendations for activities aimed at linking the past with current events in these regions.

Gender, Class, Race, and Ethnicity

The second trend, part of a larger trend in social history toward consideration of gender, class, race, and ethnicity, has also proved fruitful in producing scholarship on the war. A growing body of literature now examines the myriad ways that racial ideologies in the participating nations influenced the causes, conduct, and consequences of the war and were a crucible for forging competing notions of national identity. For those interested in the history of race in Cuba and the United States, the centennial volumes by Lisa Brock and Digna Castañeda Fuertes, *Between Race and Empire: African Americans and Cubans before the Cuban Revolution* (Philadelphia: Temple University Press, 1998) and Michael L. Krenn, ed., *Race and U.S. Foreign Policy in the Ages of Territorial and Market Expansion, 1840 to 1900* (New York: Garland Publishers, 1998) are good places to start. Brock and Castañeda Fuertes bring together nearly a dozen essays which, taken as a whole, provide a cross-cultural and transnational history of a century of pan-African and pan-American political, social, and cultural relations. The essays are ably introduced by Brock; particularly relevant to the discussions of nationalisms and the War of 1898 are Carmen Montejo Arrechea's chapter on *Minerva*, the first known magazine in Cuba dedicated to black women and published in the 1880s; Nancy Mirabal's chapter about Afro-Cubans and African-Americans in Ybor City and Tampa in the years following the war, which provides a poignant analysis of the deterioration of race relations among Cuban émigrés in the aftermath of the war; and David J. Hellwig's discussion of the African-American press and U.S. involvement in Cuba in the first decade of the twentieth century. Of particular interest in Krenn's volume are chapters by Merline Pitre on Frederick Douglass and American diplomacy in the Caribbean; by Rubin Francis Weston on racism and the imperialist campaign; on imperialism and the Anglo-Saxon by Thomas F. Gossett; on anti-imperialists, the Philippines, and the inequality of man by Christopher Lasch; on race and American expansion in Cuba and Puerto Rico by Philip W. Kennedy; on African-Americans and the quest for empire by Willard B. Gatewood, Jr.; on David Fagen, an Afro-American rebel in the Philippines, by Michael C. Robinson and Frank N. Schubert; on Booker T. Washington and the white man's burden by Louis R. Harlan; and on the opposition of "Negro" newspapers to American Philippine policy by George P. Marks III. Other recent studies that focus on the participation of African-American soldiers in the war include Frank N. Schubert, *Black Valor: Buffalo Soldiers and the Medal of Honor, 1870–1898* (Wilmington, Del.: Scholarly Resources, 1997) and Edward Van Zile Scott, *The Unwept: Black American Soldiers and the Spanish-American War* (Montgomery, Ala.: Black Belt Press, 1996).

Several excellent studies have been published on the connections between domestic and international policies. One of the best is Matthew Frye Jacobson, *Barbarian Virtues: The United States Encounters Foreign Peoples at Home and Abroad, 1876–1917* (New York: Hill and Wang, 2000). Jacobson's study explores the linkages between immigration and empire-building, which he views as "two sides of the same coin" (p. 4). For other theoretical discussions of how racial ideologies contributed to the formation of U.S. policies and national identity, see John Tebbel, *America's Great Patriotic War with Spain: Mixed Motives, Lies, and Racism in Cuba and the Philippines, 1898–1915* (Manchester Center, Vt.: Marshall Jones Co., 1996) and Michael H. Hunt, *Ideology and U.S. Foreign Policy* (New Haven: Yale University Press, 1987).

Turning to Cuba and the role of Afro-Cubans in building an independent Cuba, Aline Helg, *Our Rightful Share: The Afro-Cuban Struggle for Equality, 1886–1912* (Chapel Hill: University of North Carolina Press, 1995) documents the ways foreign powers and elite white Cubans subordinated Afro-Cubans through ideology and action. An outstanding study of race in the earlier Ten Years' War and the period leading up to the War of 1898 is Ada Ferrer, *Insurgent Cuba: Race, Nation, and Revolution, 1868–1898* (Chapel Hill: University of North Carolina Press, 1999). For an earlier view of the economic and political impact of the abolition of slavery on the independence movement, informed by extensive archival work within Cuba, see Rebecca Scott, *Slave Emancipation in Cuba: The Transition to Free Labour, 1860–1899* (Princeton: Princeton University Press, 1985). Christopher Schmidt-Nowara, *Empire and Antislavery: Spain, Cuba, and Puerto Rico, 1833–1874* (Pittsburgh, Pa.: University of Pittsburgh Press, 1999) and his "Spanish Cuba: Race and Class in Spanish Anti-Slavery Ideology," *Cuban Studies* 25 (Pittsburgh, Pa.: University of Pittsburgh Press, 1995) analyze the political interactions between Spain and her colonies that led to the abolition of slavery in Cuba and Puerto Rico during the generations before the war. On racial attitudes in Puerto Rico and Cuba in the century leading up to the war, see Jay Kinsbruner, *Not of Pure Blood: The Free People of Color and Racial Prejudice in Nineteenth-Century Puerto Rico* (Durham, N.C.: Duke University Press, 1996). A superb older study of the intersection of race, class, and gender in nineteenth-century Cuba is Verena Martínez Alier, *Marriage, Class and Colour in Nineteenth Century Cuba: A Study of Racial Attitudes and Sexual Values in a Slave Society* (Cambridge: Cambridge University Press, 1974).

Racial ideologies affected the ways that Latin American elites related to each other, to the United States, and to Spain; as well as the ways that Spaniards viewed their colonies. This topic has been relatively absent from the U.S. historiography. See Mónica Quijada, "Latinos y anglosajones: El 98 en el fin de siglo sudamericano," *Hispania* [Madrid] 57, no. 2 (1997): 589–609 on the responses of Latin American governments to the war and the ideologies underlying the war.

A number of recent studies are challenging the traditional historiography of the war by introducing new insights about the roles of gender, women, and notions of masculinity and femininity into the debates about American identity, but much work has yet to be done on these topics in relation to the various sites of the war. Kristin L. Hoganson's *Fighting for American Manhood: How Gender Politics Provoked the Spanish-American and Philippine-American Wars* (New Haven: Yale University Press, 1998) is a model for studying the dynamics of gender and discourse in national policy circles. On gender and war, see also Miriam Cooke and Angela Woollacott, eds., *Gendering War Talk* (Princeton: Princeton University Press, 1993) and Cynthia Enloe, *Bananas, Beaches, and Bases: Making Feminist Sense of International Politics* (Berkeley: University of California Press, 1990). Felix V. Matos-Rodríguez and Linda C. Delgado, eds., *Puerto Rican Women's History: New Perspectives* (Armonk, N.Y.: M. E. Sharpe, 1998) begins the work of recovering the protagonism of Puerto Rican women in that region. See also Eileen J. Findlay, "Love in the Tropics: Marriage, Divorce, and the Construction of Benevolent Colonialism in Puerto Rico, 1898–1910," in Gilbert Joseph, Catherine LeGrand, and Ricardo Salvatore, eds., *Close Encounters of Empire: Writing the Cultural History of U.S.–Latin American Relations* (Durham, N.C.: Duke University Press, 1998), 139–72, and her "Domination, Decency, and Desire: The Politics of Sexuality in Ponce, Puerto Rico, 1870–1920" (Ph.D. diss., University of Wisconsin, 1995). Sonya Michel and Robyn Muncy, eds., *Engendering America: A Documentary History, 1865 to the Present* (Dubuque, Iowa: McGraw-Hill, 1999) provides powerful examples and interpretations of primary documents regarding shifting notions of masculinity and femininity in America at the end of the nineteenth century. Ruth Roach Pierson and Nupur Chaudhuri, eds., *Na-*

tion, Empire, Colony: Historicizing Gender and Race (Bloomington: Indiana University Press, 1998), based on a conference of the International Federation for Research in Women's History, includes a collection of case studies which analyze the ways that gender intersects discourses of race, ethnicity, class, and nation; these provide useful theoretical frameworks for researching gender and the War of 1898. On manhood in the war years, see Gail Bederman, *Manliness and Civilization: A Cultural History of Gender and Race in the United States, 1880–1917* (Chicago: University of Chicago Press, 1995), and Michael Kimmel, *Manhood in America: A Cultural History* (New York: Free Press, 1996).

On U.S. women and American foreign policy, see Edward P. Crapol, ed., *Women and American Foreign Policy: Lobbyists, Critics, and Insiders*, 2d ed. (Wilmington, Del.: Scholarly Resources, 1992); Judith Papachristou, "American Women and Foreign Policy, 1898–1905: Exploring Gender in Diplomatic History," *Diplomatic History* 14 (fall 1990): 493–501; and Rebecca Brooks Edwards, "Gender in American Politics, 1880–1900" (Ph.D. diss., University of Virginia, 1995). For an understanding of the multifaceted roles of women in American culture in the war period, see Anne Ruggles Gere, *Intimate Practices: Literacy and Cultural Work in U.S. Women's Clubs, 1880–1920* (Champaign: University of Illinois Press, 1997). Gere discusses the ways that clubwomen from different class, religious, and racial backgrounds related to the articulation of a new nation through their engagement with projects such as Americanization, consumer culture, and redefining womanhood. Robyn Muncy, *Creating a Female Dominion in American Reform, 1890–1935* (New York: Oxford University Press, 1991) analyzes female activism in the Progressive Era; and Carrie A. Foster, *The Women and the Warriors: The U.S. Section of the Women's International League for Peace and Freedom, 1915–1946* (Syracuse, N.Y.: Syracuse University Press, 1995) provides a case study of WILPF, established in part by former leaders of the Anti-Imperialist League. For a discussion of the role of women in Cuba's independence movement, see Raquel Vinat de la Mata, "A cien años de una experiencia: Participación femenina en la lucha independentista cubana, 1895–1898," in Manuel López Díaz, comp., *Cuba: La Guerra de 1898* (San José, Costa Rica: Facultad Latinoamericana de Ciencias Sociales-FLACSO, 1999), 151–70. On Cuban women in the period immediately following the war, see K. Lynn Stoner, *From the House to the Streets: The Cuban Woman's Movement for Legal Reform, 1898–1940* (Durham, N.C.: Duke University Press, 1991).

Several recent studies shed light on the role of workers in the war period. Labor historian Joan Casanovas uses regional and national Spanish, Cuban, and U.S. sources to document the role of urban labor in the disintegration of the relationship between Cuba and Spain in *Bread, or Bullets! Urban Labor and Spanish Colonialism in Cuba, 1850–1898* (Pittsburgh, Pa.: University of Pittsburgh Press, 1998). An interesting analysis of the machinists in the Spanish navy may be found in Antonio de la Vega Blasco, "Los maquinistas del 98," *Revista de Historia Naval* [Spain] 9, no. 33 (1991): 43–54. For a discussion of U.S. labor's relationship with incipient labor movements in Puerto Rico and Cuba in the aftermath of the war, see Joseph Bedford, "Samuel Gompers and the Caribbean: The AFL, Cuba, and Puerto Rico, 1898–1906," *Labor's Heritage* 6, no. 4 (1995): 4–25. For a study of the Spanish anarchists and the war, see Rafael Nuñez Florencio, "Los anarquistas españoles y americanos ante la guerra de Cuba," *Hispania. Revista española de historia* 51 (September–December 1991): 1077–1092.

The aforementioned works aside, traditional historiography and much of the new scholarship have tended to focus on the causes, conduct, and consequences of the war as related to the role of the presidency, diplomacy, big business, the military, the press and public opinion, and the debates over imperialism fueled by the war.

U.S.-Latin American Relations

Numerous new works analyze U.S.-Latin American relations and situate the war of 1898 at the beginning or within the trajectory of the history of U.S. foreign policy. For an overview of the war as initiating an interventionist trend in Latin America, see Mark T. Gilderhus, *The Second Century: U.S.-Latin American Relations since 1889* (Wilmington, Del.: Scholarly Resources, 2000) and Ivan Musicant, *The Banana Wars: A History of United States Military Intervention in Latin America from the Spanish-American War to the Invasion of Panama* (New York: Macmillan Publishing Co., 1990). Musicant argues that U.S. interventions in Latin America have stemmed from geo-strategic interests, particularly "the need to create a Caribbean bulwark shielding the Atlantic approaches to America's hemispheric jugular vein, the isthmus and canal of Panama." For an understanding of the war as part of a longer continuum of U.S. foreign policies, see the excellent political history by Lars Schoultz, *Beneath the United States: A History of U.S. Policy toward Latin America* (Cambridge: Harvard University Press, 1998). Lester Langley, *The Americas in the Age of Revolution, 1750–1850* (New Haven: Yale University Press, 1996); Leopoldo Zea, *The Role of the Americas in History*, ed. Amy A. Oliver, trans. Sonja Karsen (Savage, Md.: Rowman & Littlefield, 1992); and James E. Lewis, *The American Union and the Problem of Neighborhood: The United States and the Collapse of the Spanish Empire, 1783–1829* (Chapel Hill: University of North Carolina Press, 1998) examine the early relationships between the Americas. Thomas M. Leonard, ed., *United States-Latin American Relations, 1850–1903: Establishing a Relationship* (Tuscaloosa: University of Alabama Press, 1999) includes a series of essays focusing on the relationships between the United States and individual Latin American countries in the second half of the nineteenth century.

A number of excellent cultural studies of the Americas have been published in recent years that illustrate the connections between art and empire. See Edward W. Said, *Culture and Imperialism* (New York: Vintage Books, 1994); Joseph, LeGrand and Salvatore, *Close Encounters Empire*; Leslie Bethell, ed., *A Cultural History of Latin America: Literature, Music, and the Visual Arts in the 19th and 20th Centuries* (New York: Cambridge University Press, 1998); Amy Kaplan and Donald E. Pease, eds., *Cultures of United States Imperialism* (Durham, N.C.: Duke University Press, 1993); and Robert W. Rydell, *All the World's a Fair: Visions of Empire at American International Expositions, 1876–1916* (Chicago: University of Chicago Press, 1984). For the ongoing impact of the war on Latin American artists, see *Cien años después... Cien artistas contemporáneos: reflexiones en torno a la presencia norteamericana* (San Juan, Puerto Rico: Comité de los Cien, 1998). Manuel Méndez Saavedra, *1898: La guerra hispanoamericana en caricaturas* (San Juan, Puerto Rico: Comisión Puertorriqueña para la Celebración del Quinto Centenario del Descubrimiento de América y Puerto Rico [Gráfica Metropolitana], 1992) contains a broad selection of cartoons on the war from U.S., Puerto Rican, Spanish, and other European and Latin American sources.

A particularly hot topic in U.S. historiography in recent years has been the impact of the war of 1898 on U.S.-Cuban relations. See Jules Benjamin, *The United States and the Origins of the Cuban Revolution: An Empire of Liberty in an Age of National Liberation* (Princeton: Princeton University Press, 1990); Jorge Ibarra, *Prologue to Revolution: Cuba, 1898–1958* (Boulder, Colo.: Lynne Rienner, 1998); José M. Hernández, *Cuba and the United States: Intervention and Militarism, 1869–1933* (Austin: University of Texas Press, 1993); and Louis A. Pérez, Jr., *Cuba and the United States: Ties of Singular Intimacy* (Athens, Ga.: University of Georgia Press, 1997).

SPANISH SCHOLARSHIP

Throughout the 1990s, Spain hosted a phenomenal number of scholarly gatherings, many of which were marked by reconsideration not only of the Spanish (both national and regional) role in the war, but of American and Pacific dimensions of the war as well. See Octavio Ruiz-Manjón and Alicia Langa, eds., *Los significados del 98* (Madrid: Universidad Complutense, 1999); Miguel Luque Talaván, Juan J. Pacheco Onrubia, and Fernando Palanco Aguado, eds., *1898: España y el Pacífico: Interpretación del pasado, realidad del presente* (Madrid: Asociación Española de Estudios del Pacífico, 1999); Antonio Gutiérrez Escudero and María Luisa Laviana Cuetos, coords., *España y las Antillas: el 98 y más* (Sevilla: Diputación de Sevilla, Cultura y Deportes, 1999); María José Alvarez Maurín et al., eds., *Fin de Siglo: Crisis y nuevos principios* (León: Universidad de León, 1999); Consuelo Naranjo Orovio, Miguel Angel Puig-Samper, and Luis Miguel García

Mora, eds., *La nación soñada: Cuba, Puerto Rico y Filipinas ante el 98: Actas del congreso internacional celebrado en Aranjuez del 24 al 28 de abril de 1995* (Aranjuez [Madrid]: Doce Calles, [1996]); Jorge Uría González, ed., *Asturias y Cuba en torno al 98. Sociedad, economía, política y cultura en la crisis de entresiglos* (Barcelona: Labor, 1994); Demetrio Ramos and Emilio de Diego, eds., *Cuba, Puerto Rico y Filipinas en la perspectiva del 98* (Madrid: Editorial de la Universidad Complutense, 1997); José Luis Abellán et al., *El 98 iberoamericano* (Madrid: Editorial Pablo Iglesias, 1998); and *Actas del congreso sobre 1898 de la Asociación Española de Historia Contemporánea*, 2 vols. (Sevilla, 2000). See also the special issue of *Revista de Occidente*, 202–203 (March 1998) entitled *1898: ¿Desastre nacional o impulso modernizador?* and the monograph of *Cuadernos Hispanoamericanos* 577–578 (July–August 1998) entitled *El 98 visto desde América.*

As the war was the defining moment that marked the definitive eclipse of Spanish colonial power, the late 1990s also witnessed a bevy of publications that revisit the Spanish defeat and the multiple Spanish perspectives on the war. For a well-written analysis of the war against the context of Spanish politics and the Latin American independence wars earlier in the nineteenth century, see Sebastian Balfour's *The End of Spanish Empire, 1898–1923* (Oxford: Clarendon Press, 1997). Numerous articles by Sylvia L. Hilton address different dimensions of Spain's engagement with the Western Hemisphere. Her essay, "Democracy Goes Imperial: Spanish Views of American Policy in 1898," in David K. Adams and Cornelius A. Van Minnen, eds., *Reflections on American Exceptionalism* (Staffordshire, England: Ryburn Pub., Keele University Press, 1994), 97–128, succinctly reviews the Spanish historiography on the war. For a discussion of Spanish federalists and their relationship to the United States, see her "Los Estados Unidos como modelo: Los federalistas españoles y el mito americano durante la crisis colonial de 1895–1898," *Ibero-americana pragensia* 32 (1998): 11–29. Hilton, "¿'Modernos cartagineses' o 'una nación patriota'?: Los Estados Unidos y su capacidad militar en la retórica republicana española de 1895–1899," in *Los significados del 98*, eds. Octavio Ruiz-Manjón and Alicia Langa (Madrid; Universidad Complutense, 1999), 119–48, analyzes the splits and power struggles within Spain's national body politic with regard to questions of honor, valor, values, and civil-military relations.

For Spanish perspectives on the diplomatic negotiations of the war, see Cristóbal Robles Muñoz, *1898: diplomacia y opinión* (Madrid: Consejo Superior de Investigaciones Científicas, 1991); Juan Pan-Montojo (coord.), José Alvarez Junco et al., *Más se perdió en Cuba: España, 1898 y la crisis de fin de siglo* (Madrid: Alianza Editorial, 1998); and Julián Companys Monclus, *España en 1898: entre la diplomacia y la guerra*, prologue by Carlos Seco Serrano (Madrid: Ministerio de Asuntos Exteriores, 1991).

Rosario Sevilla Soler, ed., "En torno al '98,' " *Anuario de estudios americanos* 50, no. 1 (1998) includes fifteen essays in Spanish on various aspects of the war, the press, and the social, economic, and political context of Spain and the Antilles at the end of the nineteenth century. Juan Pablo Fusi and Antonio Niño, eds., *Antes del "desastre": Orígenes y antecedentes de la crisis del 98* (Madrid: Marcial Pons, 1998) includes essays on the roots of the "Disaster." For a discussion of the legacy of the war on Spanish-Cuban relations, see Alejandro García Alvarez and Consuelo Naranjo Orovio, "Cubanos y españoles después del 98: De la confrontación a la convivencia pacífica," *Revista de Indias* 58, no. 212 (1998): 101–29.

Internal Spanish politics and the war has sparked considerable academic interest in the past decade. See Emilio de Diego, dir., *1895: La guerra en Cuba y la España de la Restauración* (Madrid: Editorial Complutense, 1996); Pedro Laín Entralgo and Carlos Seco Serrano, eds., *España en 1898. Las claves del Desastre* (Madrid: Galaxia Gutenberg, 1998); Regina Mezei, "Carlism and the Spanish-American War: The Role of Pretender Carlos VII," *Mediterranean Studies* 6 (1996): 113–28; George L. Vásquez, "Altamira, the Generation of 1898, and the Regeneration of Spain," *Mediterranean Studies* 5 (1995): 85–100; and Octavio Ruiz, "Spain on the Threshold of a New Century: Society and Politics before and after the Disaster of 1898," *Mediterranean Historical Review* [Great Britain] 13, nos. 1–2 (1998): 7–27. Spanish regional interests related to the war are considered in Ludger Mees, "De la marcha de Cádiz al árbol de Gernika: El país vasco ante la guerra y la crisis del 98," *Studia Histórica. Historia Contemporánea* [Spain] 15 (1997): 239–64.

For a review of the multiple reconstructions of meaning which the Spaniards have given to the war at a national level, see the earlier essay by Martin Blinkhorn, "Spain: The 'Spanish Problem' and the Imperial Myth," *Journal of Contemporary History* 15 (1980): 5–25.

SCHOLARSHIP ON CUBA

Several new works take up Cuban perspectives of the War of 1898 (in addition to those previously mentioned). For the latest Cuban scholarship on the war, Manuel López Díaz, comp., *Cuba: La guerra de 1898* (San José, Costa Rica: Facultad Latinoamericana de Ciencias Sociales-FLACSO, 1999) includes chapters by Oscar Zanetti Lecuona on Spanish commercial interests in Cuba; by Gloria García Rodríguez on Cuban society at the end of the nineteenth century; on Cuban autonomy by Mildred de la Torre Molina; on General Weyler's policies of *reconcentración* by Francisco Pérez Guzmán and Manuel López Díaz; on various military aspects of the war by Yoel Cordobí Núñez, Yolanda Díaz Martínez, and Gustavo Placer Cervera; on female participation in the independence struggle by Raquel Vinat de la Mata; on Cuba's new status as a North American "neocolony" by Hernán Pérez Concepción; and on José Martí by José Cantón Navarro. *Debates americanos* 4 (July–December 1997) likewise includes articles on Cuba's war for independence from a wide range of personal and analytical perspectives and themes, particularly with regard to Cuban culture and the international context of the war, as well as a round-table discussion among Cuban historians. In that monograph on "La sociedad cubana. Mas allá del 98," contributors include Enrique Baltar Rodríguez, José Tabares del Real, Áurea Matilde Fernández Muñiz, Hilda Otero Abreu, Francisco Pérez Guzmán, Fe Iglesias García, Oílda Hevia Lanier, Eusebio Leal Spengler, Luis Toledo Sande, Rolando Rodríguez, Cintio Vitier, Mons. Carlos Manuel de Céspedes, Rafael Cepeda, Miguel Barnet, Salvador Bueno, María Teresa Linares, Francisca López Civeira, Ana Cairo Ballester, Rolando García Blanco, Ana M. De la O and Adrián López, Zoila Lapique Becali, Carmen Almodóvar Muñóz, and Heriberto Hernández. Contributions to conferences at Cuba's Casa de las Américas over the course of the 1990s have been published periodically in *Casa de las Américas.* See, for example, the presentations from the Casa de las Américas conference, "Los 98: Historia de un siglo," beginning in issue no. 210 (1998). The journal also published contributions to conferences held elsewhere in Latin America, such as "Hacia la comprensión del 98: representaciones finiseculares de España y Latinoamérica," organized by the Centro de Investigación en Identidad y Cultura Latinoamericanas and the Escuela de Filología, Lingüística y Literatura of the University of Costa Rica in San José—see *Casa de las Américas* 213 (October–December 1998). See the insightful essays and useful historiographic survey in Pérez, *Essays on Cuban History.* A brief but useful essay on Cuban historiography prior to the 1960s is Duvon C. Corbitt, "Cuban Revisionist Interpretations of Cuba's Struggle for Independence," *Hispanic American Historical Review* 43 (August 1963): 395–404.

Relatively few new studies have focused on the role of the Cuban exile community in influencing U.S. public opinion. An exception is Lillian Guerra, "Contradictory Identities, Conflicted Nations: Cuban Émigrés in the United States and the Last War for Independence (1895–1898)," in this volume, and her "Crucibles of Liberation in Cuba: José Martí, Nationalisms and the Search for Social Unity" (Ph.D. diss., University of Wisconsin-Madison, 2000), which break new ground in this area. Earlier studies include Marshall M. True, "Revolutions in Exile: The Cuban Revolutionary Party, 1891–1898" (Ph.D. diss., University of Virginia, 1965); George W. Auxier, "The Propaganda Activities of the Cuban *Junta* in Precipitating the Spanish-American War, 1895–1898," *Hispanic American Historical Review* 19 (1939): 286–305; Fernando Serrano Suárez, "Notas para un estudio de la prensa revolucionaria cubana en el exilio, 1878–1887," *Aportes. Revista de historia del siglo XIX* 7 (March 1988): 28–43; and Raymond A. Detter, "The Cuban Junta and Michigan: 1895–1898," *Michigan History* 48, no. 1 (1964): 35–46. The latter discusses the role of the Cuban exile community in fomenting a climate in favor of recognition of Cuban belligerancy and independence.

Primary sources abound on this topic: see Leon Primelles, ed., *La revolu-*

ción del 95 según la correspondencia de la delegación cubana en Nueva York, 5 vols. (Havana: Editorial Habanera, 1932–37); and Partido Revolucionario Cubano, *Correspondencia diplomática de la delegación cubana en Nueva York durante la guerra de independencia de 1895 a 1898*, 5 vols., ed. José Agustín Martínez (Havana: Imprenta del Archivo Nacional, 1943–46). For a view of pro-independence activities in Paris, see Paul Estrade, *La colonia cubana de París, 1895–1898: el combate patriótico de Betances y la solidaridad de los revolucionarios franceses* (Havana: Editorial de Ciencias Sociales, 1984). See Horatio Rubens, *Liberty: The Story of Cuba* (New York: Brewer, Warren & Putnam, 1932) for a first-hand account of Cuban exile activities by the legal counsel of the junta in New York.

On the relationship between Cuban culture in Cuba and in the United States, see Louis A. Pérez, Jr., *On Becoming Cuban: Identity, Nationality, and Culture* (Chapel Hill: University of North Carolina Press, 1999); and Gustav Pérez Firmat, *Life on the Hyphen: The Cuban-American Way* (Austin: University of Texas Press, 1994).

The war and the wave of immigration to the island which it provoked influenced Cuban and Puerto Rican nationalism in a variety of unforeseen ways, particularly in patterns of migration and immigration. For a study of U.S. migration to Cuba and continued U.S. efforts to annex Cuba in the period after the war, see Carmen Diana Deere, "Here Come the Yankees! The Rise and Decline of United States Colonies in Cuba, 1898–1930," *Hispanic American Historical Review* 78, no. 4 (1998): 729–65. Other studies of emigration include S. Kaplan, R. Moncarz, and J. Steinberg, "Jewish Emigrants to Cuba: 1898–1960," *International Migration* [Switzerland] 28, no. 3 (1990): 295–310, which analyzes the exodus of Jews from Eastern Europe and the Soviet Union to Cuba in search of new commercial opportunities and respite from harsh conditions in their homelands; Dominga González Suárez, "Síntesis histórica de la política inmigratoria," *Universidad de La Habana* [Cuba] 229 (1987): 15–38, which analyzes the influx of Spaniards, Haitians, Jamaicans, and others into Cuba in the first two decades after the war; and Juan Pérez de la Riva, "La población de Cuba, la guerra de independencia y la inmigración del siglo XX," *Estudios de historia social* [Spain] 1–4 (1988): 397–405, which documents how, despite dramatic mortality and exile rates during the independence wars, Cuba more than recovered its population through immigration and increased fertility rates. For an earlier study of the Spanish migration to Cuba in the aftermath of the war, see Michael Kenny, "Twentieth Century Expatriates in Cuba: A Sub Culture," *Anthropological Quarterly* 34, no. 2 (April 1961): 85–93.

PUERTO RICAN PERSPECTIVES

The centennial is producing new scholarship in Puerto Rico as well. Symbolic of the efforts to broaden the scope of analysis to include a variety of national (if not international) viewpoints is Luis E. González Vales, ed.,

1898: Enfoques y perspectivas: Simposio Internacional de Historiadores en torno al 1898: Cuba, España, Estados Unidos, Filipinas, y Puerto Rico (San Juan, Puerto Rico: Academia Puertorriqueña de la Historia, 1997). For the historiography of the war as it has been depicted in Puerto Rico, see Carmelo Rosario Natal, *El 1898 puertorriqueño en la historiografía: ensayo y bibliografía crítica* (San Juan: Academia Puertorriqueña de la Historia, 1997). Juan E. Hernández-Cruz, *La invasión de Puerto Rico: consideraciones histórico-sociológicas*, 1st ed. (San Germán, Puerto Rico: Editorial Xaguey, 1992) looks at the context for the war in Puerto Rico. Recent books by Olga Jiménez de Wagenheim, *Puerto Rico: An Interpretive History from Pre-Columbian Times to 1900* (Princeton, N.J.: Markus Wiener Publications, 1998); Francisco A. Scarano, *Puerto Rico: cinco siglos de historia* (Bogota: McGraw-Hill Interamericana, 1993); and Kal Wagenheim and Olga Jiménez de Wagenheim, *The Puerto Ricans: A Documentary History* (Princeton, N.J.: Markus Wiener Publishers, 1993) chart the development of the island from its precolonial days through its period as a Spanish colonial possession until its acquisition by the United States. See also the forthcoming book by Francisco Scarano, *Puerto Rico: Colony and Nation* (Philadelphia, Pa.: Temple University Press, 2001), and Felix V. Matos and Linda C. Delgado, eds., *Puerto Rican Women's History: New Perspectives* (Armonk, N.Y.: M.E. Sharpe, 1998).

For an understanding of the legacies of the war on current relations between the United States and Puerto Rico, see especially José Luis González, *Puerto Rico: The Four-Storeyed Country* (Princeton, N.J.: Markus Wiener Publishers, 1997); J. Trías Monge, *Puerto Rico: The Trials of the Oldest Colony in the World* (New Haven: Yale University Press, 1997); Ronald Fernández, *The Disenchanted Island: Puerto Rico and the United States in the Twentieth Century*, 2nd ed. (Westport, Conn.: Praeger, 1996); and Irene Fernández Aponte, *El cambio de soberanía en Puerto Rico: otro '98*, Colección Independencia de Iberoamérica (Madrid: Editorial MAPFRE, 1992). Lillian Guerra's *Popular Expression and National Identity in Puerto Rico: The Struggle for Self, Community, and Nation* (Gainesville: University Press of Florida, 1998) analyzes elite and popular class conceptions of national identity, focusing in particular on the multiple appropriations of the figure of the Spanish-based *jíbaro*, or peasant, as a national symbol. Stuart B. Schwartz, "The Hurricane of San Ciriaco: Disaster, Politics, and Society in Puerto Rico, 1899–1901," *Hispanic American Historical Review* 72, no. 3 (1992): 303–34 offers a fascinating study of the ways that natural disaster solidified a relationship between the U.S. military government in Puerto Rico and the landed class and created a context that inhibited options for Puerto Rican independence. See also the provocative study by Luis Gervasio García, "El otro es uno: Puerto Rico en la mirada norteamericana de 1898," *Revista de Indias* 57, no. 211 (1997): 729–59.

PHILIPPINE PERSPECTIVES

Several new books have been published which offer a revisionist social history of the Philippine-American War, begun following the signing of the Treaty of Paris, which ceded the Philippine Islands to the United States. For an overview of the Spanish, U.S., and Filipino historiography of the Philippine Revolution of 1896–1902, see the brief but useful chapter by Bernardita Reyes Churchill, "The Philippines and the Historiography of 1898: Perspectives and Critical Bibliography," in Luque Talaván, *1898*, 289–302. On the legacies of war, see Maria Serena I. Diokno, ed., *Voices and Scenes of the Past: The Philippine-American War Retold* (Quezon City: The José W. Diokno Foundation, 1999); Luis Francia and Angel Velasco Shaw, ed., *Vestiges of War: The Philippine-American War and Its Aftermath* (Pasig City: Anvil Press, 2000); and H. W. Brands, *Bound to Empire: The United States and the Philippines* (New York: Oxford University Press, 1992). On Filipino efforts to influence U.S. policies, see Jim Zwick, "The Anti-Imperialist League and the Origins of Filipino-American Oppositional Solidarity," *Amerasia Journal* 24, no. 2 (summer 1998): 65–87. On questions of international law, see Luis Eugenio Togores Sánchez, "Imperialismo, relaciones internacionales y derecho internacional en Extremo Oriente (Filipinas), 1830–1898/1914," *Quinto centenario* 16 (1990): 141–72. For an overview of the U.S. debates over extending the war to the Philippines, see Ephraim Smith, "William McKinley's Enduring Legacy: The Historiographical Debate on the Taking of the Philippine Islands," in Bradford, *Crucible*, 205–49; Walter L. Williams, "United States Indian Policy and the Debate over Philippine Annexation: Implications for the Origins of American Imperialism," *The Journal of American History* 66 (1979): 810–31; and the now classic Daniel B. Schirmer, *Republic or Empire: American Resistance to the Philippine War* (Cambridge: Schenkman Publishing Company, 1972). On the Philippine resistance movement, see Teodoro Agoncillo, *The Revolt of the Masses: The Story of Bonifacio and the Katipunan* (Quezon City: University of Philippines, 1956); and on the divisions between Philippine elites favoring U.S. rule and the nationalists, see Reynaldo H. Imperial, "Collaboration-Resistance Pull in the Philippine-American Ward (1898–1902) in Samar," *Leyte-Samar Studies* [Philippines] 19, no. 1 (1985): 81–102; and Jim Zwick's chapter in this volume.

GUAM

For studies on the impact of the war on Guam, see Don A. Farrell, "The Partition of the Marianas: A Diplomatic History, 1898–1919," *Isla: A Journal of Micronesian Studies* [Guam] 2, no. 2 (1994): 273–301, which examines the partition of the Mariana Islands (including Guam) by the competing colonial powers between 1898 and 1919; Robert Rogers, *Des-*

tiny's Landfall: A History of Guam (Honolulu: University of Hawai'i Press, 1995); Anne Perez Hattori, "Bodily Harm: Rereading Naval Discourses on Guam, 1898–1841," *Isla: A Journal of Micronesian Studies* [Mangilao, Guam], 1998; Pedro C. Sanchez, *Guahan Guam: The History of Our Island* (Agaña, Guam: Sanchez Publishing House, 1988); and Deborah Wei and Rachael Kamel, *Resistance in Paradise*, 109–30.

THEMATIC CONCERNS

Role of McKinley and Roosevelt

Theodore Roosevelt's war years have come under examination in three recent books. Peggy Samuels, *Teddy Roosevelt at San Juan: The Making of a President* (College Station: Texas A & M University Press, 1997) examines how Teddy Roosevelt's oft-mentioned role in the Battle of San Juan Hill supported his development as a presidential figure. Harry Paul Jeffers, *Colonel Roosevelt: Theodore Roosevelt Goes to War, 1897–1898* (New York: J. Wiley & Sons, 1996) analyzes Roosevelt's military leadership during the war, and Dale L. Walker, *The Boys of '98: Theodore Roosevelt and the Rough Riders* (New York: Forge, 1998) discusses the campaigns and history of the volunteer cavalry in the war.

No new scholarship has yet superceded the older studies of President McKinley's role found in Lewis L. Gould, *The Spanish-American War and President McKinley* (Lawrence: University Press of Kansas, 1982); Robert Dallek, *1898: McKinley's Decision* (New York: Chelsea House Publications, 1969); John Layser Offner, "President McKinley and the Origins of the Spanish-American War" (Ph.D. diss., Penn State University, 1957); Margaret Leech, *In the Days of McKinley* (New York: Harper & Brothers, 1959); and H. Wayne Morgan, *William McKinley and His America* (Syracuse, N.Y.: Syracuse University Press, 1963).

Diplomacy and the War

For an analysis of Spanish and American diplomatic efforts to avoid war, see John Offner, *An Unwanted War: The Diplomacy of the United States and Spain over Cuba, 1895–1898* (Chapel Hill: University of North Carolina Press, 1992). Offner argues that the United States and Spain wanted peace, but the Cuban nationalists were unyielding. His book emphasizes Spanish-American relations and the trans-Atlantic struggle over Cuba, and he concludes that the war was an inevitable result of the collision of Cuban nationalism with Spanish colonialism. For another view, see the recent critique by Mark Peceny, "A Constructivist Interpretation of the Liberal Peace: The Ambiguous Case of the Spanish-American War," *Journal of Peace Research* [Great Britain] 34, no. 4 (1997): 415–30. The classic study of the diplomatic efforts prior to the war is Horace Edgar Flack, *Spanish American Diplomatic Relations Preceding the War of 1898*, Johns Hopkins University Studies in History and Political Science, series 24, nos. 1 and 3 (Baltimore, January–February 1906). Ernest R. May, *Imperial Democracy: The Emergence of America as a Great Power* (New York: Harcourt Brace, 1961) continues to be a useful source for placing the war within the broader context of international politics. For legal perspectives and a history of the conduct of the belligerents, see Elbert J. Benton, *International Law and Diplomacy of the Spanish American War* (Gloucester, Mass.: Peter Smith, 1968). Primary documents on diplomatic efforts may be found in U.S. Department of State, *Papers Relating to the Foreign Relations of the United States, 1898* (Washington, D.C.: Government Printing Office, 1901).

Numerous articles and dissertations have dealt with the involvement and perceptions of governments and individuals other than those most directly involved in the war. Thomas Schoonover, "Europe, the Spanish-American War and Great Power Activity in the Caribbean and Asia," in Society for Historians of American Foreign Relations, *Newsletter* 28, no. 3 (1997): 1–27 discusses commercial and military interests of the United States and Europe as they sought control of the Central American isthmus in the years surrounding the war. Schoonover's earlier work, *The United States in Central America, 1860–1911: Episodes of Social Imperialism and Imperial Rivalry in the World System* (Chapel Hill, N.C.: Duke University Press, 1991), places the war within the broader context of geopolitical and economic rivalries over Central America. See also Lester Langley with Thomas D. Schoonover, *The Banana Men: American Mercenaries and Entrepreneurs in Central America, 1880–1930* (Lexington: University Press of Kentucky, 1994). For general perspectives from Europe, see Luis Alvarez Gutiérrez, "Los imperios centrales ante el progresivo deterioro de las relaciones entre España y los Estados Unidos," *Hispania* [Madrid] 57, no. 2 (1997): 435–78; Markus M. Hugo, "La Guerra de 1898 y su contexto internacional. Tendencias historiográficas y publicaciones con motivo del Centenario," in *Notas* 17, vol. 6 (1999): 2–16; Francis Roy Bridge, "Great Britain, Austria-Hungary, and the Concert of Europe on the Eve of the Spanish-American War," *Mitteilungen des Österreichischen Staatsarchivs* [Austria] 44 (1996): 87–108, which describes joint European efforts to prevent the war and the national political considerations behind their failure to do so; and Zbigniew Kwiecien, "The Far Eastern Issues in the American-Spanish Peace Negotiations in Paris in 1898," *American Studies* [Poland] 9 (1990): 37–58. On the German press and the war, see Luis Alvarez Gutiérrez, "La diplomacia alemana ante el conflicto hispano-norteamericano de 1897–1898: Primeras tomas de posición," *Hispania* [Madrid] 54, no. 1 (1994): 201–56; and Markus M. Hugo, "Germany and the War of 1898" (Ph.D. diss., University of Giessen, Germany, forthcoming).

Studies of British relations with Spain and Europe during the war include

Rosario de la Torre del Río, "1895–1898: Inglaterra y la búsqueda de un compromiso internacional para frenar la intervención norteamericana en Cuba," *Hispania* [Madrid] 57, no. 2 (1997): 515–49. See also her earlier book, *Inglaterra y España en 1898* (Madrid: EUDEMA, Ediciones de la Universidad Complutense de Madrid, 1988). For other perspectives, see Luis Alvarez Gutiérrez, "Tanger en la guerra hispanonorteamericana de 1898," *Boletín de la Real Academia de la Historia* [Spain] 195, no. 1 (1998): 81–131.

Diplomatic, military, and economic support from Latin American countries (or lack thereof) for Cuban independence continues to be the subject of scholarly debate. On Latin American perspectives on the war, see Sergio Vilaboy, "La revolución independentista de Cuba y la Guerra de 1898 desde la perspectiva de América Latina," *Contrastes. Revista de Historia Moderna* [Murcia] 7–8 (1991–93): 65–83; and Francisco Corral, "El 98 en Paraguay: Rafael Barret," and Ignacio García, "La colonia española en Buenos Aires y la Guerra de Cuba," both in Manuel Alcántara, ed., *América Latina, realidades y perspectivas* (Salamanca: Ediciones Universidad de Salamanca, 1997): 74–103 and 190–218. On Mexican perspectives on the war, see Rafael Rojas, "La política mexicana ante la guerra de independencia de Cuba (1895–1898)," *Historia mexicana* [Mexico] 45, no. 4 (1996): 783–805; and Salvador Morales, "Visión mexicana del 98," Agustín Sánchez, "La crisis del 98 y las relaciones hispanomexicanas," and Sara Ortelli, "La colonia española de México frente al conflicto del 98," *Cuadernos hispanoamericanos* [Madrid] 577–78 (1998): 23–43, 45–58, and 73–85. An especially helpful overview on Latin American relations (governmental and nongovernmental) may be found in Foner, *Spanish-Cuban-American War*, 1:151–62. Fredrick B. Pike explains the relative lack of Hispanic support for Cuban independence in part as a function of a particularly effective propaganda campaign waged by Spain. See his *Hispanismo: 1898–1936: Spanish Conservatives and Liberals and Their Relations with Spanish America* (Notre Dame, Ind.: Notre Dame University Press, 1971).

Economics of War

Oscar Zanetti Lecuona, *Comercio y poder. Relaciones cubano-hispano-norteamericanas en torno a 1898* (La Habana-Santafé de Bogotá: Fondo Editorial Casa de las Américas-Ministerio de Relaciones Exteriores de Colombia, 1998) received the Casa de las Américas Prize for the Outstanding Essay on the Impact of 1898 on the Americas and the Hispanic World and analyzes the ways in which the development of commercial ties between Cuba, Spain, and the United States set the stage for the war. David M. Pletcher, *The Diplomacy of Trade and Investment: American Economic Expansion in the Hemisphere, 1865–1900* (Columbia: University of Missouri Press, 1998) analyzes U.S. economic expansion throughout Latin America in the period leading up to the war. Emma A. Dávila Ruiz, "Apuntes sobre el comercio entre Puerto Rico y Gran Bretaña durante el siglo XIX," *Op. Cit. Boletín del Centro de Investigaciones Históricas* [Río Piedras, Puerto Rico] 7 (1992): 255–92 argues on the other hand, that U.S. domination of Puerto Rico began abruptly following the war. The role of U.S. business interests in the war has been the subject of much debate but relatively little recent scholarship. The recently re-issued work by Walter LaFeber, *The New Empire: An Interpretation of American Expansion, 1860–1898* (1963; reprint, Ithaca: Cornell University Press, 1998) argues that the war was the culmination of economic forces and interests. The classic study to argue that business interests were marginal to the decision to go to war is Julius Pratt, *Expansionists of 1898: The Acquisition of Hawaii and the Spanish Islands* (Baltimore: Johns Hopkins Press, 1936). Philip Foner and Richard C. Winchester summarize earlier debates on this topic in their documentary edition, *The Anti-Imperialist Reader: A Documentary History of Anti-Imperialism in the United States*, vol. 1 (New York: Holmes & Meier Publishers, 1984), esp. xx–xxv.

Military Aspects of the War

The military and political facets of the 1898 war have, on the other hand, been the focus of much new research. Joseph Smith, *The Spanish-American War: Conflict in the Caribbean and the Pacific 1895–1902* (New York: Longman, 1994) is part of the Modern Wars in Perspective series edited by B. W. Collins and H. M. Scott, which seeks to integrate military history into the academic mainstream. His well-written volume synthesizes the various interpretations of the causes, consequences, nature, and implications of U.S. intervention in the Cuban war with Spain. On the consequences of the war, particularly relating to the roles of the U.S. Navy, Army, military intelligence, and the Marines, see the essays in James C. Bradford, ed., *Crucible of Empire: The Spanish American War and Its Aftermath* (Annapolis, Md.: Naval Institute Press, 1993). David Trask, *War with Spain in 1898* (Lincoln: University of Nebraska Press, 1996) focuses mainly on the conduct of the war itself. Trask concludes, among other things, that the U.S. Army did not perform badly, that the United States did not attack the Philippines in order to acquire it, and that McKinley exerted extraordinary efforts to avoid the war with Spain. An older but important work containing primary documents relating to the military and diplomatic conduct of the war is French Ensor Chadwick, *The Relations of the United States and Spain: The Spanish-American War*, 2 vols. (New York: C. Scribner's Sons, 1909).

For revisionist analyses of the role of the U.S.S. *Maine*, see Peggy and Harold Samuels, *Remembering the Maine* (Washington, D.C.: Smithsonian Institution Press, 1995) and H. G. Rickover, *How the Battleship Maine was Destroyed* (Washington, D.C.: Department of the Navy, 1976). See also

John Edward Weems, *The Fate of the Maine* (College Station: Texas A&M University Press, 1992); and Michael Blow, *A Ship to Remember: The Maine and the Spanish-American War* (New York: Morrow, 1992). Louis A. Pérez, Jr., "The Meaning of the *Maine*," *Pacific Historical Review* 58 (1989): 293–322 provides a still useful overview of the historiographic debates over the *Maine*. For a Spanish point of view, see Guillermo G. Calleja Leal, "La voladura del Maine," *Revista de historia militar* 34, no. 69 (1990): 163–96.

Abundant first-hand accounts by participants and witnesses to the war continue to be published. Pictorials of the war may be found in Donald M. Goldstein, *The Spanish-American War: The Story and Photographs* (Washington, D.C.: Brassey's, 1998). Michael E. Stevens, ed., *Letters from the Front, 1898–1945* (Madison: State Historical Society of Wisconsin, 1992); A. B. Fever, *Santiago Campaign of 1898: A Soldier's View of the Spanish-American War* (Westport, Conn.: Praeger, 1993); and Frank Harper, ed., "*Just Outside of Manila": Letters from Members of the First Colorado Regiment in the Spanish American and Philippine-American Wars*, Colorado Historical Society, monograph 7 (Denver, 1991) provide eyewitness accounts from diaries, scrapbooks, memoirs, and regimental histories. See also Jack Shulimson et al., ed., *Marines in the Spanish-American War, 1895–1899* (Washington, D.C.: History and Museums Division, Headquarters, U.S. Marine Corps, 1998); Jack Shulimson, *The Marine Corps' Search for a Mission, 1880–1898* (Lawrence: University Press of Kansas, 1993); and A. B. Feuer, *The Spanish-American War at Sea: Naval Action in the Atlantic* (Westport, Conn.: Praeger, 1995). James Moorhead Perry, ed., *Arrogant Armies: Great Military Disasters and the Generals Behind Them* (New York: John Wiley, 1996) includes a chapter on Major General William R. Shafter and the Spanish-American War.

For Spanish military views, see José Antonio Plaza, *El maldito verano del 98: los 112 días de la guerra con los Estados Unidos* (Madrid: Temas de Hoy, 1997); Javier Figuero and Carlos G. Santa Cecilia, *La España del desastre* (Barcelona: Plaza & Janés, 1997); Antonio Téllez Molina, "La marina de guerra española frente al desastre del 98: Una aproximación al testimonio de sus combatientes," *Revista de historia naval* [Spain] 8, no. 30 (1990): 39–49; and *Memoria del 98: de la guerra de Cuba a la semana trágica* (Madrid: El País, with the collaboration of the Centro Hispano, 1997).

A recently published memoir from the Puerto Rican Esteban López Jiménez is Luce and Mercedes López-Baralt, eds., *Crónica del '98: El testimonio de un médico puertorriqueño* (Madrid: Ediciones Libertarias, 1998). On the role of Puerto Ricans in the war, see María de los Angeles Castro Arroyo, " '¿Que pelear si los de Madrid no quieren?' Una versión criolla de la guerra del 98 en Puerto Rico," *Revista de Indias* [Madrid] 57, no. 211 (1997): 657–94. Newly published Cuban accounts include Calixto García Iñiguez, *Calixto García Iñiguez: pensamiento y acción militares*, comp. José

Miguel Abreu Cardet and Elia Sintes Gómez (La Habana: Editorial de Ciencias Sociales, 1996). For a discussion of Cuban military activities during the war, see César García del Pino, *La acción naval de Santiago de Cuba* (Havana: Editorial de Ciencias Sociales, 1988). For an account from the Philippines, see José de Arcilla, ed., "The Fall of Manila: Excerpts from a Jesuit Diary," *Philippine Studies* [Philippines] 37, no. 2 (1989): 192–214.

The War, Imperialism, and Anti-Imperialism

While the debates over imperialism were the subject of extensive analysis in the past, they produced relatively little new scholarship in the 1990s. The primary exception is the work of Jim Zwick. See his chapter in this volume as well as his pioneering work on the internet, *Anti-Imperialism in the United States, 1898–1935* and related websites at <http://www.BoondocksNet.com>. Fortunately, some excellent writings, including documentary editions of primary sources (some at Zwick's website), are available from earlier years. One of the best secondary works is Philip Foner, *The Spanish-Cuban-American War and the Birth of American Imperialism, 1895–1902*, 2 vols. (New York: Monthly Review Press, 1972). Foner suggests that the U.S. entry into Cuba's war against Spain inaugurated a new imperialist phase in U.S. foreign relations. He provides an in-depth discussion of the economic causes of the war both within Cuba and in the United States, the appeal of the war for the U.S. public, the contribution of Cuban military forces to the U.S. victory over Spain, and the Latin American context in which the Cuban struggle for independence took place. The opposition to U.S. intervention in the war spanned the political spectrum and was marked by its heterogeneity. For primary sources, see Theodore P. Greene, ed., *American Imperialism in 1898: Problems in American Civilization* (Boston: D. C. Heath and Company, 1955). Gems in Greene's volume include J. A. Hobson's still fresh "Imperialism," William L. Langer's "Critique of Imperialism," Charles A. Beard's "Territorial Expansion Connected with Commerce," Samuel F. Bemis's "The Great Aberration of 1898," Joseph E. Wisan's "The Cuban Crisis as Reflected in the New York Press," and, on the Philippines, essays by Henry Cabot Lodge and Carl Schurz. Philip S. Foner and Richard C. Winchester, *The Anti-Imperialist Reader: Volume I: From the Mexican War to the Election of 1900* (New York: Holmes & Meier Publishers, 1984) reviews the literature on anti-imperialism and provides a treasure-trove of lesser-known speeches, letters, editorials, and position papers by labor, blacks, middle-class groups and individuals, and the Anti-Imperialist League. See also E. Berkeley Tompkins, *Anti-Imperialism in the United States: The Great Debate* (Philadelphia: University of Pennsylvania Press, 1970); Robert L. Beisner, *Twelve against Empire: The Anti-Imperialists, 1898–1900* (New York: McGraw-Hill Book Company, 1968); and Fred Harvey Harrington, "The Anti-Imperialist

Movement in the United States, 1898–1900," *Mississippi Valley Historical Review* 22 (1935): 211–30.

Göran Rystad, *Ambiguous Imperialism: American Foreign Policy and Domestic Politics at the Turn of the Century* (Stockholm: Esselte Studium, 1975) studies the links between U.S. electoral politics and the debates over imperialism. For conflicting interpretations of the role of U.S. progressives in foreign policy issues at the beginning of the twentieth century, see Robert David Johnson, *The Peace Progressives and American Foreign Relations* (Cambridge: Harvard University Press, 1995); William E. Leuchtenburg, "Progressivism and Imperialism: The Progressive Movement and American Foreign Policy 1898–1916," *Mississippi Valley Historical Review* 39, no. 3 (December 1952): 483–504; Thomas Paterson, "California Progressives and Foreign Policy," *California Historical Society Quarterly* 47, no. 4 (1968): 329–42; and I. Dementyev, *USA: Imperialists and Anti-Imperialists (The Great Foreign Policy Debate at the Turn of the Century)* (Moscow: Progress Publishers, 1979). On U.S. socialists, see H. H. Quint, "American Socialists and the Spanish-American War," *American Quarterly* (summer 1958): 131–41.

The Role of the Press and Public Opinion

Numerous scholars have studied the relationship between the rise of yellow journalism in the United States at the end of the nineteenth century and interventionist tendencies in the population at large, but relatively few new studies have examined the role of the U.S. press in the formation of public opinion toward the war. Recent U.S. studies tend to focus on the general role of the press, unlike the multiple studies of local and regional newspapers produced in past decades (often in dissertations that never saw publication). Marion Tuttle Marzolf, *Civilizing Voices: American Press Criticism, 1880–1950* (New York: Longman, 1991) provides a thoughtful account of the shifting roles of the press beginning in the 1880s. In Rodger Streitmatter, ed., *Mightier than the Sword: How the News Media Have Shaped American History* (Boulder, Colo.: Westview Press, 1997), the editor includes a case study on the Spanish-American War which gives the media considerable credit for fueling war hysteria among the U.S. populace. Joyce Milton, *The Yellow Kids: Foreign Correspondents in the Heyday of Yellow Journalism* (New York: Harper and Row, 1989) provides a good overview of the journalistic context of the day. Classic earlier works on this theme include George Bronson Rea, *Facts and Fakes about Cuba: A Review of Various Stories Circulated in the United States Concerning the Present Insurrection* (New York: G. Munro's Sons, 1897); Marcus M. Wilkerson, *Public Opinion and the Spanish-American War: A Study in War Propaganda* (Baton Rouge: Louisiana State University Press, 1932); Joseph E. Wisan, *The Cuban Crisis as Reflected in the New York Press (1895–1898)* (New York: Columbia University Press, 1934); and Charles H. Brown, *The Cor-*

respondent's War: Journalists in the Spanish-American War (New York: Scribner, 1967).

While new studies on the impact or representation of the war in the media have been conspicuously absent from recent U.S. literature, in Spain and Europe, this subfield continues to draw the attention of scholars, although again, to a somewhat lesser extent than in earlier years. The best single source representing a broad spectrum of new scholarship in this field is the collection of essays dealing with public opinion and the press in the Netherlands, the Dutch East Indies, Spain, Germany, Ulster, Russia, France, Portugal, Italy, Austria and Britain by Sylvia L. Hilton and Steve J. S. Ickingrill, eds., *European Perceptions of the Spanish-American War of 1898* (New York: Peter Lang, 1999). See also Manuel Leguineche, *Yo pondré la guerra: Cuba 1898, la primera guerra que se inventó la prensa* (Buenos Aires: Aguilar, 1998). For an overview of the literature related to the press and attitudes about the war, see Sylvia Hilton, "The Spanish-American War of 1898: Queries into the Relationship between the Press, Public Opinion and Politics," *Revista Española de Estudios Norteamericanos*, no. 7 (1994): 73–87; and Rosario Sevilla Soler, "¿'Opinión pública' frente a 'opinión publicada'? 1898: La cuestión cubana," *Revista de Indias* 58, no. 212 (1998): 255–76. See also Nieves Bolado Argüello, *La independencia de Cuba y la prensa: apuntes para la historia* (Torrelavega [Bilbao]: Ayuntamiento de Torrelavega, Artes Gráficos Quinzaños, 1991).

Newspapers in Madrid and Seville have also been subject to recent scrutiny, although again to a lesser extent than in previous years. On the press in Seville, see Rosario Sevilla Soler, *La guerra de Cuba y la memoria colectiva: La crisis del 98 en la prensa sevillana* (Madrid: Consejo Superior de Investigaciones Científicas, 1996).

Literary Impact of the War

The year 1898 marked something of a literary touchstone in Spain, Latin America, and the United States. A handful of U.S. authors—Julia Ward Howe, Bliss Carman, Richard Hovey, Gertrude Atherton, Brooks Adams, Thomas Nelson Page, and Julian Hawthorne—could be counted among the pro-expansionist authors, but by far the majority of leading U.S. intellectuals sided with the anti-imperialists. The anti-imperialists included prominent intellectuals such as William Dean Howells, Mark Twain [Samuel B. Clemens], Henry Blake Fuller, Ambrose Bierce, Stephen Crane, Finley Peter Dunne, William Lloyd Garrison, E. K. Godkin, Lincoln Steffens, William Graham Sumner, Thomas Bailey Aldrich, Hamlin Garland, and Thomas Wentworth Higginson. For an overview of the topic and selections of the writings, see Philip S. Foner, *The Anti-Imperialist Reader, vol. II: The Literary Anti-Imperialists* (New York: Holmes & Meier Publ., 1984), especially his intro., pp. xiii–lxvii; and Fred Harvey Harrington, "Literary Aspects of

American Anti-Imperialism, 1898–1902," *New England Quarterly* 10 (1937): 650–67.

A separate literature, much of it new, exists on Mark Twain, one of the most articulate of the U.S. anti-imperialists. See Jim Zwick, *Mark Twain's Weapons of Satire: Anti-Imperialist Writings on the Philippine-American War* (Syracuse, N.Y.: Syracuse University Press, 1992); Shelley Fisher Fishkin, ed., *Historical Guide to Mark Twain* (New York: Oxford University Press, 2001); Jim Zwick, "Mark Twain's Anti-Imperialist Writings in the 'American Century,' " in *Vestiges of War: The Philippine-American War and Its Aftermath*, ed. Luis Francia and Angel Velasco Shaw (Pasig City: Anvil Press, 2000); and the older Philip S. Foner, *Mark Twain: Social Critic*, 2nd ed. (New York: International Publishers, 1966). The University of California Press has published twenty-three of the anticipated seventy volumes of *The Works and Papers of Mark Twain* (see the Mark Twain Project at the Bancroft Library at http://www.lib.berkeley.edu/BANC/MTP/).

In Spain, the war unleashed a literary movement that came to be called the "Generation of '98." Authors of this movement included Angel Ganivet, Miguel de Unamuno, Azorín, José Ortega y Gasset, Pío Baroja, Vicente Blasco Ibáñez, Ramón María del Valle-Inclán, and Antonio and Manuel Machado y Ruiz. Their writings were marked by reflections on Spain's decline as an imperial power, a search for a new national identity, and the desire to modernize Spain's political system. The dozen essays in John P. Gabriele, ed., *Divergencias y unidad, perspectivas sobre la generación del '98* (Madrid: Editorial Orígenes, 1990) analyze the generation of 1898 as a historiographic concept and the work of individual authors of that generation. Conrad Kent and María Dolores de la Calle, eds., *Visiones Salmantinas, (1898–1998)* (Salamanca, España: Universidad de Salamanca; Ohio: Ohio Wesleyan University, 1998), based on a conference in Salamanca, offers a range of essays on the impact of the writers and artists of the Generation of '98, Spanish-U.S. and Spanish-Latin American relations at the end of the nineteenth century, and the role of Salamanca then and now. *Ecos de la Generación del 98 en la del 27* (Madrid: Ediciones Caballo Griego para la Poesía, 1998) includes the papers presented at the "Jornadas sobre Ecos de la Generación del 98 en la del 27" conference held in Lisbon, Portugal, in 1998. See also Leonardo Romero Tobar, ed., *El camino hacia el 98. (Los escritores de la Restauración y la crisis del fin de siglo)* (Madrid: Fundación Duques de Soria: Visor, 1998). Aníbal González, ed., *1898–1998: Balance de un siglo*, special issue of *Revista Iberoamericana* 64, nos. 184–85 (July–December 1998) analyzes the literary production on both sides of the Atlantic with essays on both the Generation of '98 and the Latin American modernists. Enrico Mario Santí, "Cuba, Spain, and '98: Narcissism, Melancholy, and the Crisis of Historical Memory," *Cuban Studies* 28 (Pittsburgh, Pa.: University of Pittsburgh Press, 1998) offers a postcolonial reading of the work of the Spanish Generation of '98.

For Latin America, the war marked a crisis of conscience among many intellectuals, who anguished over defining new relationships with both Spain and the United States. In Latin America, the end of the nineteenth century witnessed the emergence of the modernist movement, in which the Nicaraguan poet Rubén Darío and the Cuban intellectual José Martí were the primary figures. While modernist literature of the end of the nineteenth century has traditionally been seen as subscribing to the tenets of "art for art's sake," it acquired a clearer social dimension in the wake of the war. See Luis Quintana Tejera, "La Generación del 98 y el modernismo literario latinoamericano como expresión de la forma hispana de una crisis universal de valores," *Cuadernos americanos* 2, no. 74 (March–April 1999): 114–23.

Questions of nationalism and American (in the broader sense of the term) identity permeated Latin American literature at the end of the nineteenth century. See especially the chapters by Sylvia Molloy, Francine Masiello, and Julio Ramos in Doris Sommer, ed., *The Places of History: Regionalism Revisited in Latin America* (Durham, N.C.: Duke University Press, 1999). An excellent overview of the period leading up to the war may be found in Julio Ramos, *Desencuentros de la modernidad en América Latina. Literatura y política en el siglo XIX* (Mexico, Fondo de Cultura Económica, 1989), forthcoming in a revised, updated translation by John D. Blanco, *Divergent Modernities: Culture and Politics in Nineteenth-Century Latin America* (Durham, N.C.: Duke University Press, 2001).

Key primary texts for the period include José Martí, "Nuestra América" (1891); Rubén Darío, "El triunfo de Calibán," *El cojo ilustrado* no. 163 (1898); Darío, "A Roosevelt" (1904); José Enrique Rodó, "Ariel" (1900); César Zumeta, "El continente enfermo"; Rufino Blanco Fombona, "La americanización del mundo"; and Manuel Ugarte, "El porvenir de la América Latina" (Valencia: F. Sempere y Compañía [1911]). See Maurice Belrose, "Latinidad vs. imperialismo yanqui en *El Cojo Ilustrado*, 1898–1903," *Casa de las Américas* 211 (April–June 1998): 72–77 for a discussion of the ideological and spiritual struggle undertaken by these and other intellectuals.

Less well known than the modernist poetry, short stories, and essays, but also part of a Latin American anti-imperialist tradition launched during the war years, are the novels by Máximo Soto Hall, *El problema* [1899] (Quito: "El Comercio", 1906) and *El árbol enfermo* [1920] (3rd ed., San Jose, Costa Rica: Trejos Hermanos, 1930); and Carlos Gagini's *La caída del Aguila* (San Jose: Editorial Costa Rica, 1973). For a discussion of these novels, see Juan Durán Luzio, "Estados Unidos versus Hispanoamérica: En torno a la novela del 98," *Casa de las Américas* [Cuba] 26, no. 153 (1985): 121–27.

As José Martí was the leading Cuban intellectual exponent of independence, I focus here primarily on new scholarship about him and his writings. Jeffrey Belnap and Raúl Fernández, *José Martí's "Our America": From National to Hemispheric Cultural Studies* (Durham, N.C.: Duke University

Press, 1998) grew in part from a conference in 1995 at the University of California Humanities Research Institute at UC Irvine, " 'Our America' and the Gilded Age: José Martí's Chronicles of Imperial Critique." The essays contained therein constitute a significant contribution in their focus on the tension between national and global perspectives found in the journalistic writings of Martí. Carmen Alemany Bay, Ramiro Muñoz, and José Carlos Rovira, eds., *José Martí: Historia y literatura ante el fin del siglo XIX* (Alicante, Spain: Universidad de Alicante, with Casa de las Américas, 1997) includes chapters by the editors, Enrique Marini-Palmieri, Benito Varela Jacome, Fina García Marruz, Andrés Sorel, Ivan A. Schulman, Teodosio Fernández, Roberto Fernández Retamar, and Cintio Vitier. Luis Angel Argüelles, comp. and prol., *Martí y México. Historia y cultura* (Mexico; UNAM, Coordinación de Humanidades, 1998) is a compilation of texts thematically organized around Martí's vision of Mexico (his adopted second *patria*) and a century of Mexican interpretations of Martí and his writings. On the legacies of Martí for Latin America, see Julio Rodríguez-Luis, *Re-Reading José Martí (1853–1895): One Hundred Years Later* (Albany, N.Y.: State University of New York Press, 1999). On the role of José Martí in the evolution of Cuban nationalism, see the previously mentioned Guerra, "Crucibles of Liberation in Cuba"; and the classic Gerald E. Poyo, "*With All, and for the Good of All." The Emergence of Popular Nationalism in the Cuban Communities of the United States, 1848–1898* (Durham, N.C.: Duke University Press, 1989). Deborah Shnookal and Mirta Muñiz, *José Martí Reader: Writings on the Americas* (Melbourne [Australia]: Ocean Press, 1999) provides a fresh English translation of a selection of the writings, letters, and poetry of José Martí, particularly those dealing with his observations of the "other" America (that is, the United States of America).

Martí, like many of his other contemporaries of the time (Ramón Betances, Eugenio María de Hostos, Gregorio Luparón) believed that the best protection against Spanish colonialism and U.S. imperialism could be found in the resuscitation of Simón Bolívar's dreams of Spanish American unity. On this topic, see Ricaurte Soler, "José Martí: Bolivarismo y antimperialismo," *Casa de las Américas* 23, no. 138 (1983): 39–46; and Salvador Morales, "Bolívar en Martí," *Islas* [Cuba] 76 (1983): 21–29.

On the position of Cuban intellectuals in the aftermath of the war, see Enrique Ubieta Gómez, "Panhispanismo o panamericanismo: controversia sobre identidad cultural (1900–1922)," *Ensayos de identidad* (La Habana: Letras Cubanas, 1993): 11–80. For the literary legacies of the war in Cuban literature, see Jorge Fornet, "El síndrome del 98 en la literatura cubana," *Casa de las Américas* 205 (October–December 1996).

The War of 1898 has perhaps had the most enduring impact on Puerto Rico; its legacies there remain vivid in the cultural arena, where issues of national identity and political status are inextricably intertwined. Two recent books on one of Puerto Rico's key intellectual figures of the times are Manuel Maldonado-Denis, *Eugenio María de Hostos y el pensamiento social iberoamericano* (Mexico: Fondo de Cultura Económica, 1992); and Eugenio María de Hostos, *Estímulos de vida para cada día: (pensamientos)*, ed. Vivian Quiles-Calderin (San Juan, Puerto Rico: Instituto de Cultura Puertorriqueña, 1998). See also Arcadio Díaz Quiñones, *La memoria rota: ensayos sobre cultura y política* (Río Piedras: Ediciones Huracán, 1993); and Evelyn DeJesus, "Manuel Zeno Gandía frente al 1898: La Guerra Hispanoamericana" (Ph.D. diss., New York University, 1986). Several recent short-story collections grapple with the continuing complexities of Puerto Rican national identity. See Joy L. De Jesús, ed., *Growing up Puerto Rican* (New York: Morrow, 1997); and Esmeralda Santiago, *When I Was Puerto Rican* (New York: Vintage Books, 1993). Puerto Rican literature of the last century is also marked by fictional works that reconstruct the period of the war. See Silvia Alvarez Curbelo, "Despedidas," *Revista de Indias* 57, no. 211 (1997): 783–99 for a reconstructed "farewell" narrative based on Puerto Rican texts from the war period. See also José Luis González, *La llegada: crónica con "ficción"* (Río Piedras, Puerto Rico: Ediciones Huracán, 1980), and his *Literatura y sociedad en Puerto Rico: de los cronistas de Indias a la generación del 98* (Mexico: Fondo de Cultura Económica, 1976).

VIDEO AND WEB RESOURCES

A wonderful teaching tool with an abundance of references to both primary sources online and websites on different aspects of the War of 1898 is Michelle D. Walker, "Multiple Intelligences and the World Wide Web: A New Approach to Teaching about War," reprinted from the Organization of American Historians (OAH) *Magazine of History* 12 (spring 1998): 44–47 at http://veritas.ucs.indiana.edu/~oah/magazine/1898/walker.html.

Another website of particular interest is the Library of Congress's "The World of 1898: The Spanish-American War," at http://lcweb.loc.gov/rr/hispanic/1898/, a site that provides brief overviews, bibliographies, chronologies, and links to a variety of fascinating related resources, including the American Memory Project's "The Spanish-American War in Motion Pictures," featuring 68 motion pictures produced between 1898 and 1901 of the Spanish-American War and the subsequent Philippine Revolution. The New York Public Library hosted from 28 March through 29 August 1998 a special exhibit, "War in Perspective: Public Appeals, Memory, and the Spanish-American Conflict," portions of which may be found online at http://www.nypl.org/research/chss/epo/spanexhib/index.html. Abstracts, art images, and conference papers from the more than 150 presenters at the "1848/1898@1998 Transhistoric Thresholds" conference held at Arizona State University in December 1998 to mark the 150th and 100th anniversary of the Mexican-American War and the War of 1898, respectively, may be found at www.asu.edu/clas/hrc/1848cd. Gary D. Keller and Cordelia

Candelaria, eds., *The Legacy of the Mexican and Spanish-American Wars: Legal, Literary, and Historical Perspectives* (Tempe, Ariz.: Bilingual Review/ Press, 2000) contains a selection of eight papers from that conference; a conference CD-Rom is forthcoming from Bilingual Review/Press at Arizona State University.

Several excellent films on the War of 1898 are now available on video. A videocassette release of the 1997 History Channel program on the subject is Sammy Jackson, producer/director, *The Spanish American War: Birth of a Super Power* (100 mins.) (New York: A&E Television Networks, 1997). Hugh Purcell produced a two-part video series, *Destiny of Empire: The Spanish-American War of 1898* (Princeton, N.J.: Films for the Humanities and Sciences, 1998), which includes two programs on the causes, characters, consequences, and conduct of the war: " 'Remember the Maine': The Roots of the Spanish-American War" (50 mins.) and "The Spanish-American War: A Conflict in Progress" (52 mins.). A somewhat older motion picture produced by Robert Saudek, *The Lure of Empire: America Debates Imperialism, 1898–1901* (New York: Learning Corp. of America, 1974), includes dramatic reenactments of congressional hearings on U.S. intervention in the Philippines following the U.S. victory in Cuba. *Latin America: Intervention in Our Own Backyard* (26 mins.), produced by Anthony Potter Productions in association with Reeves Entertainment Group (Washington, D.C.: PBS Video, 1989), is based on a 1978 television program and provides an overview of four decades of U.S. intervention in Latin America beginning with the War of 1898 until World War II.

Raquel Ortiz and Sharon Simon, prod., "Mi Puerto Rico" (87 mins.) (Berkeley: University of California Extension Center for Media and Independent Learning, 2000) is a prize-winning 1997 documentary which explores Puerto Rico's cultural and political struggles for identity within the context of the complex web of relations between the island and the U.S. mainland. A videorecording which focuses on the U.S.-backed intervention and subsequent annexation of Hawaii is *Act of War: The Overthrow of the Hawaiian Nation* (San Francisco, Calif.: CrossCurrent Media, National Asian American Telecommunications Association [distributor], 1993).

On the literary front, *José Martí: Cuba's Patriot-Poet*, produced by TRVE in Spanish (63 mins.) (Princeton, N.J.: Films for the Humanities & Sciences, 2000), combines documentary material with dramatizations to examine the life of this "Apostle of Cuban independence." *Generación del '98* (Princeton, N.J.: Films for the Humanities & Sciences, 1997–2000) is a three-part video series in Spanish produced by RTVE which provides in-depth programs on three of the preeminent writers of the Spanish Generation of '98: Miguel de Unamuno (55 mins.), Ramón María del Valle-Inclán (55 mins.), and Antonio Machado (60 mins.).

Index

About the Contributors

VIRGINIA M. BOUVIER is assistant professor of Latin American literature at the University of Maryland at College Park (UMCP). She is author of *Women and the Conquest of California, 1542–1840: Codes of Silence* (2001) and numerous monographs and articles on U.S.-Latin American relations. Her research interests center around imperial encounters in the Americas, human rights and justice issues, and women and gender in Latin America.

LILLIAN GUERRA is assistant professor of Latin American and Caribbean history at Bates College in Lewiston, Maine. The author of *Popular Expression and National Identity in Puerto Rico: The Struggle for Self, Community and Nation* (1998), she completed her doctoral studies at the University of Wisconsin-Madison in May 2000. Her work has focused on the development of conflicting nationalisms, the formation of the nation-state, and multiple interpretations of José Martí during the First Cuban Republic. Currently, she is working on a study of the women's movement in Havana and a regional study of labor organizing in Cuba during the early twentieth century.

SYLVIA L. HILTON teaches U.S. and Latin American history at the Complutense University of Madrid. Her chief research interests center on Native American-Hispano-Anglo borders and relations in America. Her most recent publications include (with Ignacio González Casasnovas) *Fuentes para la historia de Iberoamérica: guía de instrumentos de investigación*, 2 vols. (1995–97); (with Steve J. S. Ickringill) *European Perceptions of the Spanish-American War of 1898* (1999); and two collections of primary source texts on CD-Rom: *Las Raíces Hispánicas del Oeste de los Estados Unidos: Textos históricos* (1999) and *Viajeros estadounidenses en Iberoamérica, siglo XIX* (1999).

KRISTIN L. HOGANSON is assistant professor of history at the University of Illinois, Urbana-Champaign. She is the author of *Fighting for American Manhood: How Gender Politics Provoked the Spanish-American and Philippine-American Wars* (1998). Her current research considers how bourgeois U.S. women reacted to and promoted the globalizing trends of the late nineteenth and early twentieth centuries through their consumption, promulgation of popular geography, and "Americanizing" efforts.

LESTER D. LANGLEY was research professor at the University of Georgia, where he taught from 1970 until his retirement in 2000. He is editor of the series "The United States and the Americas" and the author of a dozen books on the Americas and United States-Latin American relations, including *America and the Americas: The United States in the Western Hemisphere* (1989) and (with Thomas Schoonover) *The Banana Man: American Mercenaries and Entrepreneurs in Central America, 1888–1930* (1994). His most recent book is *The Americas in the Age of Revolution, 1750–1850* (1996), the first of a projected two-volume comparative history of the Americas since the mid-eighteenth century. He currently lives in San Angelo, Texas.

LOUIS A. PÉREZ, JR. is the J. Carlyle Sitterson professor of history at the University of North Carolina at Chapel Hill. His principal areas of research are nineteenth- and twentieth-century Cuba, and his writings include dozens of books and articles, including *Cuba and the United States: Ties of Singular Intimacy* (1990); *Slaves, Sugar and Colonial Society: Travel Accounts of Cuba, 1801–1899* (1992); *Cuba: Between Reform and Revolution* (1995); *Essays on Cuban History: Historiography and Research* (1995); *The War of 1898: The United States and Cuba in History and Historiography* (1998); and *On Becoming Cuban: Identity, Nationality, and Culture* (1999).

FRANCISCO A. SCARANO is professor of history at the University of Wisconsin-Madison, where he also directs the Latin American, Caribbean, and Iberian Studies Program. His work has centered on the social and economic history of Puerto Rico in the larger Caribbean context, and his publications include *Sugar and Slavery in Puerto Rico: The Plantation Economy of Ponce, 1800–1850* (1984), *Inmigración y clases sociales en el Puerto Rico del siglo XIX* (1981, 1988), and *Puerto Rico: Cinco siglos de historia* (1993). His forthcoming book, *Puerto Rico: Colony and Nation*, will be published in 2001.

JIM ZWICK is an independent scholar based in Syracuse, New York. He is the author of *Militarism and Repression in the Philippines* (1982), and the editor of *Mark Twain's Weapons of Satire: Anti-Imperialist Writings on the*

Philippine-American War (1992). He has authored numerous essays about the anti-imperialist movement and Mark Twain's anti-imperialist writings, including "The Anti-Imperialist League and the Origins of Filipino-American Oppositional Solidarity," *Amerasia Journal* 24, no. 2 (summer 1998); "The 'Stereoscopic' War of 1899," in *Voices and Scenes of the Past: The Philippine-American War Retold*, ed. Maria Serena I. Diokno (1999); "Mark Twain's Anti-Imperialist Writings in the 'American Century,' " in *Vestiges of War: The Philippine-American War and Its Aftermath*, ed. Luis Francia and Angel Velasco Shaw (2000); and "Mark Twain and Anti-Imperialism," in Shelley Fisher Fishkin, ed., *Historical Guide to Mark Twain* (2001). Zwick is also the creator of *Anti-Imperialism in the United States, 1898–1935*, and related websites on the history and political and cultural legacies of U.S. imperialism at BoondocksNet.com.